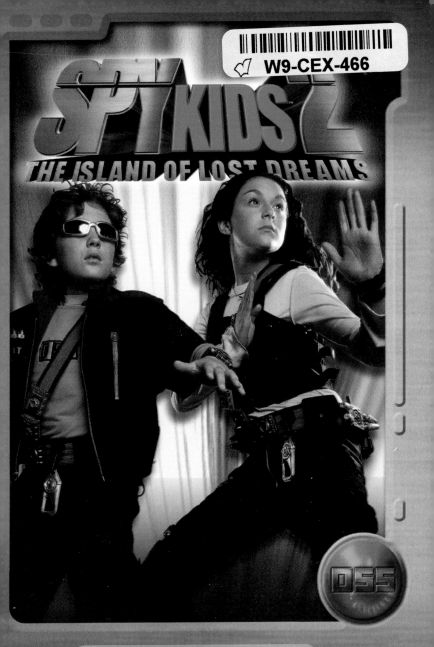

SPY KIDS 2
THE ISLAND OF LOST DREAMS

W9-CEX-466

DSS

BY ROBERT RODRIGUEZ
ADAPTED BY JAKE FORBES

Graphic Designer - Dave Snow
Cover Layout - Patrick Hook
Copy Editors - Amy Kaemon & Paul Morrissey

Senior Editor - Jake Forbes
Managing Editor - Jill Freshney
Production Manager - Jennifer Miller
Art Director - Matt Alford
VP of Production & Manufacturing - Ron Klamert
President & C.O.O. - John Parker
Publisher - Stuart Levy

Email: editor@TOKYOPOP.com
Come visit us online at www.TOKYOPOP.com

A ☻TOKYOPOP® Cine-Manga
TOKYOPOP® is an imprint of Mixx Entertainment, Inc.
5900 Wilshire Blvd. Suite 2000, Los Angeles, CA 90036

ISBN: 1-59182-234-3

First TOKYOPOP® printing: February 2003

10 9 8 7 6 5 4 3 2 1
Printed in Canada

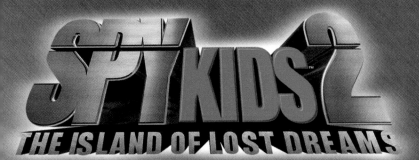

SPY KIDS 2
THE ISLAND OF LOST DREAMS

..DSS TABLE OF CONTENTS ...DSS TABLE OF CONTENTS

DSS UKATA ASSIGNMENT

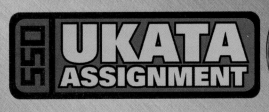

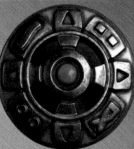

SPY KIDS 2™

DATABASE...OSS DATABASE...OSS DATA

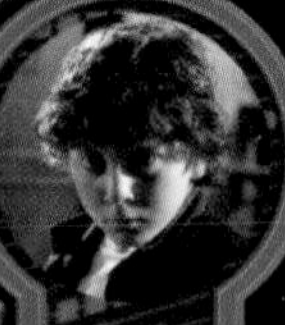

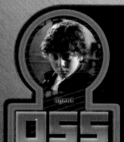

NAME:
JUNI CORTEZ

DESIGNATION:
SK1

ORGANIZATION:
OSS, SPY KIDS DIVISION

CLEARANCE:
LEVEL 2

SPECIAL SKILLS:
VOICE MIMICRY, DIPLOMACY, BALLET

BIO:
THE YOUNGEST CHILD OF SUPER-SPIES GREGORIO AND INGRID CORTEZ, JUNI TEAMED UP WITH HIS SISTER CARMEN TO STOP FEGAN FLOOP AND MINION FROM OVERTHROWING THE OSS. THEIR SUCCESS LED TO THE CREATION OF THE SPY KIDS DIVISION OF THE OSS. FOR HIS EXCELLENT PERFORMANCE AS A SPY, HE WAS NAMED THE VERY FIRST "SPY KID OF THE YEAR."

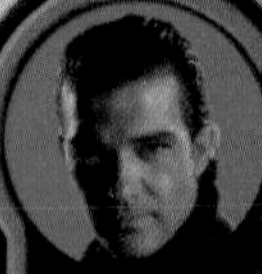

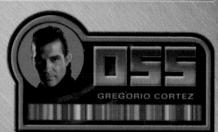

GREGORIO CORTEZ

NAME:
GREGORIO CORTEZ

BIO:
FATHER OF JUNI AND CARMEN CORTEZ. THE OSS'S TOP SPY, GREGORIO CORTEZ WAS A SHOO-IN FOR THE POSITION OF OSS DIRECTOR UNTIL FOUL PLAY LANDED DONNAGON GIGGLES IN THE BIG CHAIR.

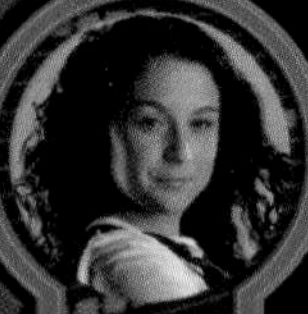

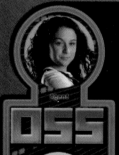

NAME:
CARMEN CORTEZ

DESIGNATION:
SK2

ORGANIZATION:
OSS, SPY KIDS DIVISION

CLEARANCE:
LEVEL 2

SPECIAL SKILLS:
COMPUTER HACKING, GYMNASTICS, SINGING

BIO:
CHARISMATIC, ATHLETIC AND INTELLIGENT, CARMEN IS A MODEL SPY. SHE SERVES THE OSS WELL, BUT SHE KNOWS THAT A GOOD SPY PUTS FAMILY FIRST. MUCH TO HER BROTHER'S DISMAY, CARMEN HAS A CRUSH ON HOT NEW AGENT GARY GIGGLES.

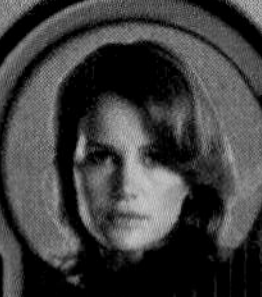

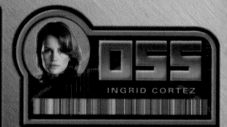

INGRID CORTEZ

NAME:
INGRID CORTEZ

BIO:
MOTHER OF JUNI AND CARMEN CORTEZ. 10 YEARS AGO, SHE WAS A SECRET AGENT WORKING AGAINST GREGORIO CORTEZ. BUT THE TWO SPIES FELL IN LOVE, AND SHE TRADED ONE LIFE OF ACTION AND ADVENTURE FOR ANOTHER: PARENTHOOD.

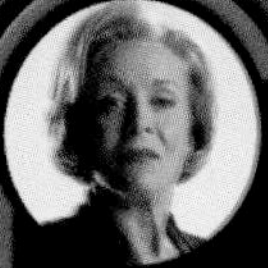

GRANDMA AND GRANDPA

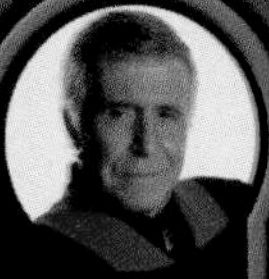

JUNI AND CARMEN'S GRANDPARENTS ON THEIR MOTHER'S SIDE. THEY LOVE THEIR DAUGHTER AND GRANDKIDS, BUT THEY NEVER GAVE GREGORIO THEIR BLESSING. HE'LL HAVE TO WORK HARD TO EARN THE RESPECT OF THESE SEASONED SPY IN-LAWS.

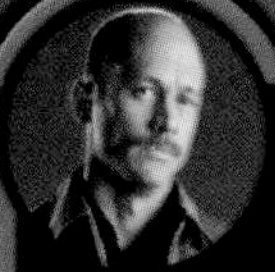

DONNAGON GIGGLES

THE NEW DIRECTOR OF THE OSS. HE SHOWS BLATANT FAVORTISM TOWARDS HIS KIDS, GARY AND GERTI, GRANTING THEM LEVEL 1 ACCESS AND GIVING THEM THE COVETED "UKATA ASSIGNMENT." THERE'S SOMETHING SUSPICIOUS ABOUT HIS INVOLVEMENT WITH THE MISSING TRANSMOOKER DEVICE.

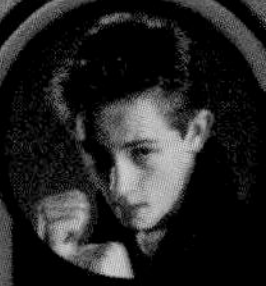

GARY GIGGLES

THE RISING STAR OF THE SPY KIDS DIVISION, GARY INSISTS ON HAVING THE LATEST GADGETS FOR EVERY MISSION. HIS DAD UPGRADED HIM TO A LEVEL 1 AGENT, WITH HIGHER ACCESS THAN THE CORTEZES, AND NAMED HIM THE NEW "SPY KID OF THE YEAR."

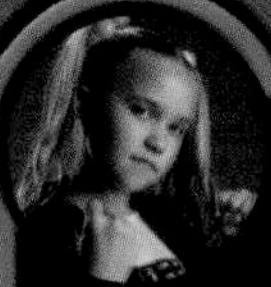

GERTI GIGGLES

THIS PRE-TEEN PRODIGY IS SMART BEYOND HER YEARS AND KNOWS MORE ABOUT COMPUTERS THAN EVEN CARMEN DOES. EVEN THOUGH SHE'S NEW TO THE OSS, SHE'S ALREADY BEEN GRANTED LEVEL 1 ACCESS BY HER FATHER, THE NEW OSS DIRECTOR. IN THE CASE OF AN EMERGENCY, HER PIGTAILS CAN BE USED AS PROPELLERS FOR A QUICK GETAWAY.

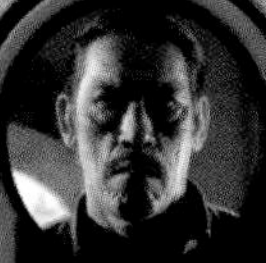

MACHETE CORTEZ

JUNI AND CARMEN'S UNCLE. HE'S A BRILLIANT INVENTOR WHO MAKES THE GADGETS THAT NO SPY SHOULD BE WITHOUT. SOME OF HIS MOST POPULAR INVENTIONS ARE THE ELECTROSHOCK GUMBALL, THE WORLD'S SMALLEST CAMERA, THE BUDDY-PACK, AND THE ALL-NEW MACHETE ELASTIC WONDER.

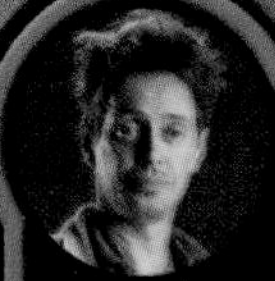

DR. ROMERO

A MAD SCIENTIST WHO CREATED THE MUTANT ANIMALS ON THE ISLAND OF LEEKE LEEKE. NOW HE LIVES TRAPPED IN HIS OWN LAB, TERRIFIED OF THE MONSTERS OUTSIDE HIS FRONT DOOR. ONLY HE KNOWS THE LOCATION OF THE REAL TRANSMOOKER DEVICE.

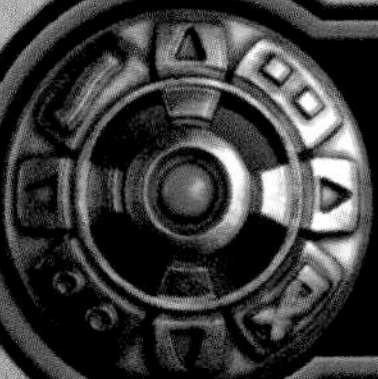

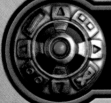

TRANSMOOKER DEVICE

A MYSTERIOUS DEVICE WITH POWER BEYOND COMPARE. IT HAS THE ABILITY TO CHANGE THE WORLD, OR EVEN DESTROY IT. THE PRESIDENT OF THE UNITED STATES HAD A PROTOTYPE MODEL, BUT THE REAL DEVICE IS LOCATED ON LEEKE LEEKE, THE ISLAND OF LOST DREAMS. IT IS HIDDEN BY A CLOAKING FIELD WHICH RENDERS THE ENTIRE ISLAND INVISIBLE TO RADAR AND PREVENTS THE USE OF ANY ELECTRONIC DEVICES ON OR NEAR THE ISLAND.

CHAPTER 1

SPY KIDS
ISLAND OF LOST DREAMS

SPY KIDS: BACK IN ACTION

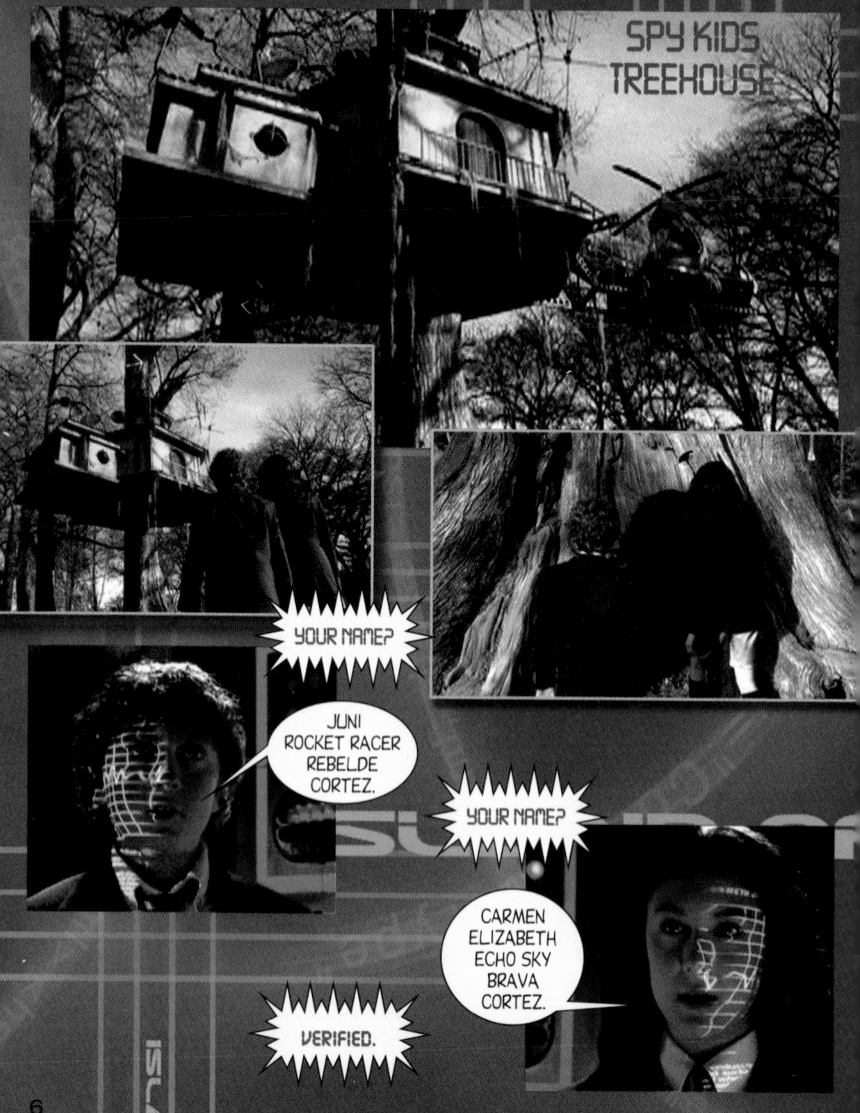
SPY KIDS TREEHOUSE
YOUR NAME?
JUNI ROCKET RACER REBELDE CORTEZ.
YOUR NAME?
CARMEN ELIZABETH ECHO SKY BRAVA CORTEZ.
VERIFIED.

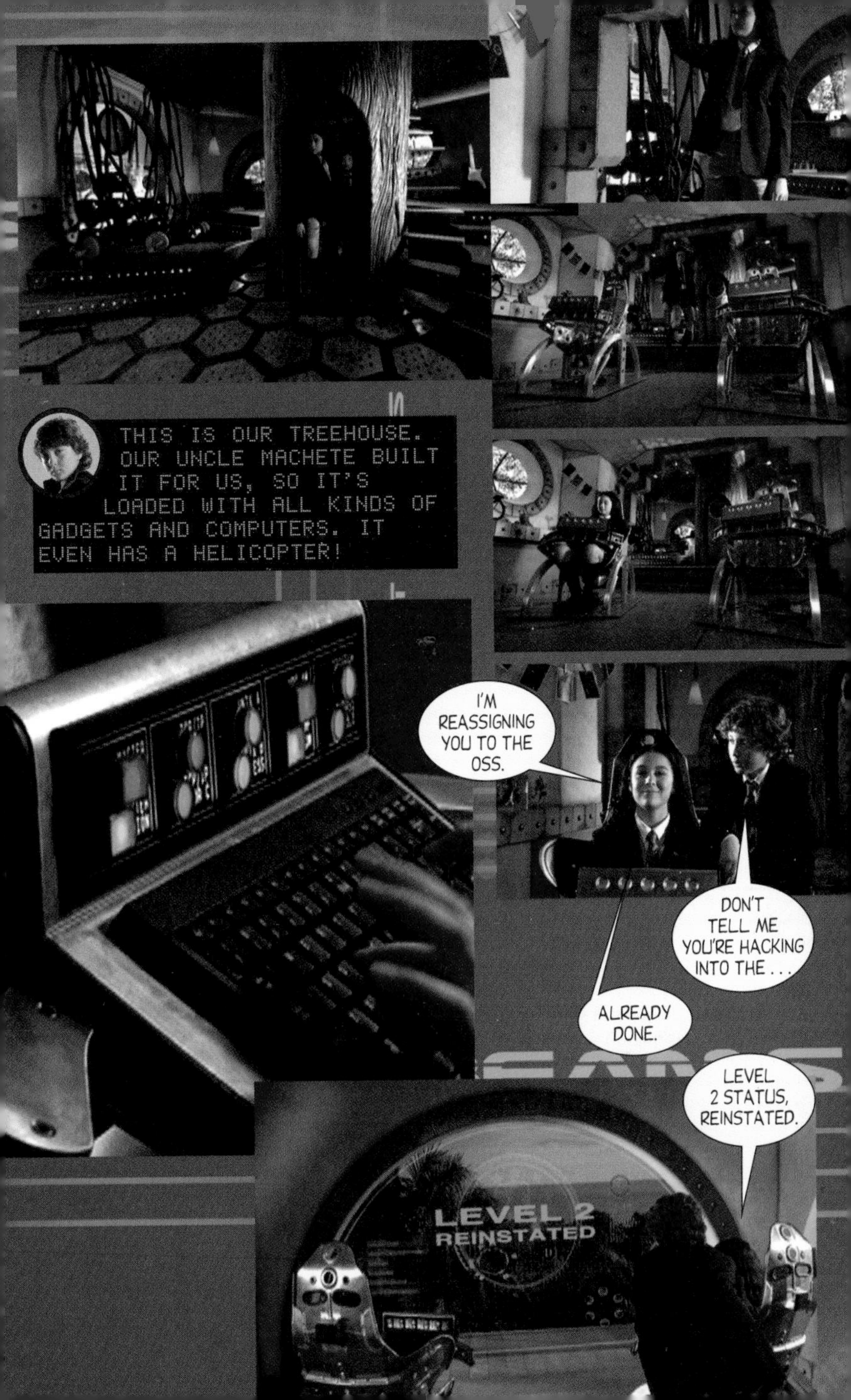
THIS IS OUR TREEHOUSE. OUR UNCLE MACHETE BUILT IT FOR US, SO IT'S LOADED WITH ALL KINDS OF GADGETS AND COMPUTERS. IT EVEN HAS A HELICOPTER!
I'M REASSIGNING YOU TO THE OSS.
DON'T TELL ME YOU'RE HACKING INTO THE . . .
ALREADY DONE.
LEVEL 2 STATUS, REINSTATED.
LEVEL 2
REINSTATED

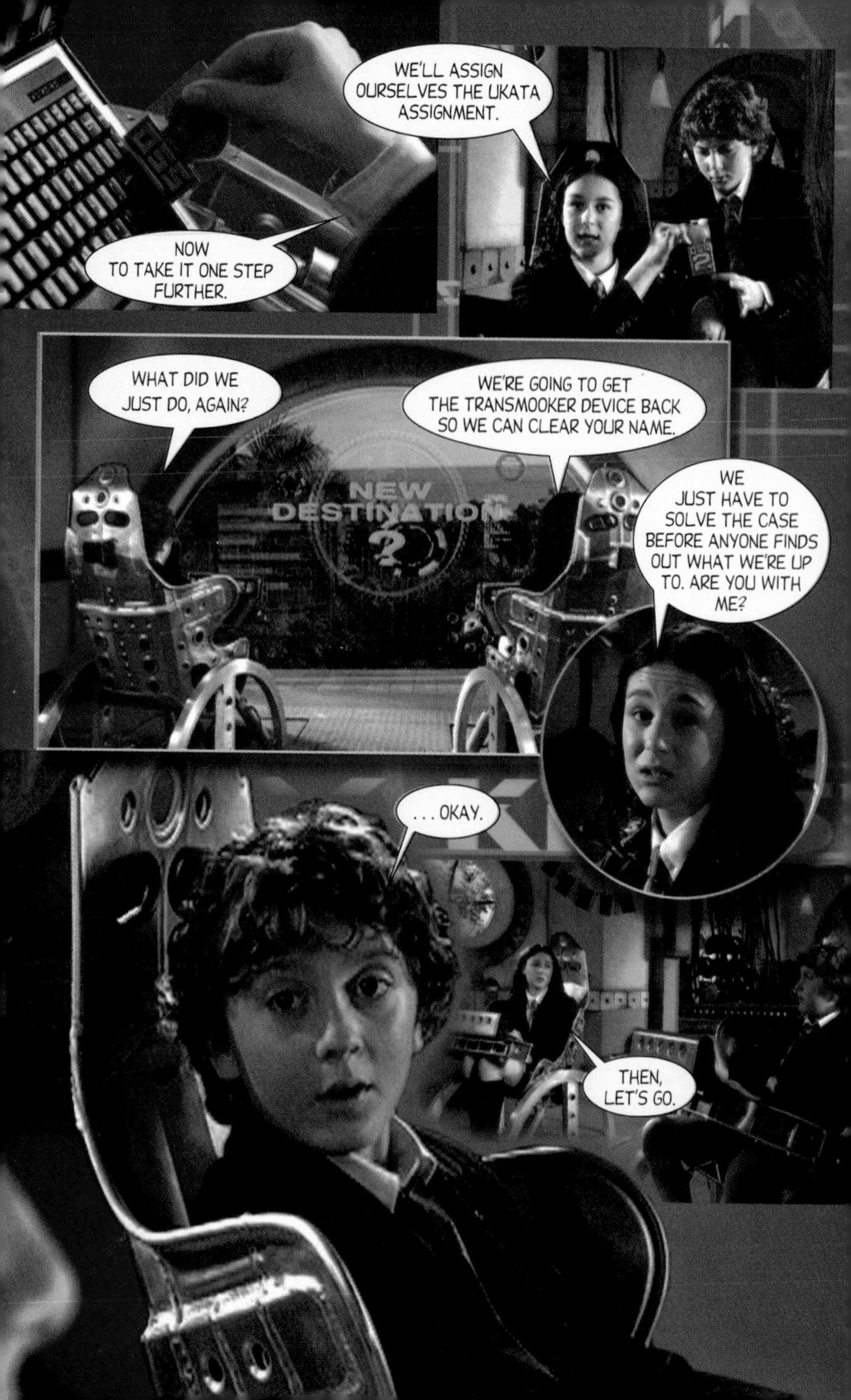
NOW TO TAKE IT ONE STEP FURTHER.
WE'LL ASSIGN OURSELVES THE UKATA ASSIGNMENT.
WHAT DID WE JUST DO, AGAIN?
WE'RE GOING TO GET THE TRANSMOOKER DEVICE BACK SO WE CAN CLEAR YOUR NAME.
NEW DESTINATION ?
WE JUST HAVE TO SOLVE THE CASE BEFORE ANYONE FINDS OUT WHAT WE'RE UP TO. ARE YOU WITH ME?
. . . OKAY.
THEN, LET'S GO.

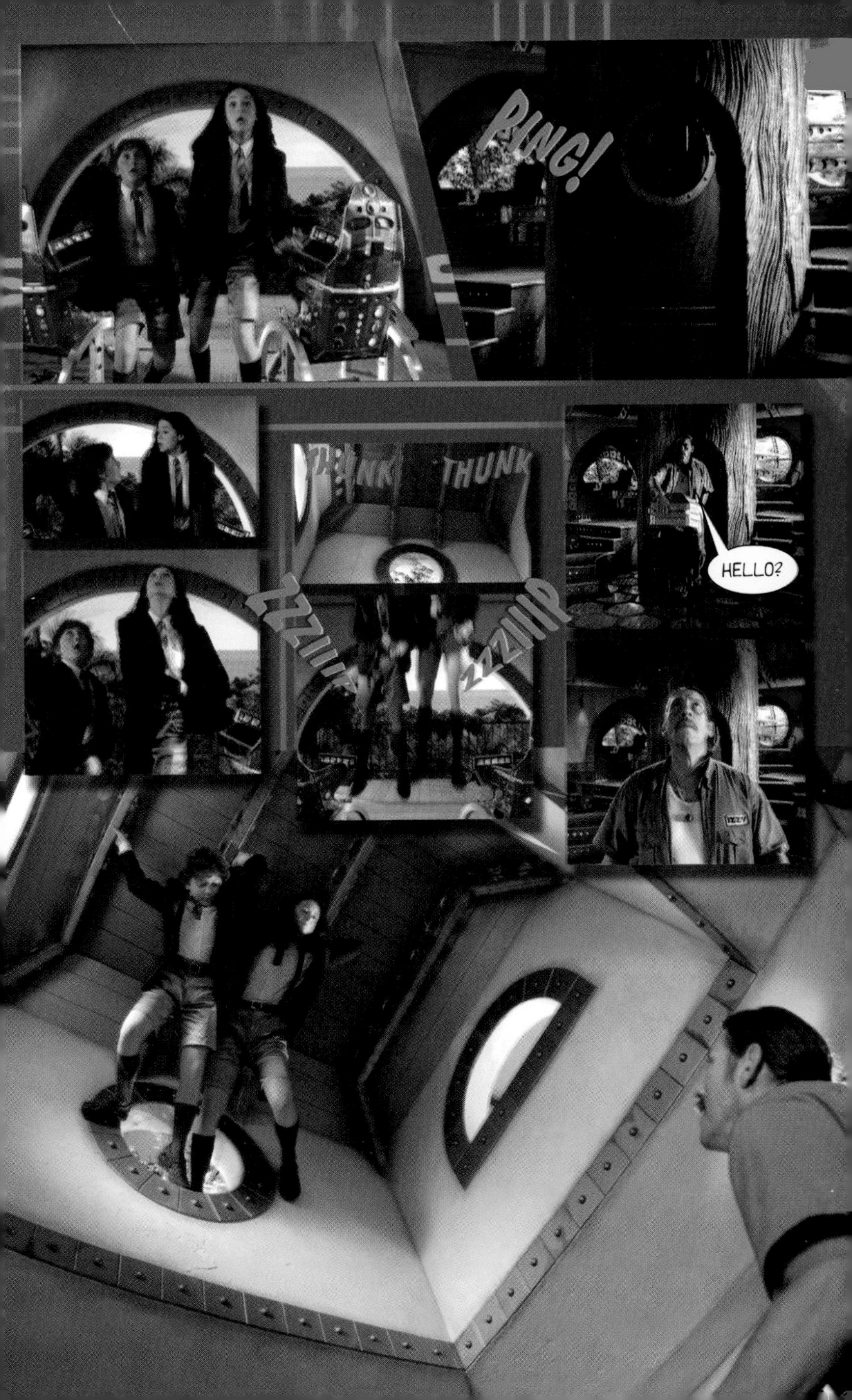
BING!
THUNK
ZZZIIIP
HELLO?

SORRY. WE THOUGHT YOU WERE SOMEONE ELSE.

GET DOWN FROM THERE!

I'VE BROUGHT YOU THE VERY LATEST IN GADGETS AND SPY GEAR.

THAT'S OUR UNCLE MACHETE. HE MAY LOOK TOUGH, BUT JUNI AND I KNOW HE'S REALLY A SOFTY. HE MAKES ALL THE COOLEST GADGETS FOR THE OSS. LET'S SEE WHAT HE BROUGHT THIS TIME!

GOOD, 'CAUSE WE'RE GONNA NEED IT.

THE VERY LATEST SPY WATCH. IT'S A TOTAL WRISTWATCH COMPUTER / COMMUNICATIONS CENTER ON YOUR WRIST. DOES EVERYTHING BUT TELL TIME.

IT DOESN'T TELL TIME?

IT'S GOT SO MUCH STUFFED INTO IT, THERE WAS NO ROOM LEFT FOR THE CLOCK.

COOL!!

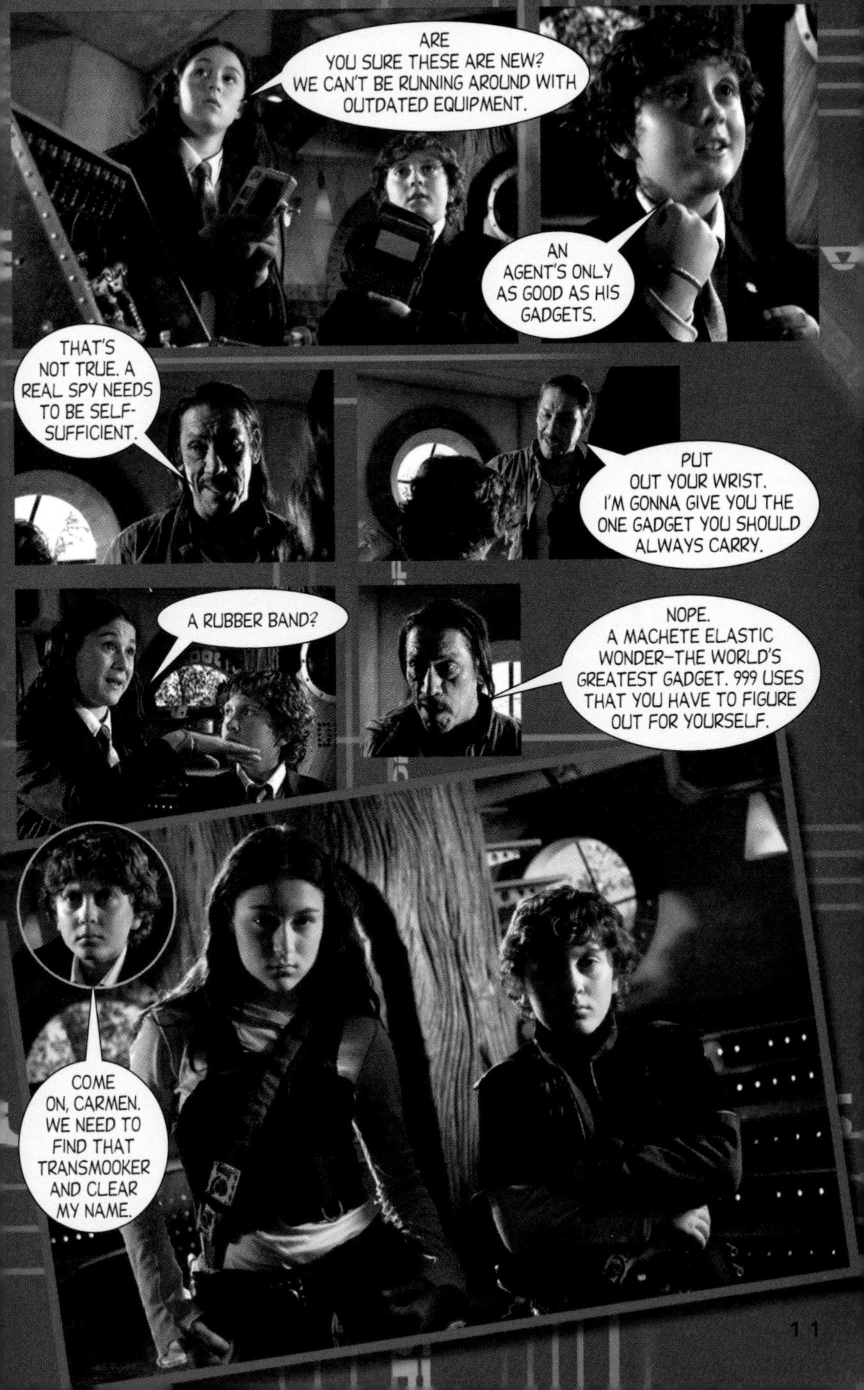
ARE YOU SURE THESE ARE NEW? WE CAN'T BE RUNNING AROUND WITH OUTDATED EQUIPMENT.
AN AGENT'S ONLY AS GOOD AS HIS GADGETS.
THAT'S NOT TRUE. A REAL SPY NEEDS TO BE SELF-SUFFICIENT.
PUT OUT YOUR WRIST. I'M GONNA GIVE YOU THE ONE GADGET YOU SHOULD ALWAYS CARRY.
A RUBBER BAND?
NOPE. A MACHETE ELASTIC WONDER—THE WORLD'S GREATEST GADGET. 999 USES THAT YOU HAVE TO FIGURE OUT FOR YOURSELF.
COME ON, CARMEN. WE NEED TO FIND THAT TRANSMOOKER AND CLEAR MY NAME.

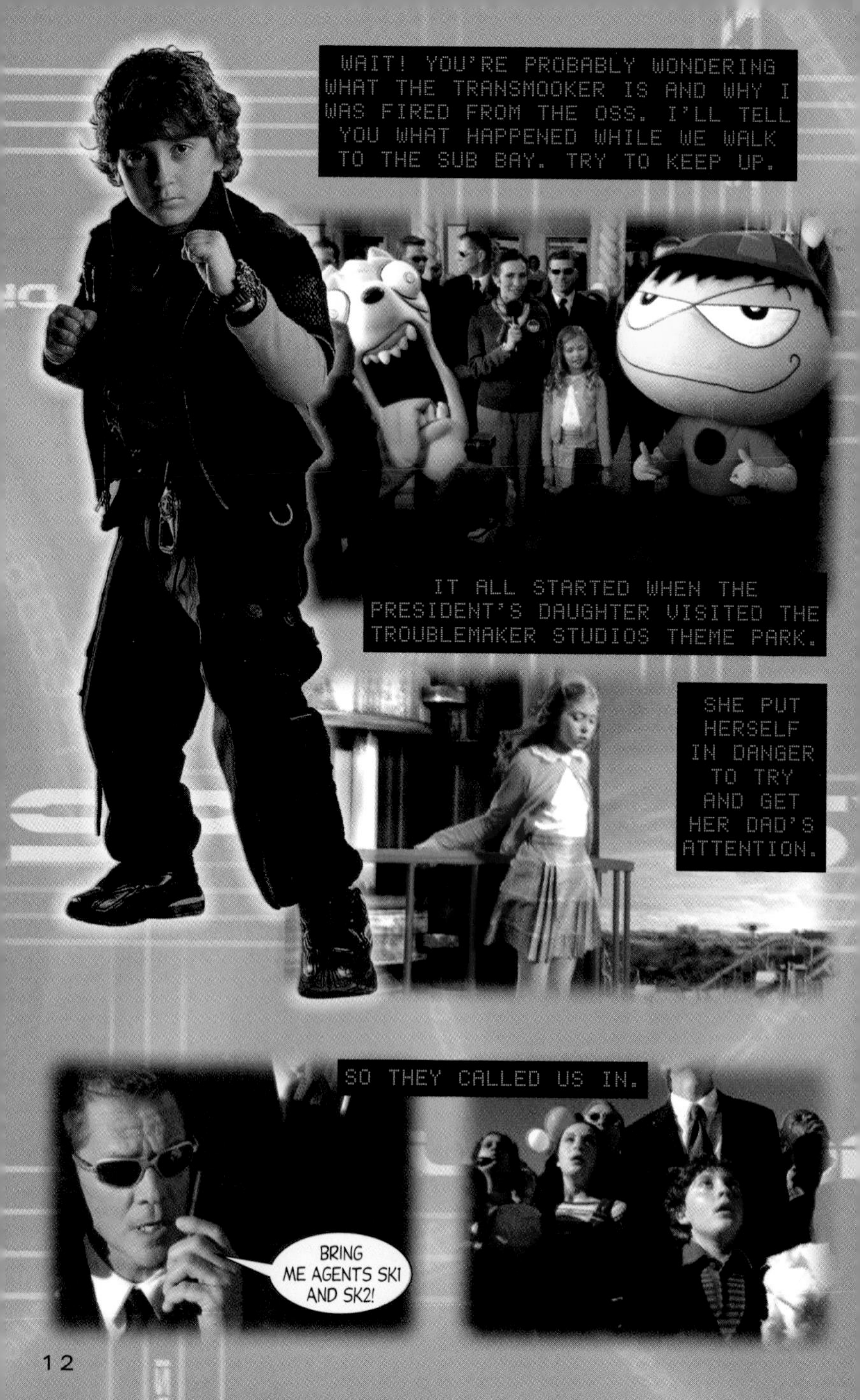
WAIT! YOU'RE PROBABLY WONDERING WHAT THE TRANSMOOKER IS AND WHY I WAS FIRED FROM THE OSS. I'LL TELL YOU WHAT HAPPENED WHILE WE WALK TO THE SUB BAY. TRY TO KEEP UP.
IT ALL STARTED WHEN THE PRESIDENT'S DAUGHTER VISITED THE TROUBLEMAKER STUDIOS THEME PARK.
SHE PUT HERSELF IN DANGER TO TRY AND GET HER DAD'S ATTENTION.
SO THEY CALLED US IN.
BRING ME AGENTS SK1 AND SK2!

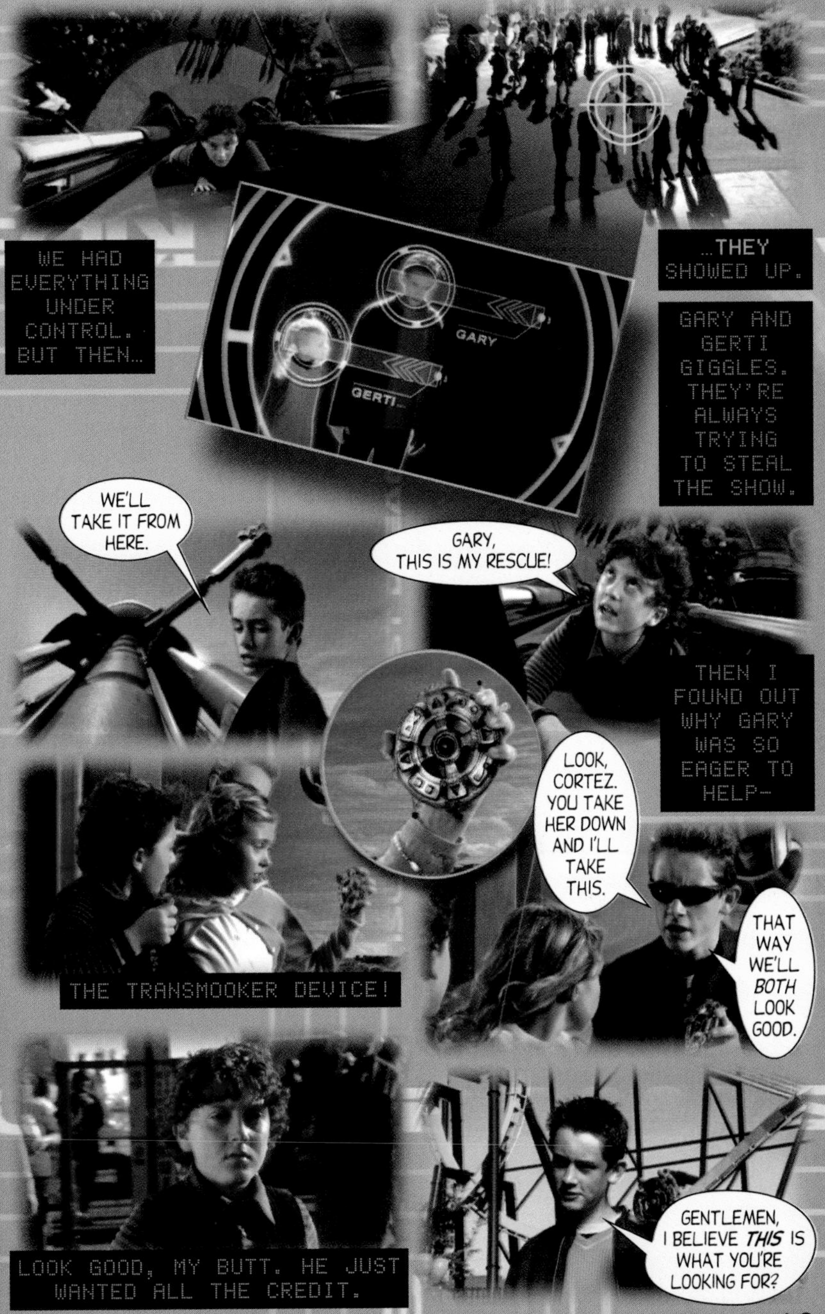
WE HAD EVERYTHING UNDER CONTROL. BUT THEN...
GARY
GERTI...
...THEY SHOWED UP.
GARY AND GERTI GIGGLES. THEY'RE ALWAYS TRYING TO STEAL THE SHOW.
WE'LL TAKE IT FROM HERE.
GARY, THIS IS MY RESCUE!
THEN I FOUND OUT WHY GARY WAS SO EAGER TO HELP-
THE TRANSMOOKER DEVICE!
LOOK, CORTEZ. YOU TAKE HER DOWN AND I'LL TAKE THIS.
THAT WAY WE'LL *BOTH* LOOK GOOD.
LOOK GOOD, MY BUTT. HE JUST WANTED ALL THE CREDIT.
GENTLEMEN, I BELIEVE ***THIS*** IS WHAT YOU'RE LOOKING FOR?

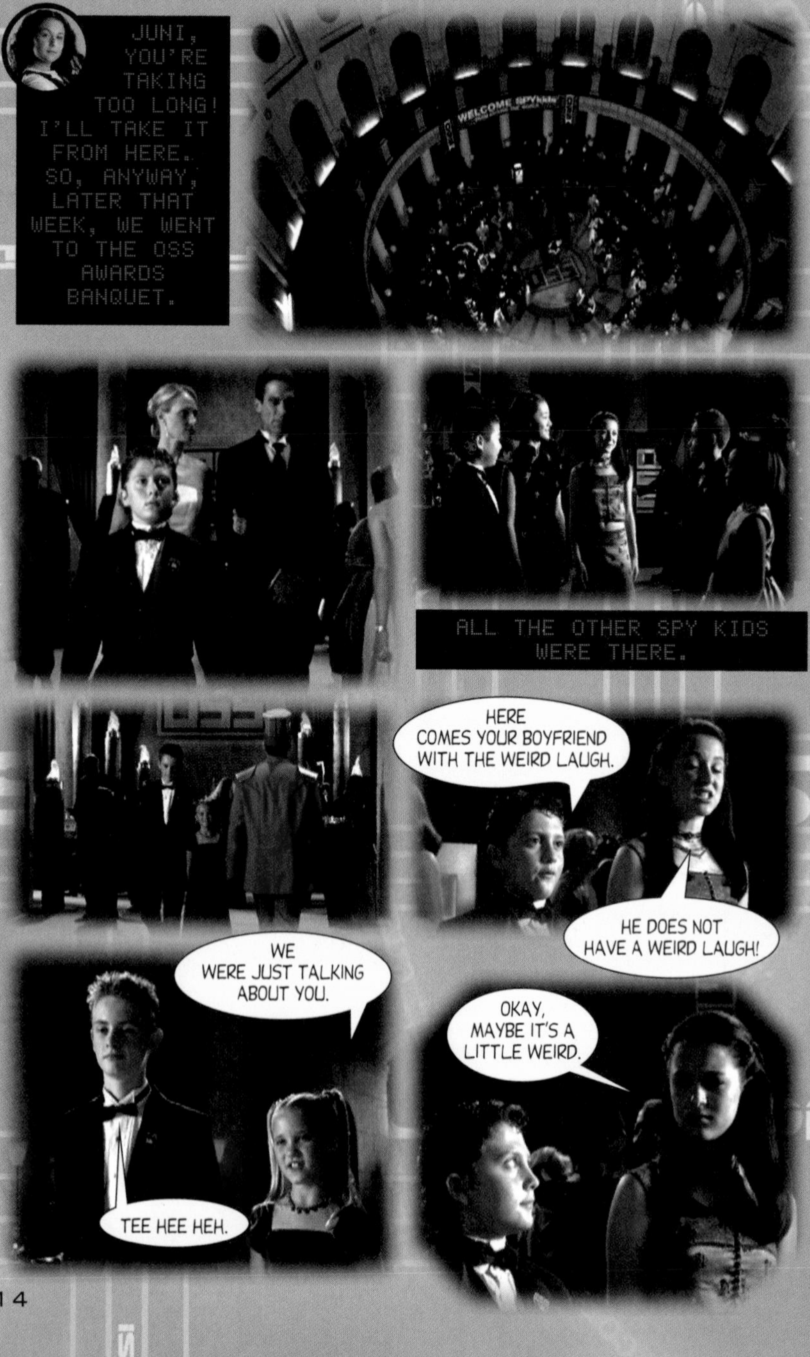
JUNI, YOU'RE TAKING TOO LONG! I'LL TAKE IT FROM HERE. SO, ANYWAY, LATER THAT WEEK, WE WENT TO THE OSS AWARDS BANQUET.
ALL THE OTHER SPY KIDS WERE THERE.
HERE COMES YOUR BOYFRIEND WITH THE WEIRD LAUGH.
HE DOES NOT HAVE A WEIRD LAUGH!
WE WERE JUST TALKING ABOUT YOU.
TEE HEE HEH.
OKAY, MAYBE IT'S A LITTLE WEIRD.

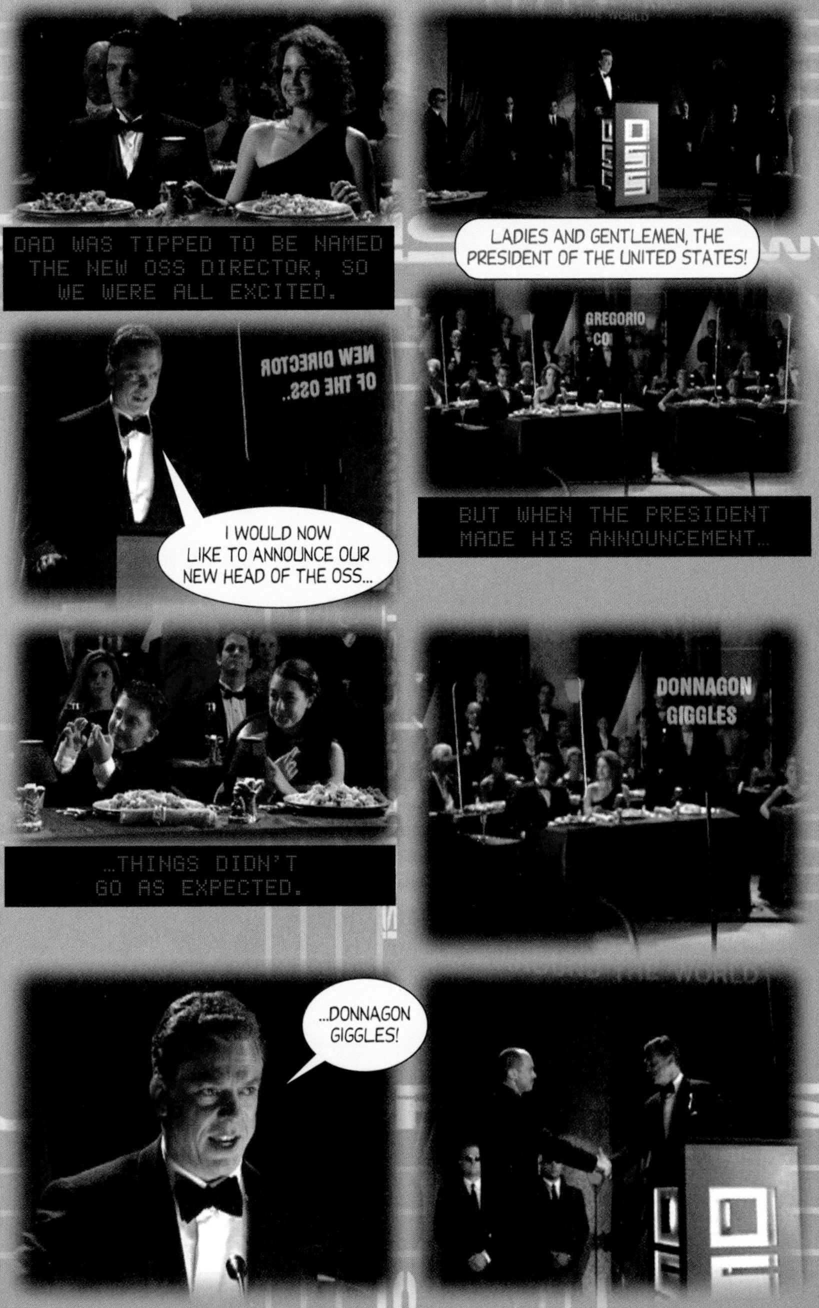
DAD WAS TIPPED TO BE NAMED THE NEW OSS DIRECTOR, SO WE WERE ALL EXCITED.
LADIES AND GENTLEMEN, THE PRESIDENT OF THE UNITED STATES!
I WOULD NOW LIKE TO ANNOUNCE OUR NEW HEAD OF THE OSS...
BUT WHEN THE PRESIDENT MADE HIS ANNOUNCEMENT...
...THINGS DIDN'T GO AS EXPECTED.
DONNAGON GIGGLES
...DONNAGON GIGGLES!

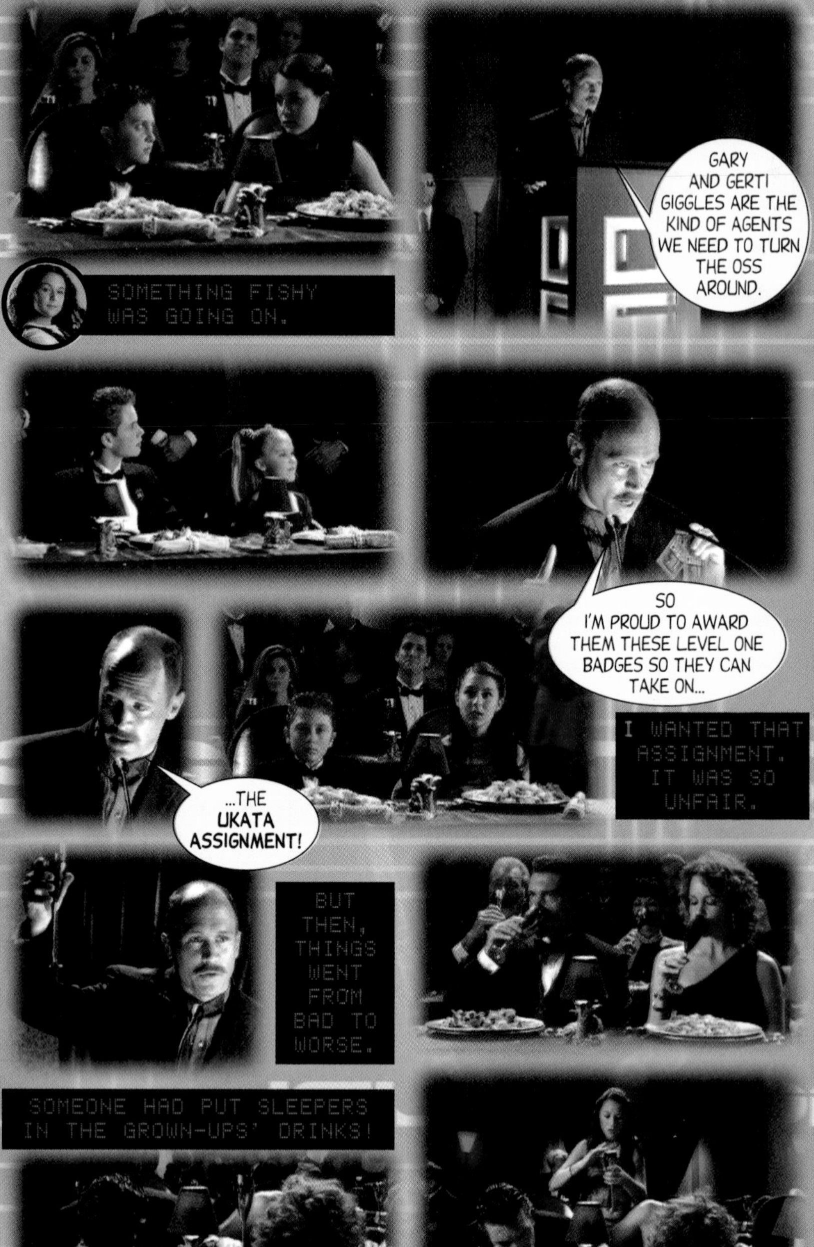
SOMETHING FISHY WAS GOING ON.
GARY AND GERTI GIGGLES ARE THE KIND OF AGENTS WE NEED TO TURN THE OSS AROUND.
SO I'M PROUD TO AWARD THEM THESE LEVEL ONE BADGES SO THEY CAN TAKE ON...
...THE UKATA ASSIGNMENT!
I WANTED THAT ASSIGNMENT. IT WAS SO UNFAIR.
BUT THEN, THINGS WENT FROM BAD TO WORSE.
SOMEONE HAD PUT SLEEPERS IN THE GROWN-UPS' DRINKS!

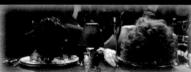

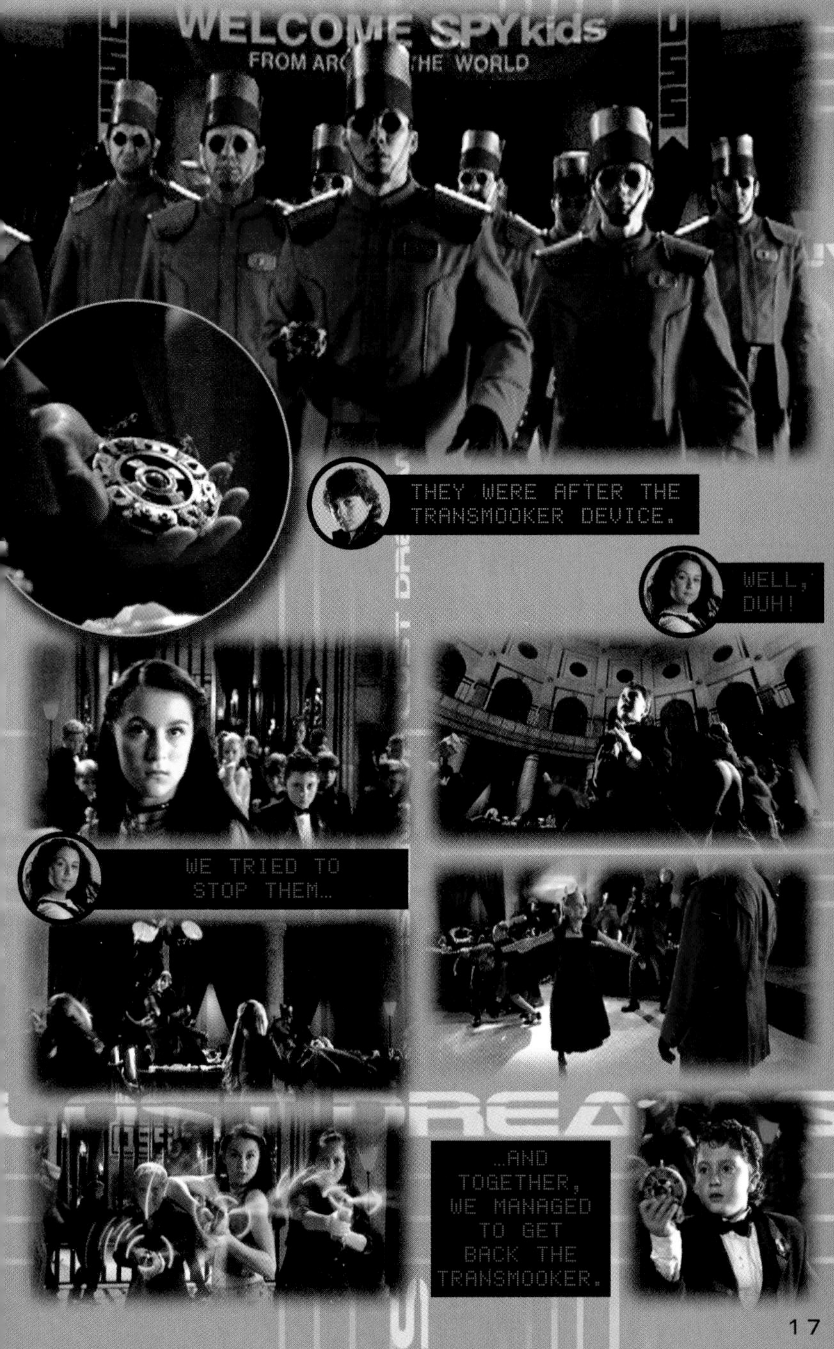

WELCOME SPYkids
THEY WERE AFTER THE TRANSMOOKER DEVICE.
WELL, DUH!
WE TRIED TO STOP THEM...
...AND TOGETHER, WE MANAGED TO GET BACK THE TRANSMOOKER.

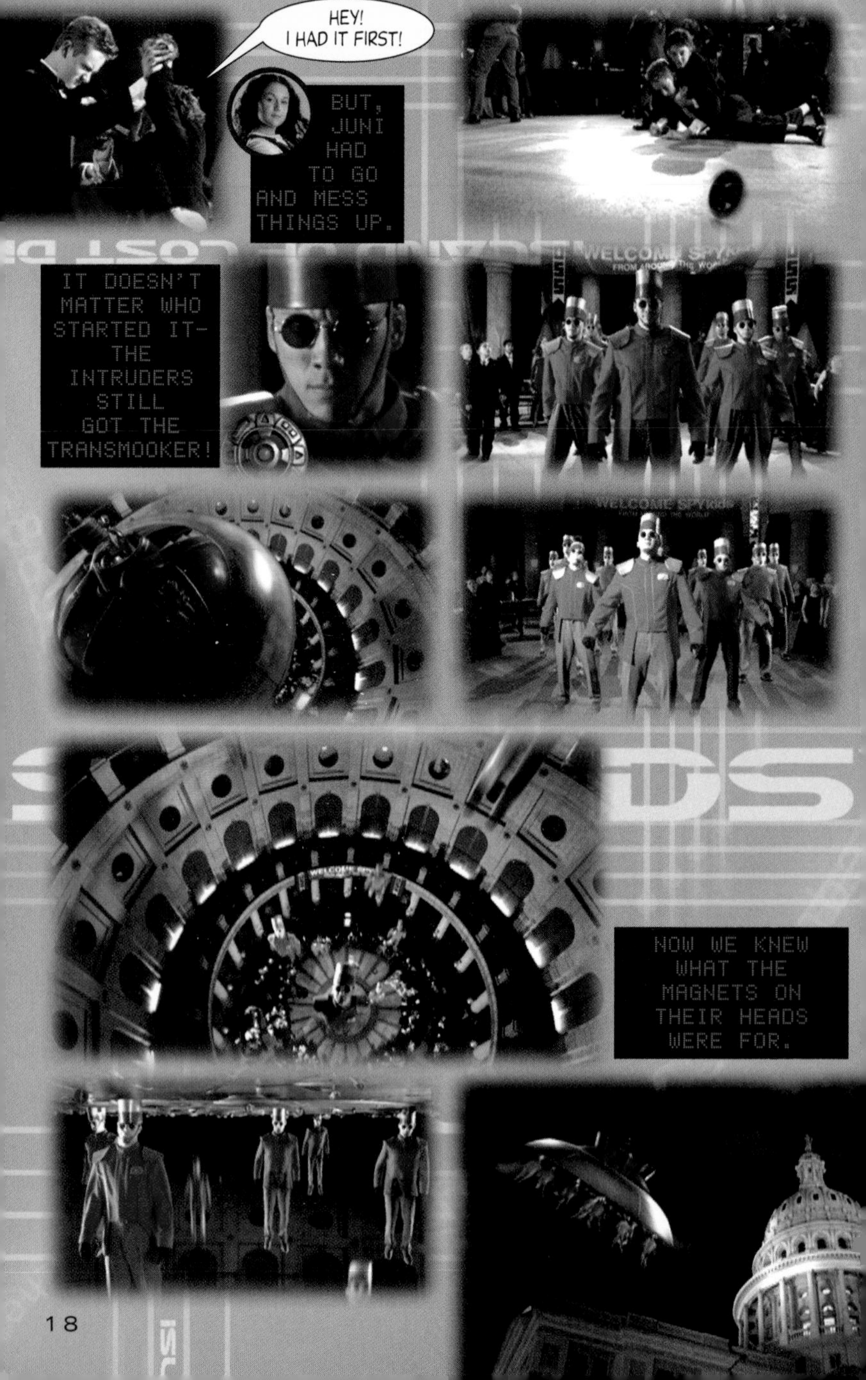
HEY! I HAD IT FIRST!
BUT, JUNI HAD TO GO AND MESS THINGS UP.
IT DOESN'T MATTER WHO STARTED IT- THE INTRUDERS STILL GOT THE TRANSMOOKER!
NOW WE KNEW WHAT THE MAGNETS ON THEIR HEADS WERE FOR.

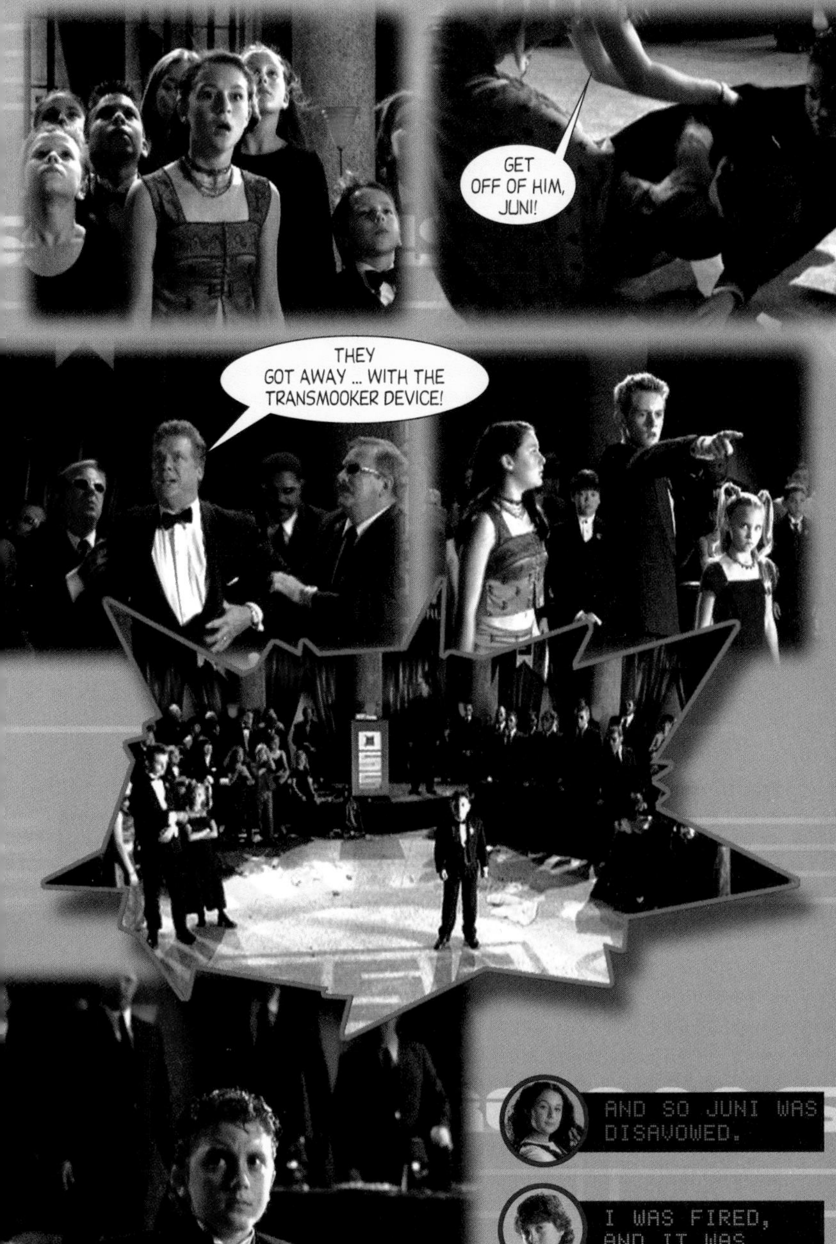
GET OFF OF HIM, JUNI!
THEY GOT AWAY ... WITH THE TRANSMOOKER DEVICE!
AND SO JUNI WAS DISAVOWED.
I WAS FIRED, AND IT WAS TOTALLY UNFAIR!

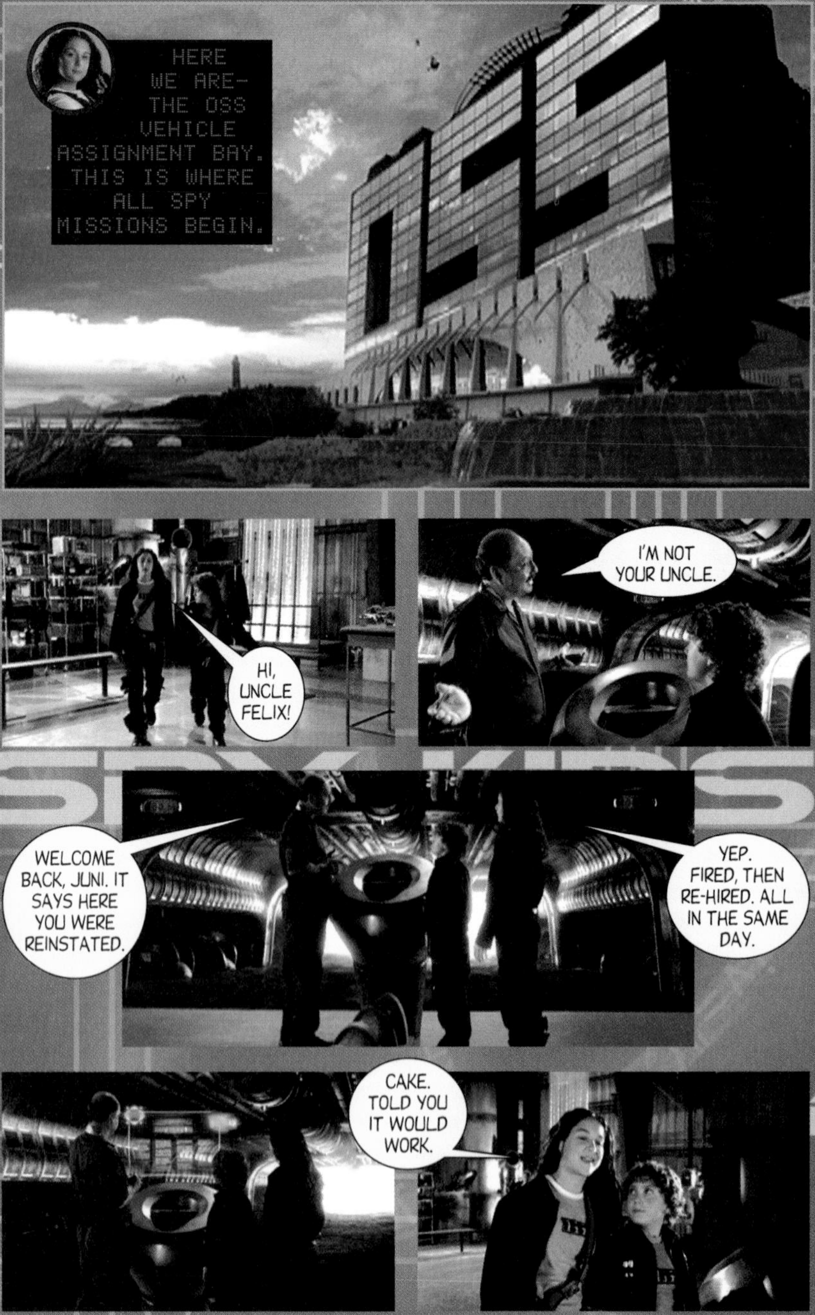
HERE WE ARE– THE OSS VEHICLE ASSIGNMENT BAY. THIS IS WHERE ALL SPY MISSIONS BEGIN.
HI, UNCLE FELIX!
I'M NOT YOUR UNCLE.
WELCOME BACK, JUNI. IT SAYS HERE YOU WERE REINSTATED.
YEP. FIRED, THEN RE-HIRED. ALL IN THE SAME DAY.
CAKE. TOLD YOU IT WOULD WORK.

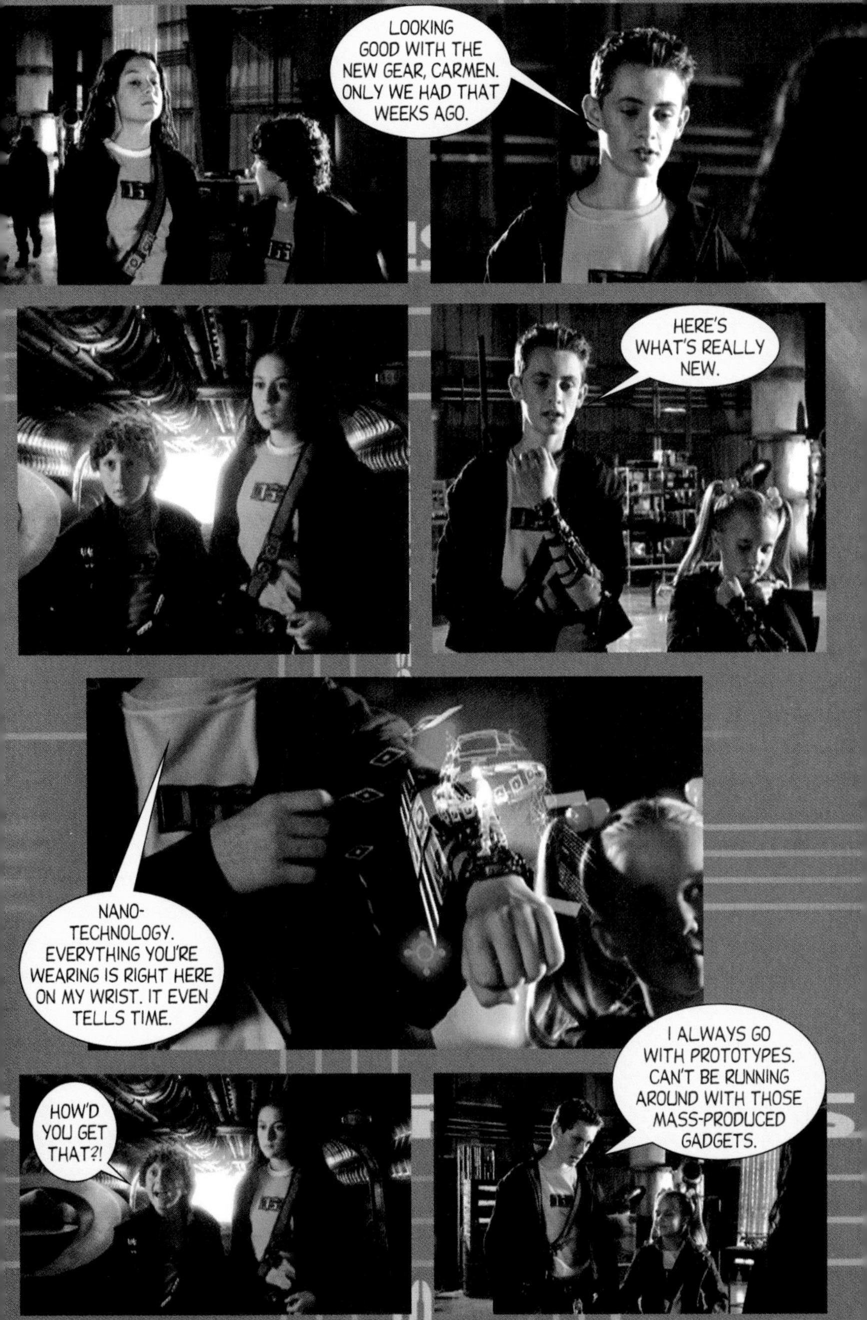
LOOKING GOOD WITH THE NEW GEAR, CARMEN. ONLY WE HAD THAT WEEKS AGO.
HERE'S WHAT'S REALLY NEW.
NANO-TECHNOLOGY. EVERYTHING YOU'RE WEARING IS RIGHT HERE ON MY WRIST. IT EVEN TELLS TIME.
HOW'D YOU GET THAT?!
I ALWAYS GO WITH PROTOTYPES. CAN'T BE RUNNING AROUND WITH THOSE MASS-PRODUCED GADGETS.

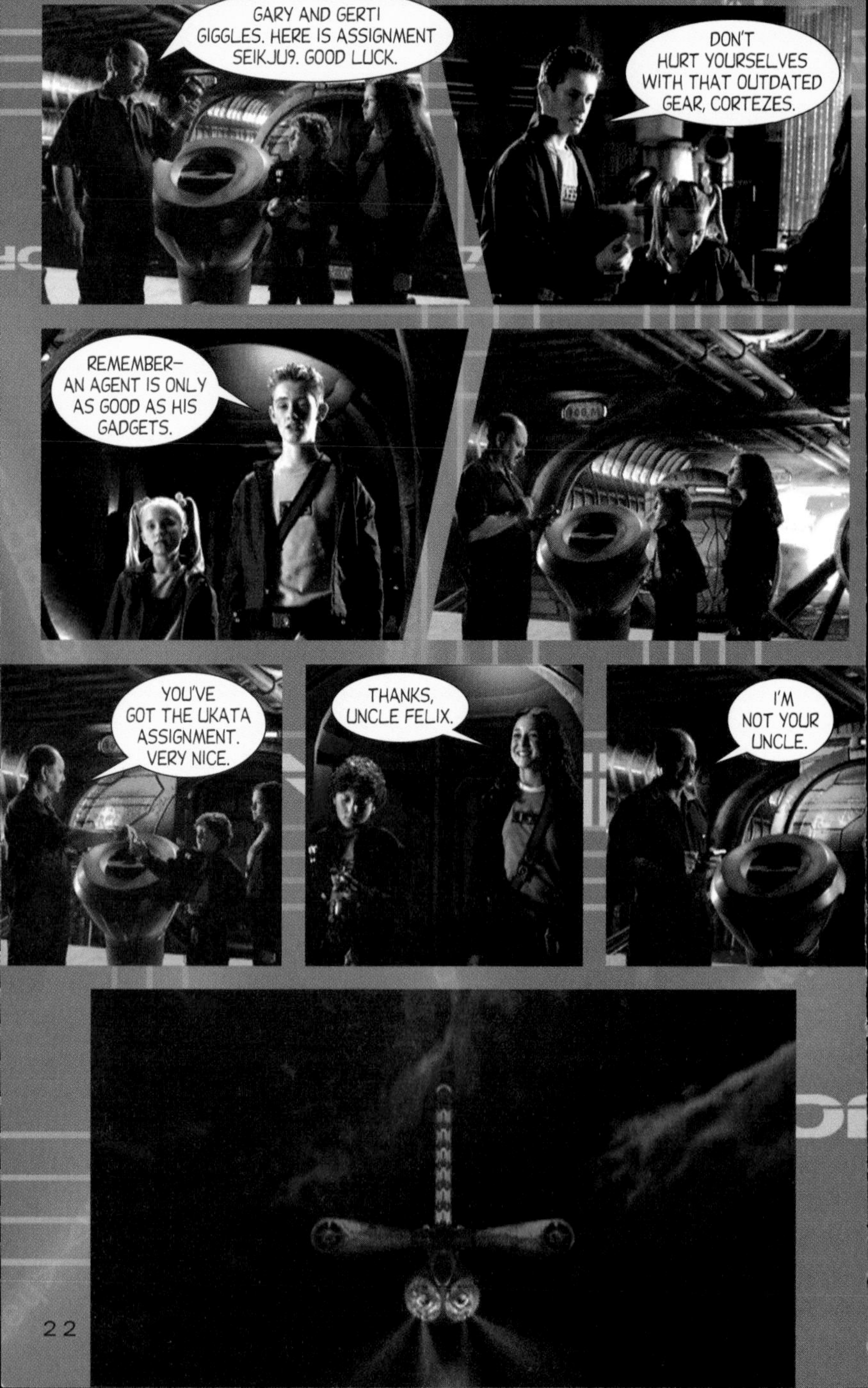
GARY AND GERTI GIGGLES. HERE IS ASSIGNMENT SEIKJU9. GOOD LUCK.
DON'T HURT YOURSELVES WITH THAT OUTDATED GEAR, CORTEZES.
REMEMBER– AN AGENT IS ONLY AS GOOD AS HIS GADGETS.
YOU'VE GOT THE UKATA ASSIGNMENT. VERY NICE.
THANKS, UNCLE FELIX.
I'M NOT YOUR UNCLE.

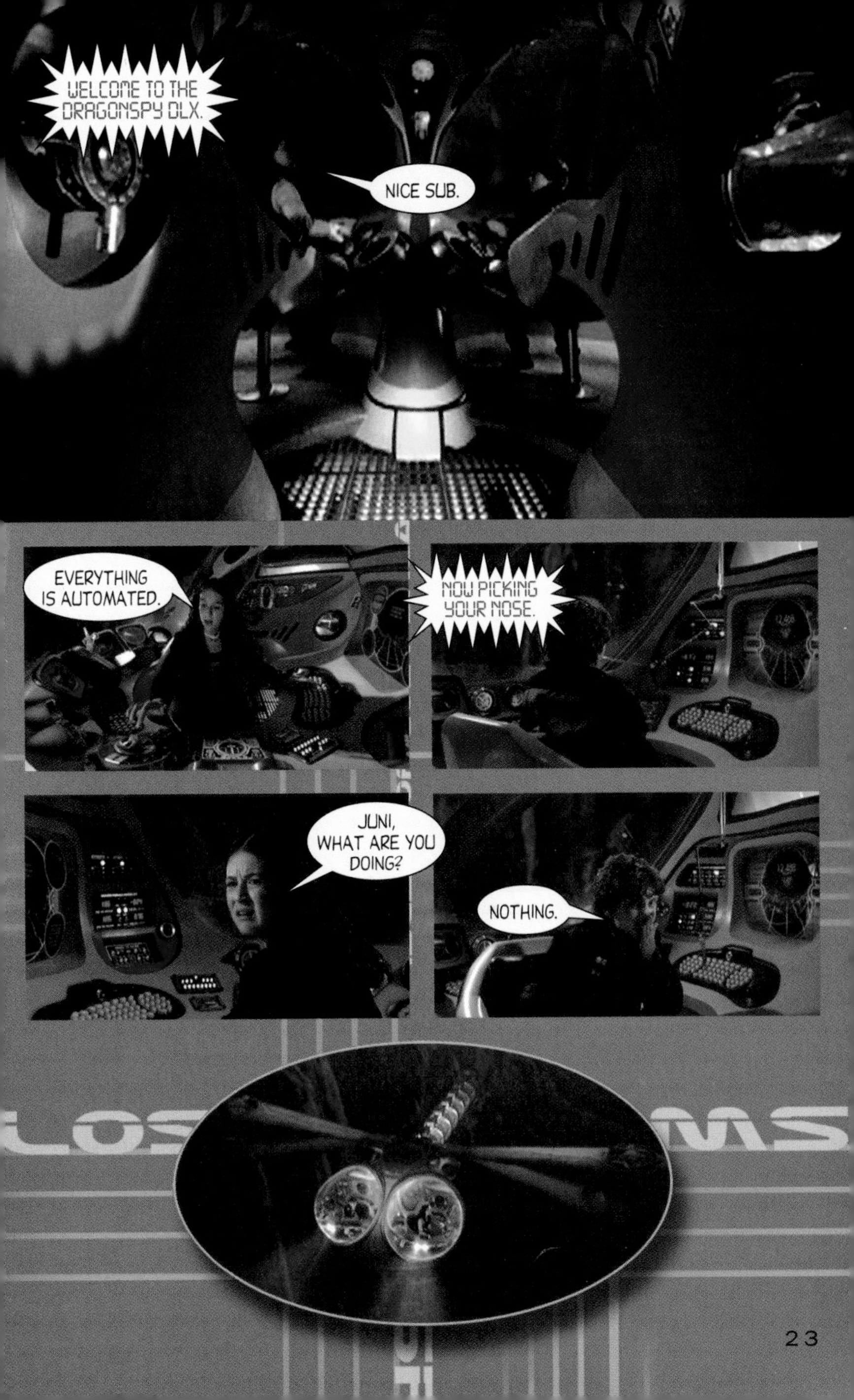
WELCOME TO THE DRAGONSPY DLX.
NICE SUB.
EVERYTHING IS AUTOMATED.
NOW PICKING YOUR NOSE.
JUNI, WHAT ARE YOU DOING?
NOTHING.

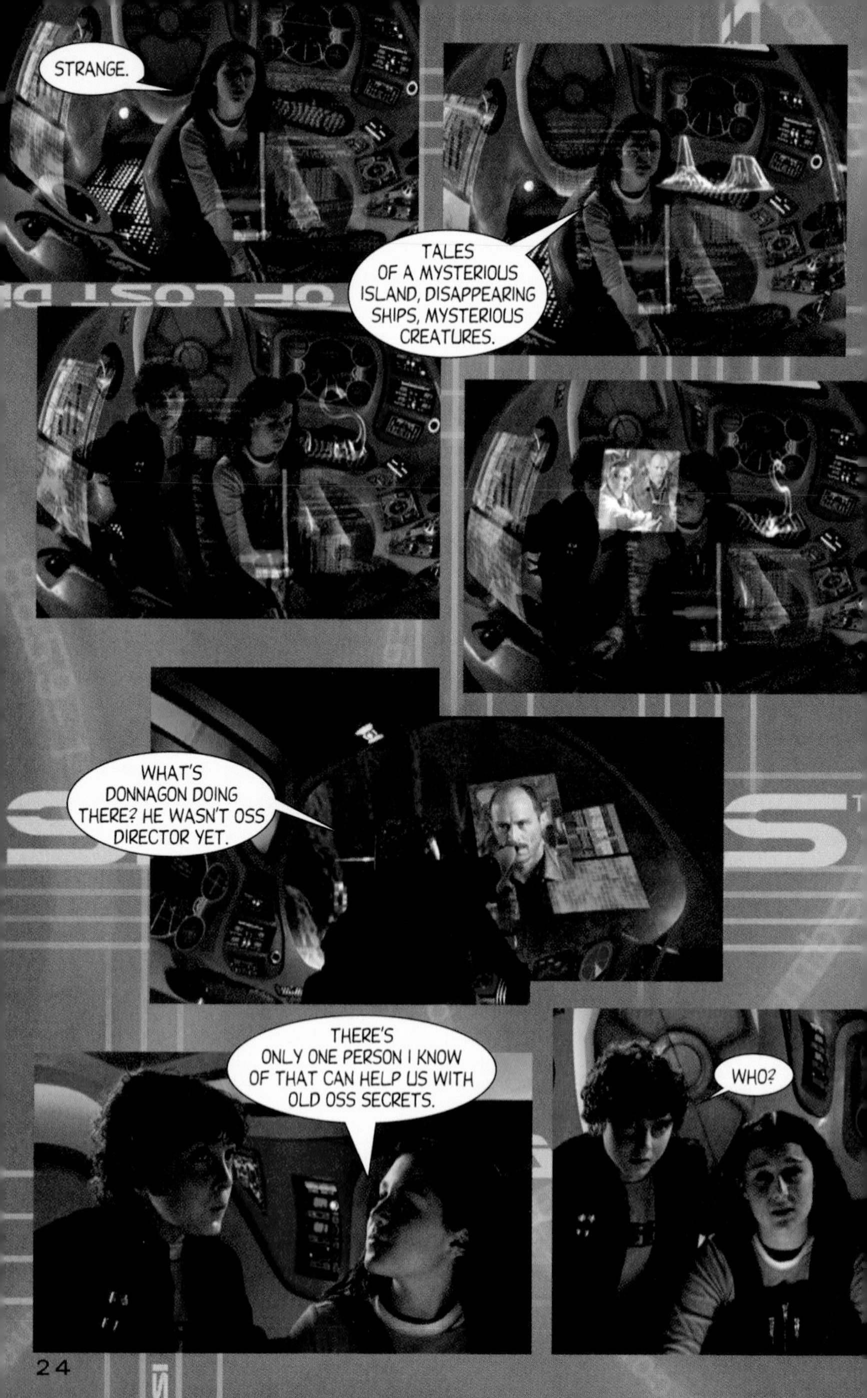
STRANGE.
TALES OF A MYSTERIOUS ISLAND, DISAPPEARING SHIPS, MYSTERIOUS CREATURES.
WHAT'S DONNAGON DOING THERE? HE WASN'T OSS DIRECTOR YET.
THERE'S ONLY ONE PERSON I KNOW OF THAT CAN HELP US WITH OLD OSS SECRETS.
WHO?

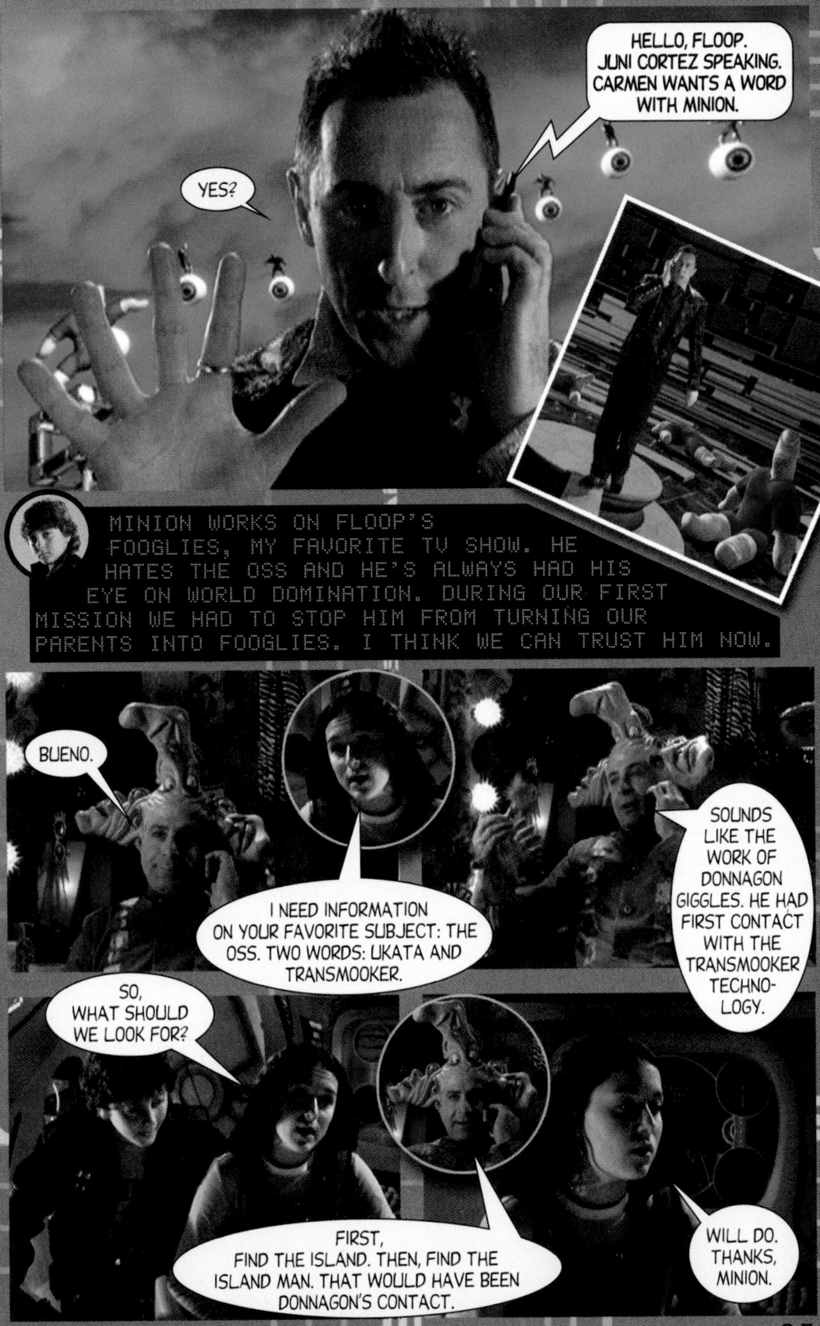
YES?
HELLO, FLOOP. JUNI CORTEZ SPEAKING. CARMEN WANTS A WORD WITH MINION.
MINION WORKS ON FLOOP'S FOOGLIES, MY FAVORITE TV SHOW. HE HATES THE OSS AND HE'S ALWAYS HAD HIS EYE ON WORLD DOMINATION. DURING OUR FIRST MISSION WE HAD TO STOP HIM FROM TURNING OUR PARENTS INTO FOOGLIES. I THINK WE CAN TRUST HIM NOW.
BUENO.
I NEED INFORMATION ON YOUR FAVORITE SUBJECT: THE OSS. TWO WORDS: UKATA AND TRANSMOOKER.
SOUNDS LIKE THE WORK OF DONNAGON GIGGLES. HE HAD FIRST CONTACT WITH THE TRANSMOOKER TECHNO-LOGY.
SO, WHAT SHOULD WE LOOK FOR?
FIRST, FIND THE ISLAND. THEN, FIND THE ISLAND MAN. THAT WOULD HAVE BEEN DONNAGON'S CONTACT.
WILL DO. THANKS, MINION.

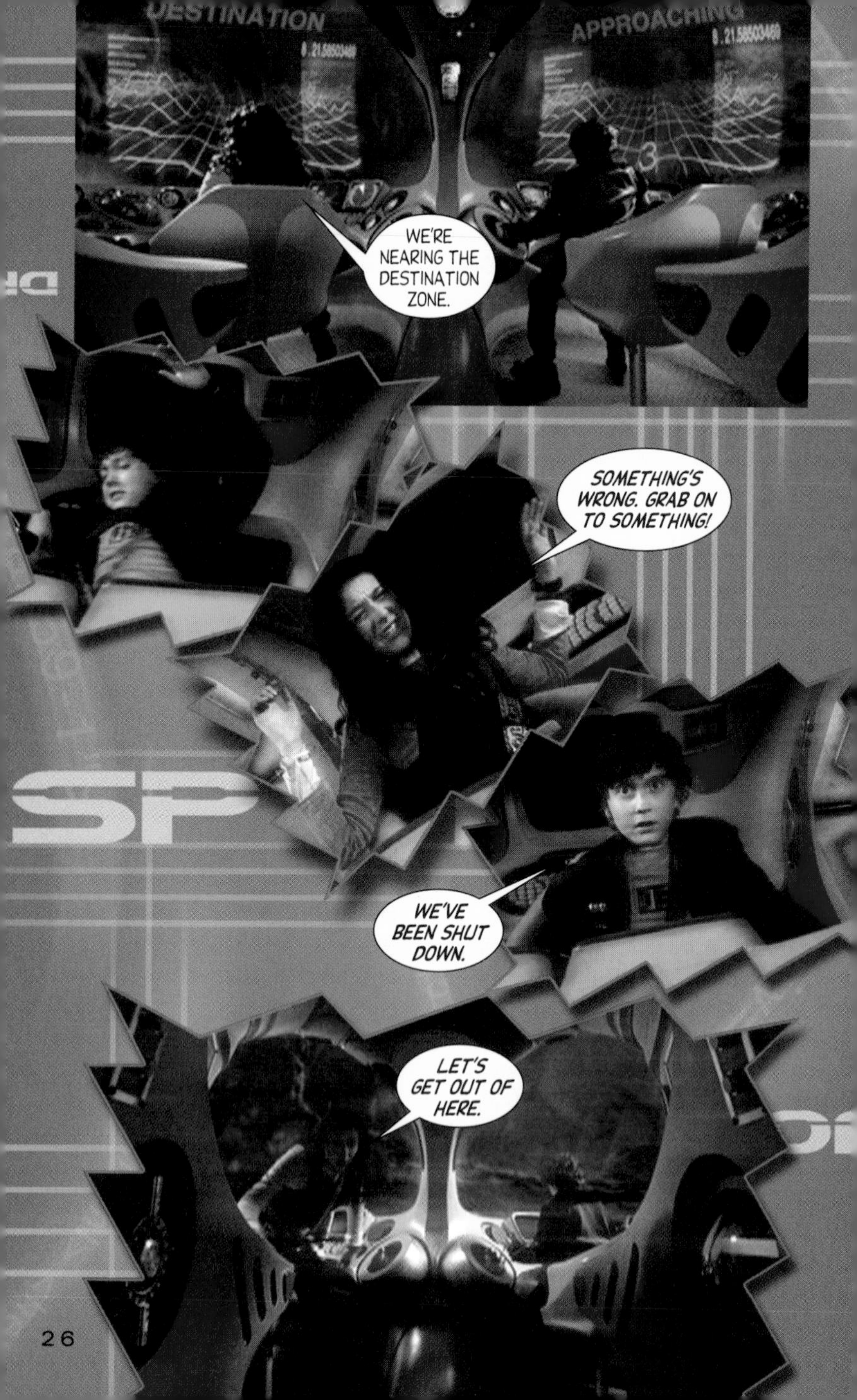
DESTINATION
APPROACHING
WE'RE NEARING THE DESTINATION ZONE.
SOMETHING'S WRONG. GRAB ON TO SOMETHING!
WE'VE BEEN SHUT DOWN.
LET'S GET OUT OF HERE.

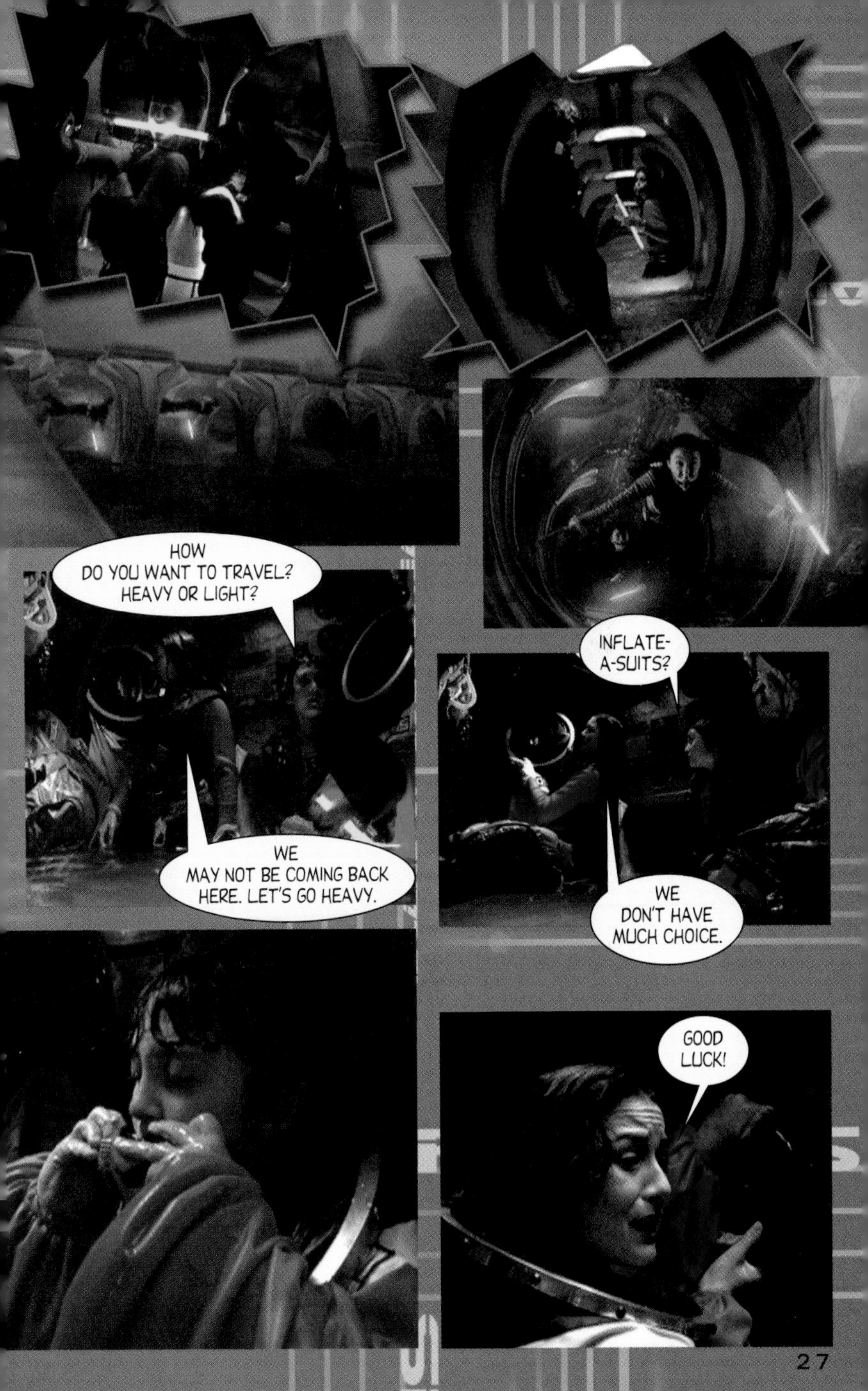
HOW DO YOU WANT TO TRAVEL? HEAVY OR LIGHT?
WE MAY NOT BE COMING BACK HERE. LET'S GO HEAVY.
INFLATE-A-SUITS?
WE DON'T HAVE MUCH CHOICE.
GOOD LUCK!

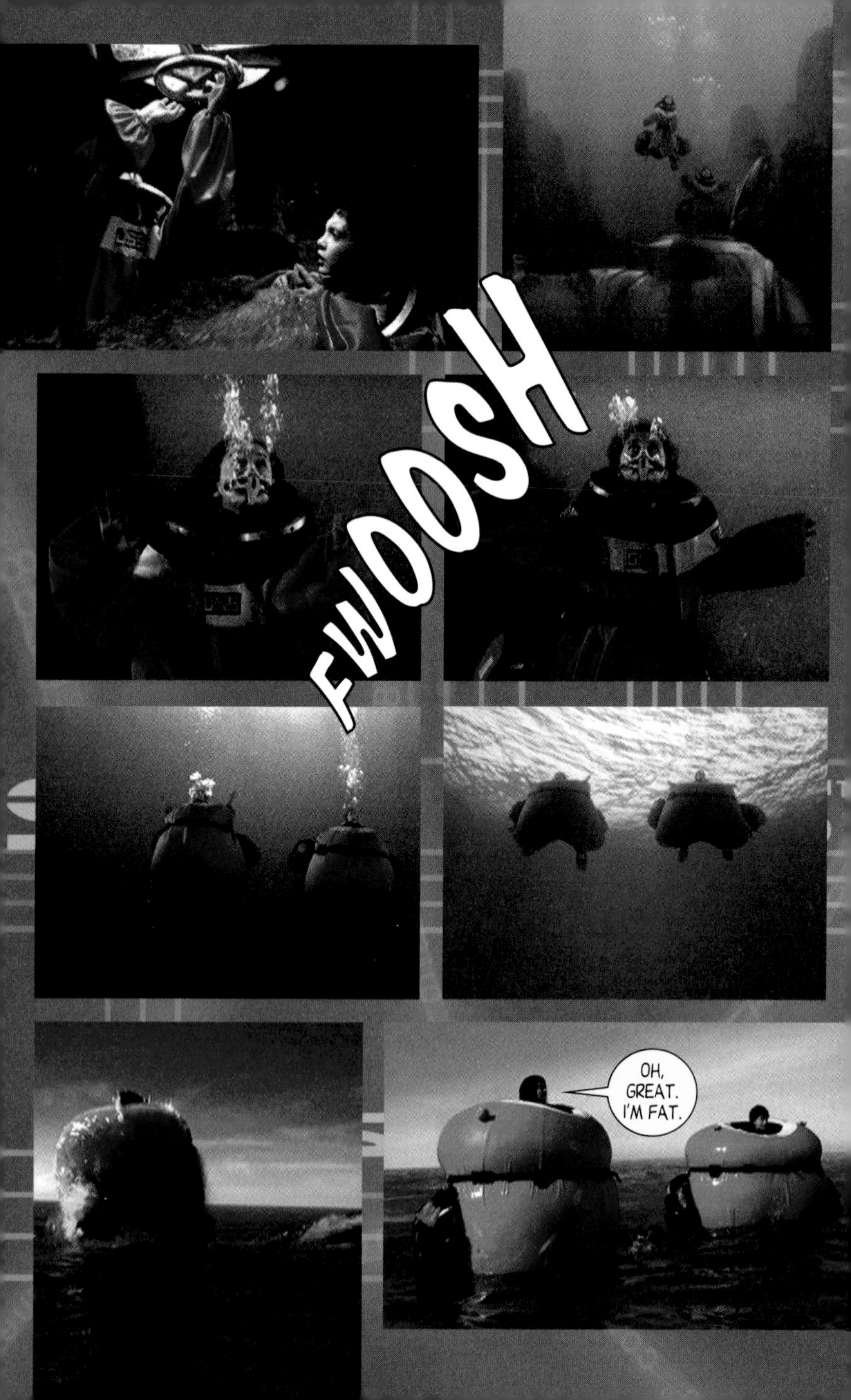
FWOOSH
OH, GREAT. I'M FAT.

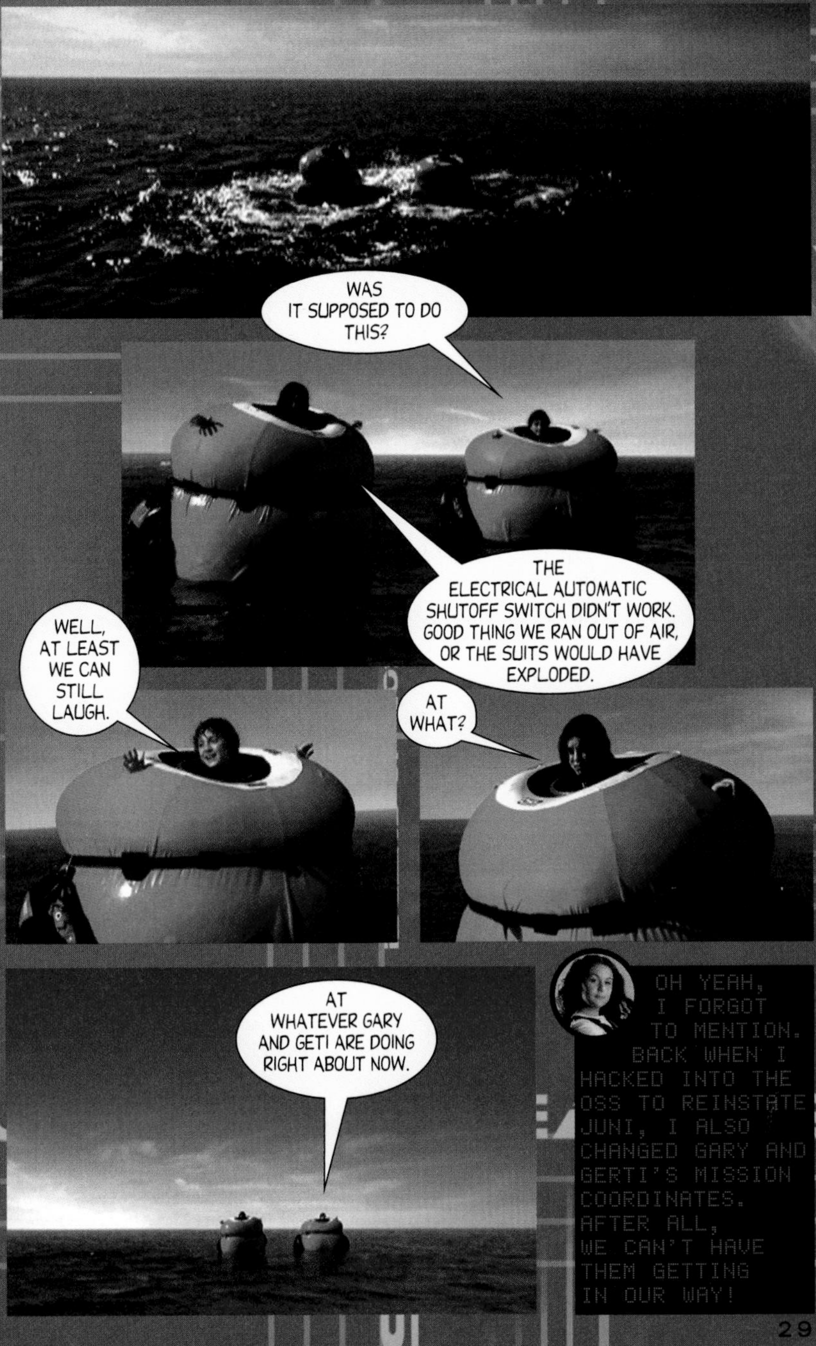
WAS IT SUPPOSED TO DO THIS?
THE ELECTRICAL AUTOMATIC SHUTOFF SWITCH DIDN'T WORK. GOOD THING WE RAN OUT OF AIR, OR THE SUITS WOULD HAVE EXPLODED.
WELL, AT LEAST WE CAN STILL LAUGH.
AT WHAT?
AT WHATEVER GARY AND GETI ARE DOING RIGHT ABOUT NOW.
OH YEAH, I FORGOT TO MENTION. BACK WHEN I HACKED INTO THE OSS TO REINSTATE JUNI, I ALSO CHANGED GARY AND GERTI'S MISSION COORDINATES. AFTER ALL, WE CAN'T HAVE THEM GETTING IN OUR WAY!

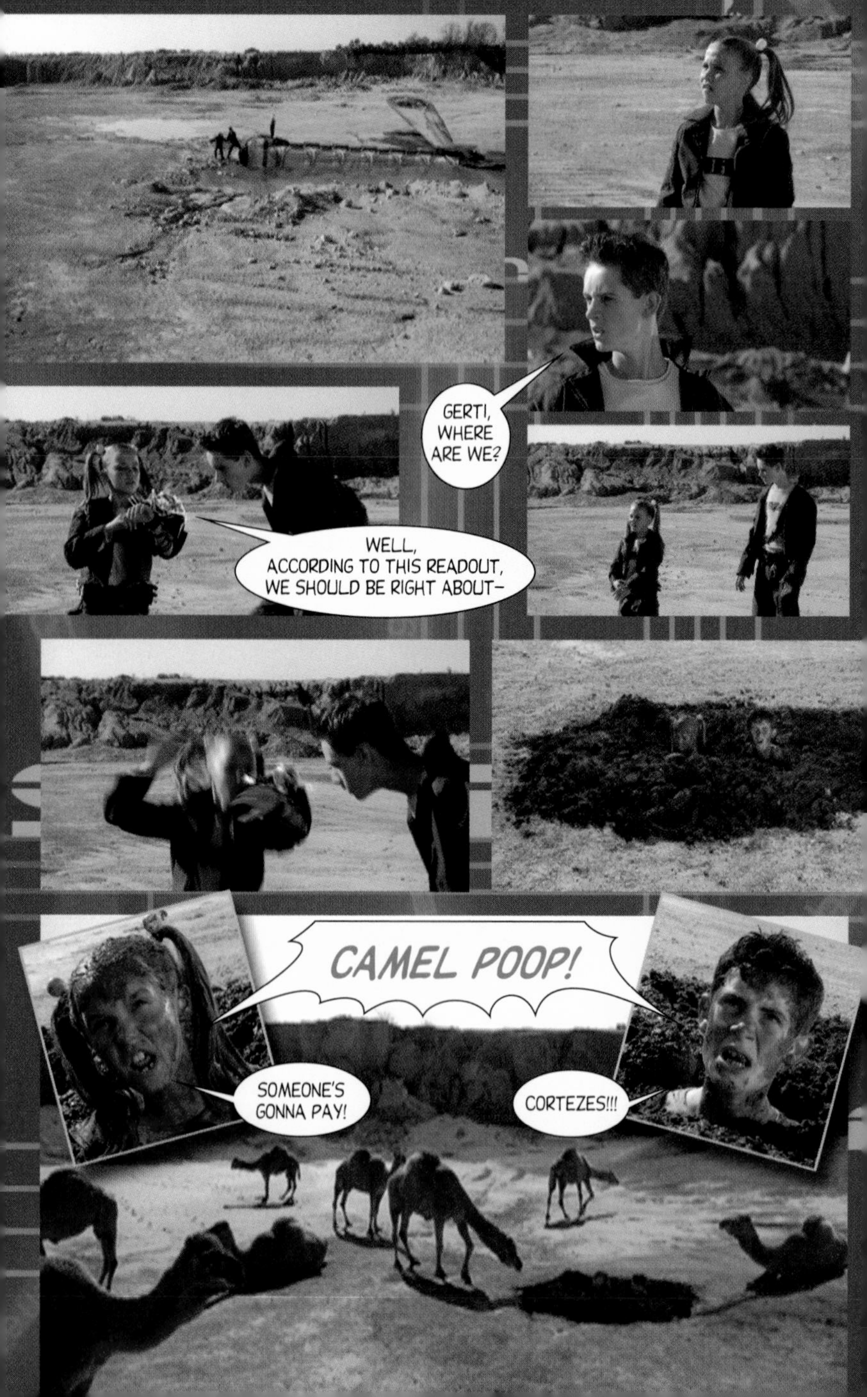
GERTI, WHERE ARE WE?
WELL, ACCORDING TO THIS READOUT, WE SHOULD BE RIGHT ABOUT—
CAMEL POOP!
SOMEONE'S GONNA PAY!
CORTEZES!!!

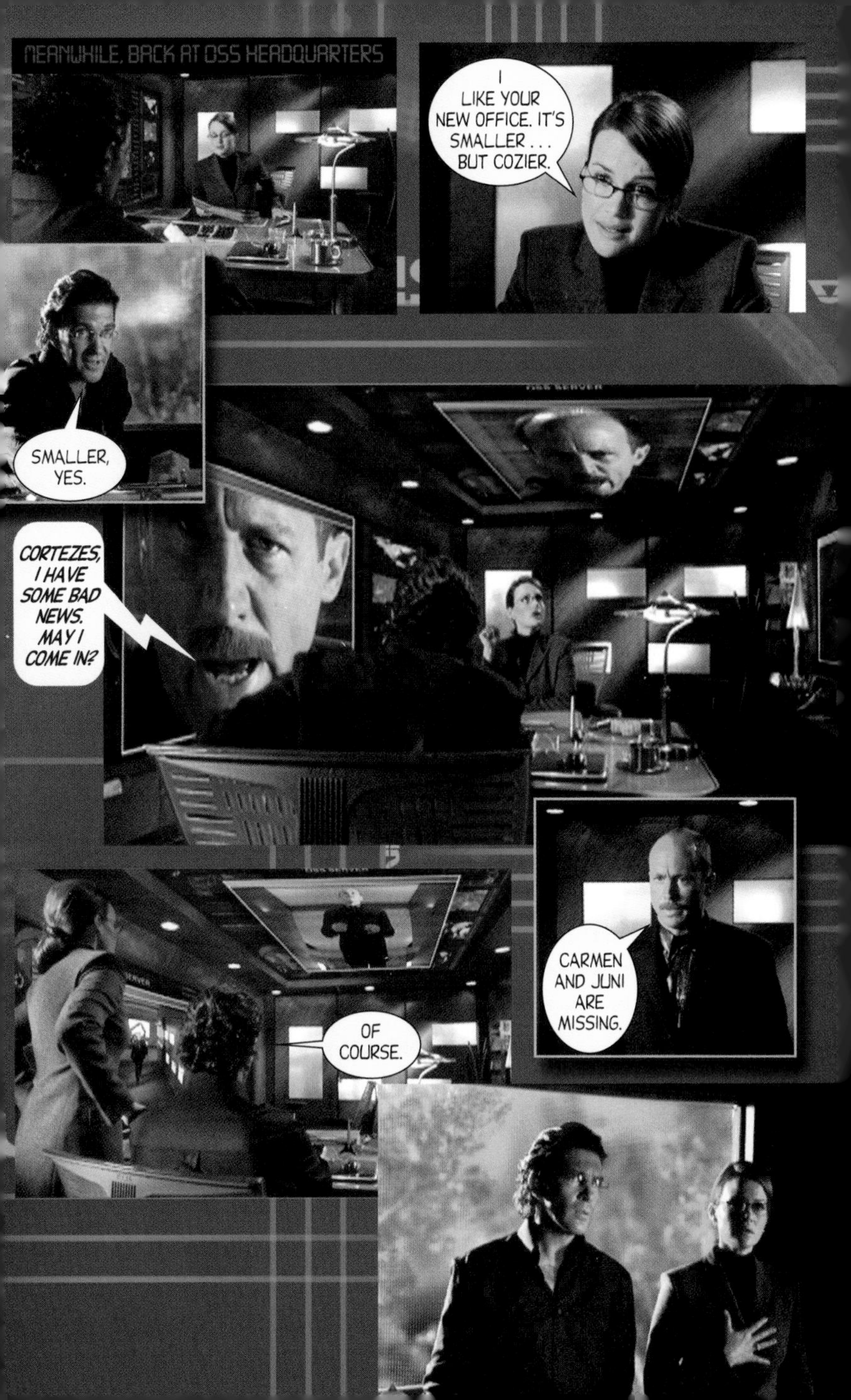
MEANWHILE, BACK AT OSS HEADQUARTERS
I LIKE YOUR NEW OFFICE. IT'S SMALLER . . . BUT COZIER.
SMALLER, YES.
CORTEZES, I HAVE SOME BAD NEWS. MAY I COME IN?
OF COURSE.
CARMEN AND JUNI ARE MISSING.

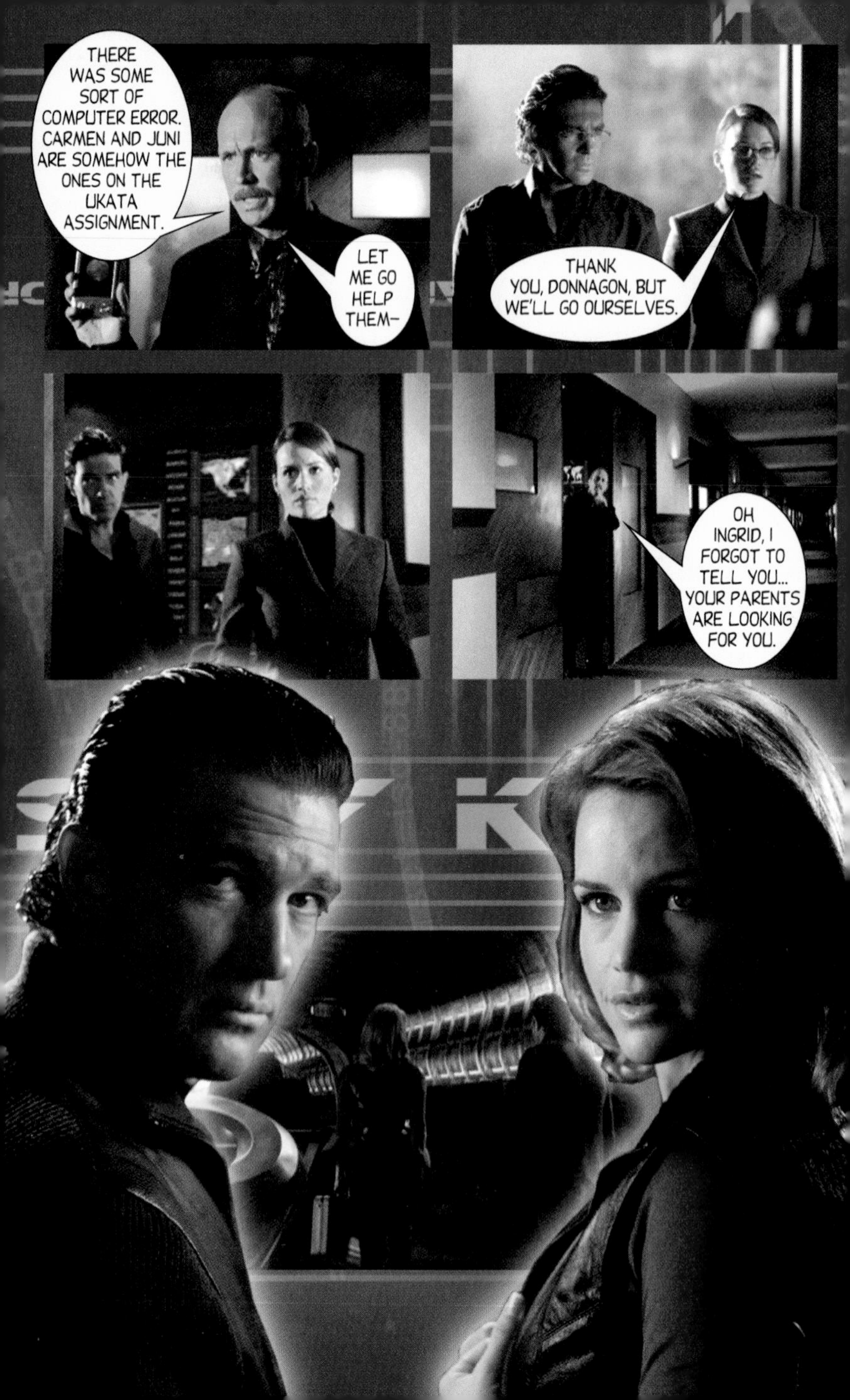
THERE WAS SOME SORT OF COMPUTER ERROR. CARMEN AND JUNI ARE SOMEHOW THE ONES ON THE UKATA ASSIGNMENT.
LET ME GO HELP THEM–
THANK YOU, DONNAGON, BUT WE'LL GO OURSELVES.
OH INGRID, I FORGOT TO TELL YOU... YOUR PARENTS ARE LOOKING FOR YOU.

CHAPTER 2

SPY KIDS

ISLAND OF LOST DREAMS

THE ISLAND OF DR. ROMERO

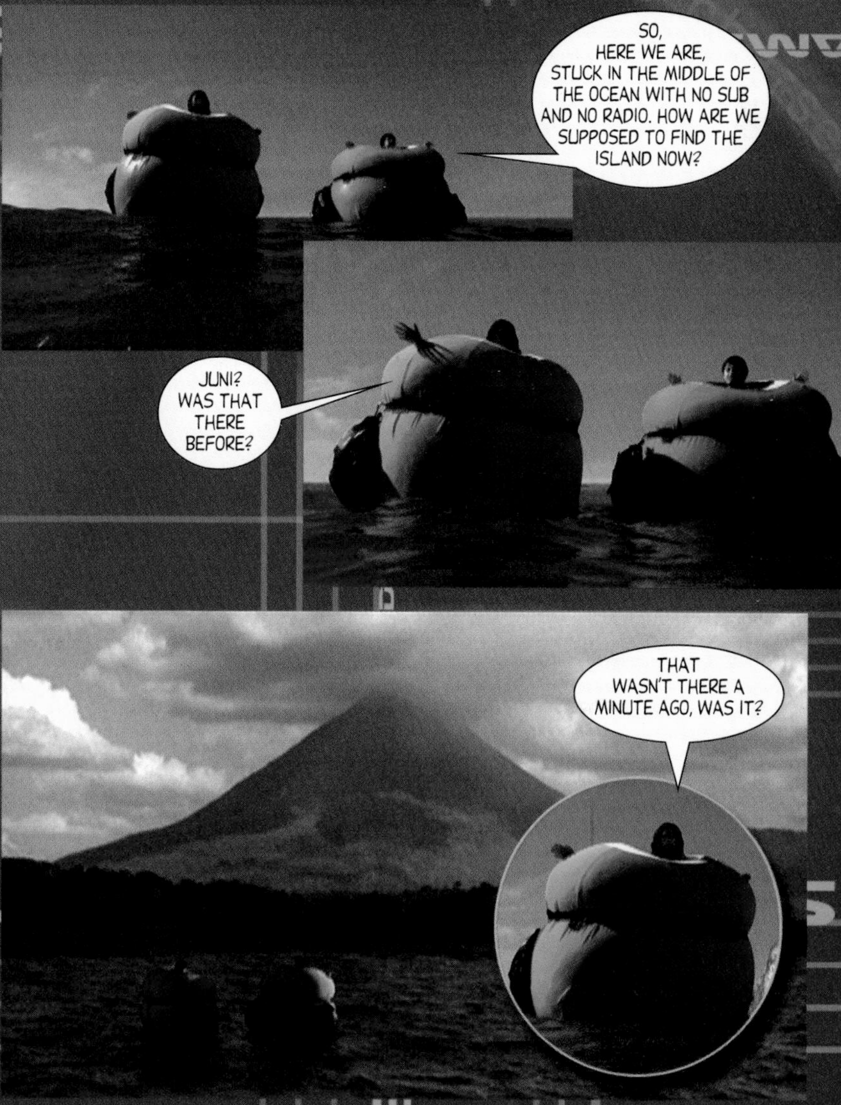
SO, HERE WE ARE, STUCK IN THE MIDDLE OF THE OCEAN WITH NO SUB AND NO RADIO. HOW ARE WE SUPPOSED TO FIND THE ISLAND NOW?
JUNI? WAS THAT THERE BEFORE?
THAT WASN'T THERE A MINUTE AGO, WAS IT?

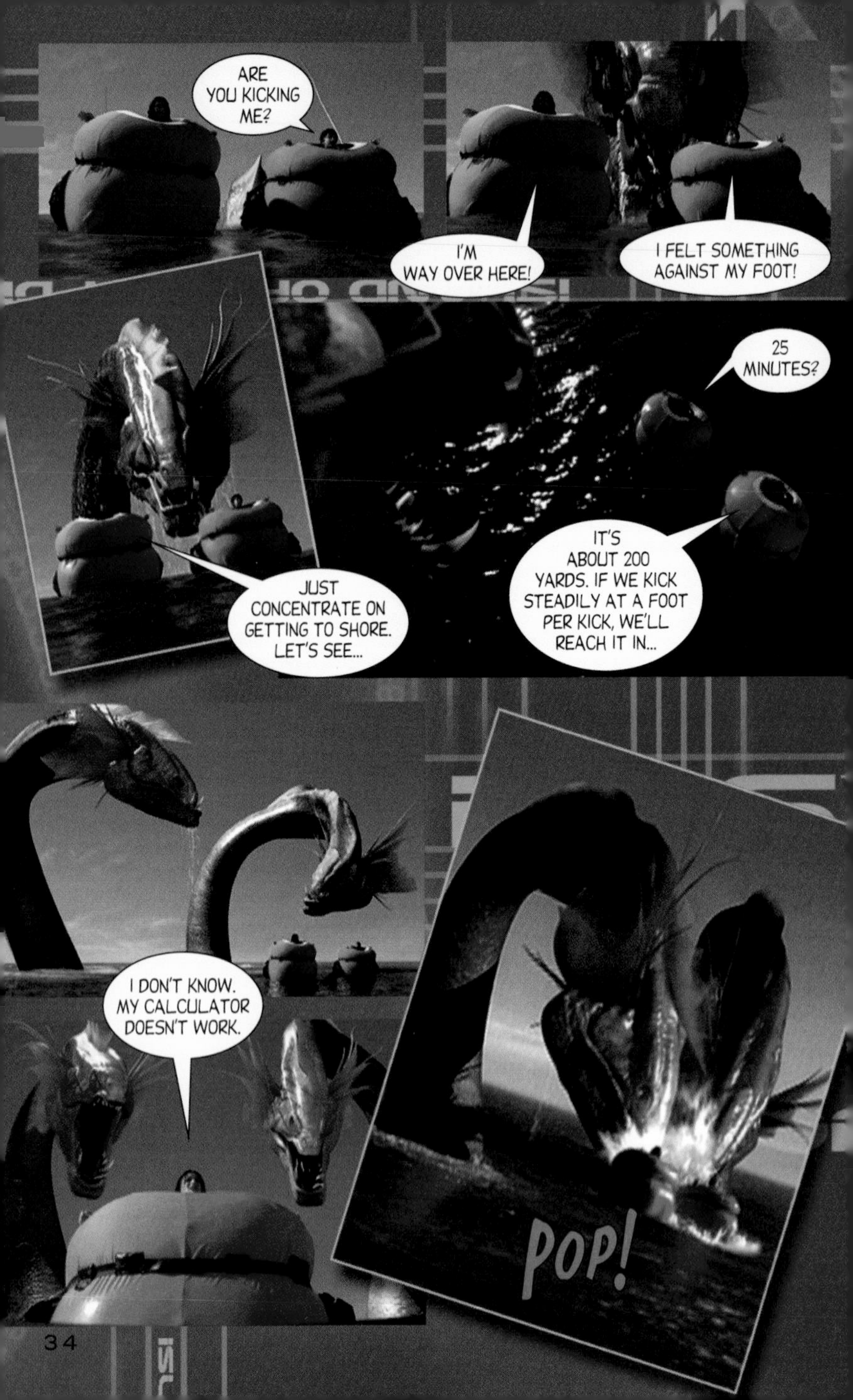

ARE YOU KICKING ME?
I'M WAY OVER HERE!
I FELT SOMETHING AGAINST MY FOOT!
JUST CONCENTRATE ON GETTING TO SHORE. LET'S SEE...
IT'S ABOUT 200 YARDS. IF WE KICK STEADILY AT A FOOT PER KICK, WE'LL REACH IT IN...
25 MINUTES?
I DON'T KNOW. MY CALCULATOR DOESN'T WORK.
POP!

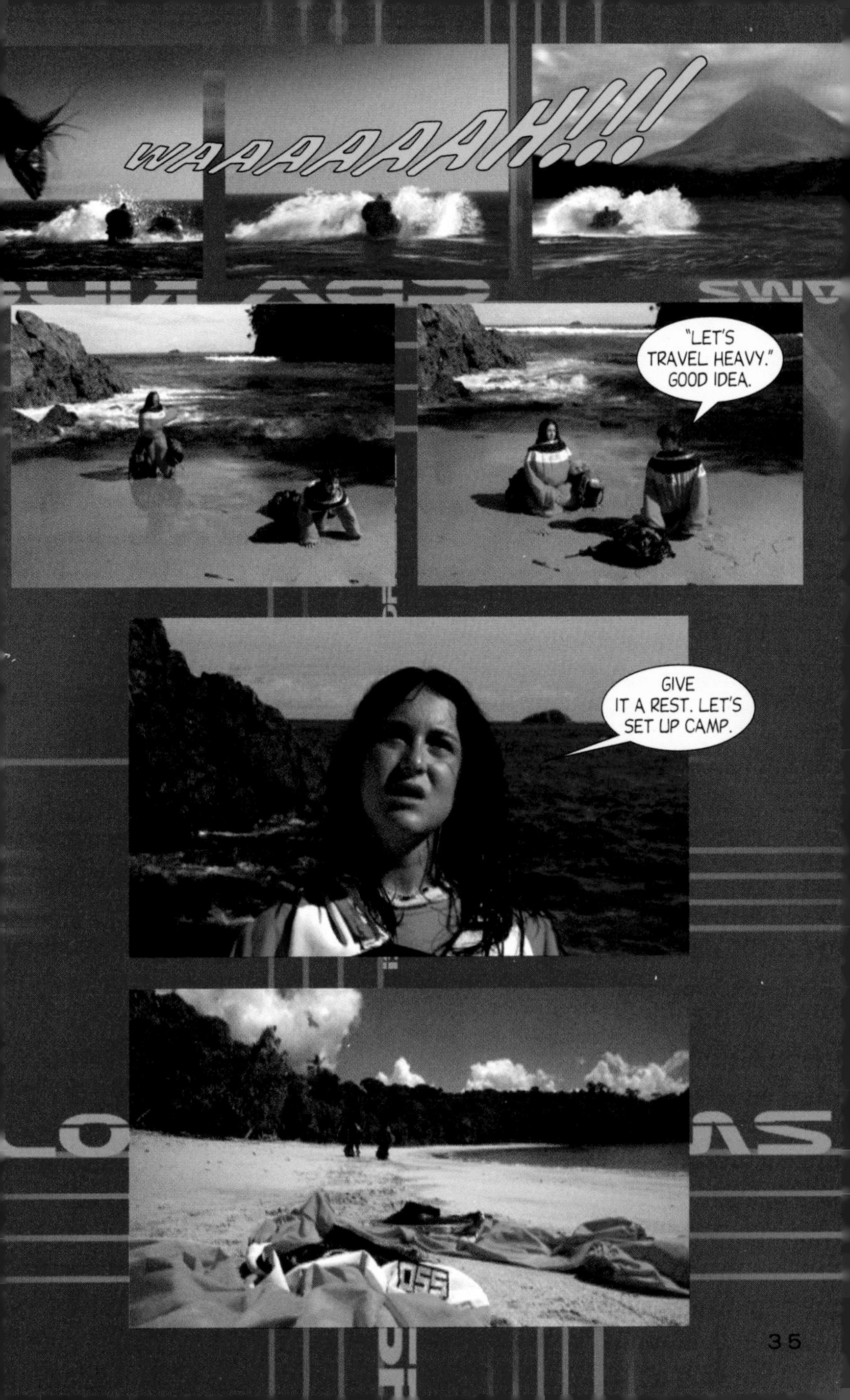
WAAAAAAAH!!!
"LET'S TRAVEL HEAVY." GOOD IDEA.
GIVE IT A REST. LET'S SET UP CAMP.

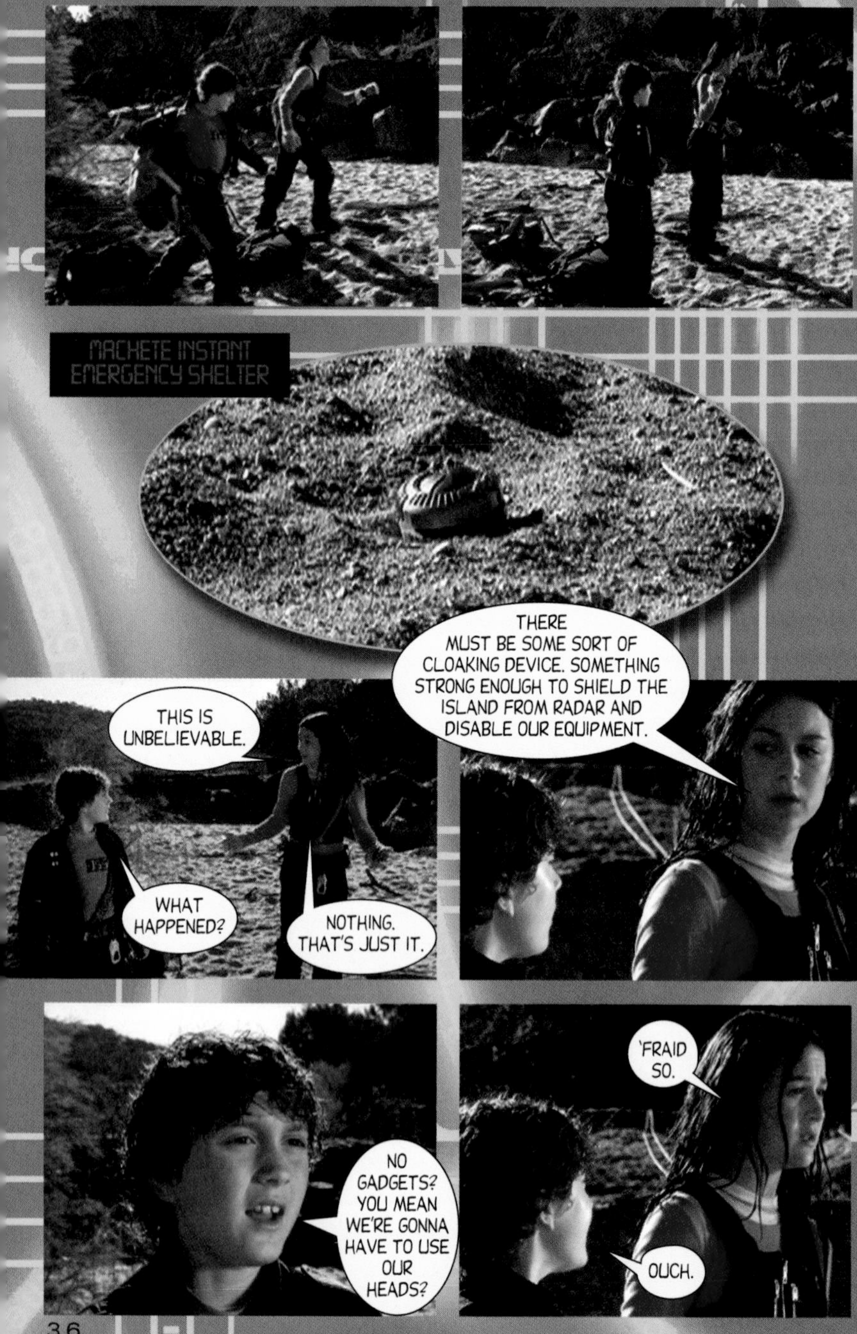
MACHETE INSTANT EMERGENCY SHELTER
THIS IS UNBELIEVABLE.
WHAT HAPPENED?
NOTHING. THAT'S JUST IT.
THERE MUST BE SOME SORT OF CLOAKING DEVICE. SOMETHING STRONG ENOUGH TO SHIELD THE ISLAND FROM RADAR AND DISABLE OUR EQUIPMENT.
NO GADGETS? YOU MEAN WE'RE GONNA HAVE TO USE OUR HEADS?
'FRAID SO.
OUCH.

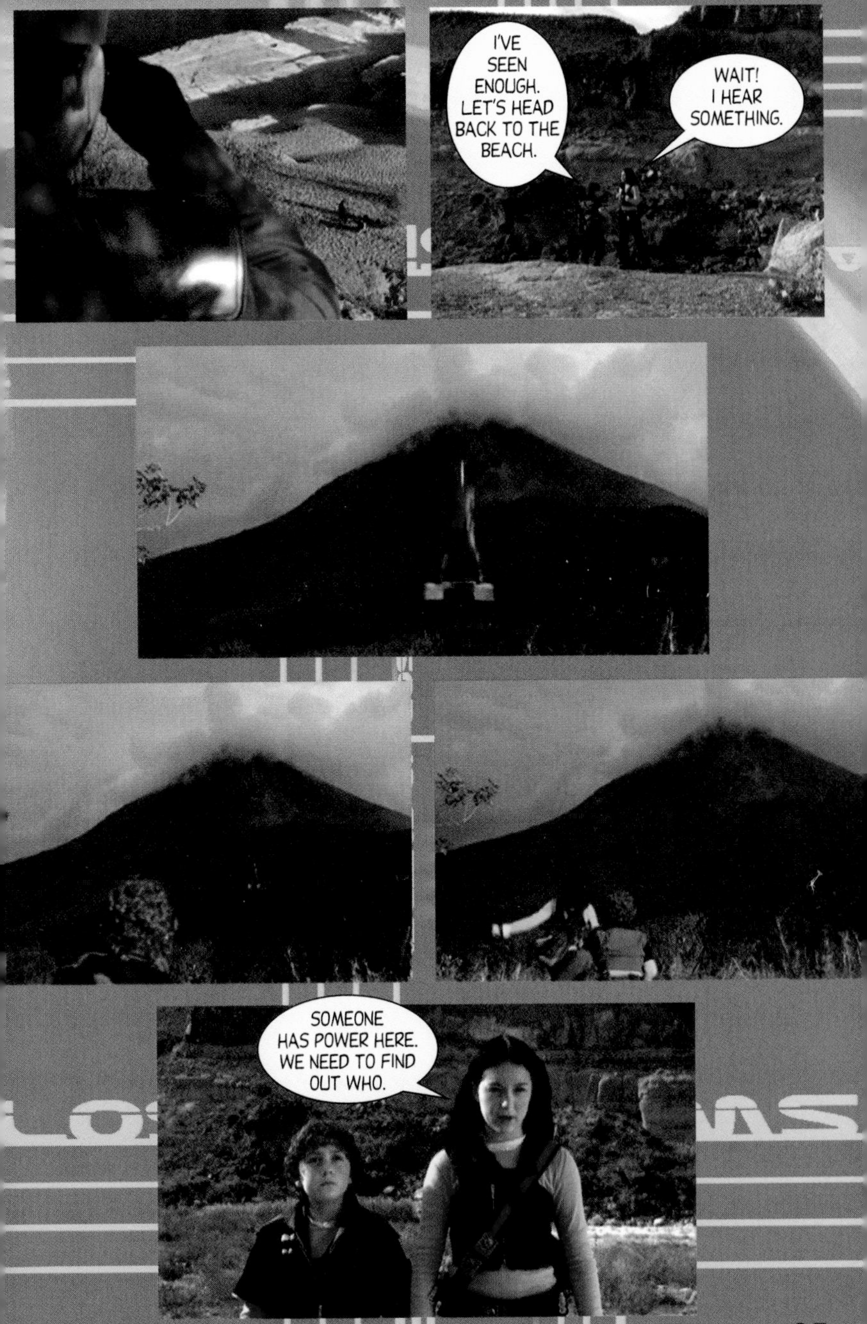
I'VE SEEN ENOUGH. LET'S HEAD BACK TO THE BEACH.
WAIT! I HEAR SOMETHING.
SOMEONE HAS POWER HERE. WE NEED TO FIND OUT WHO.

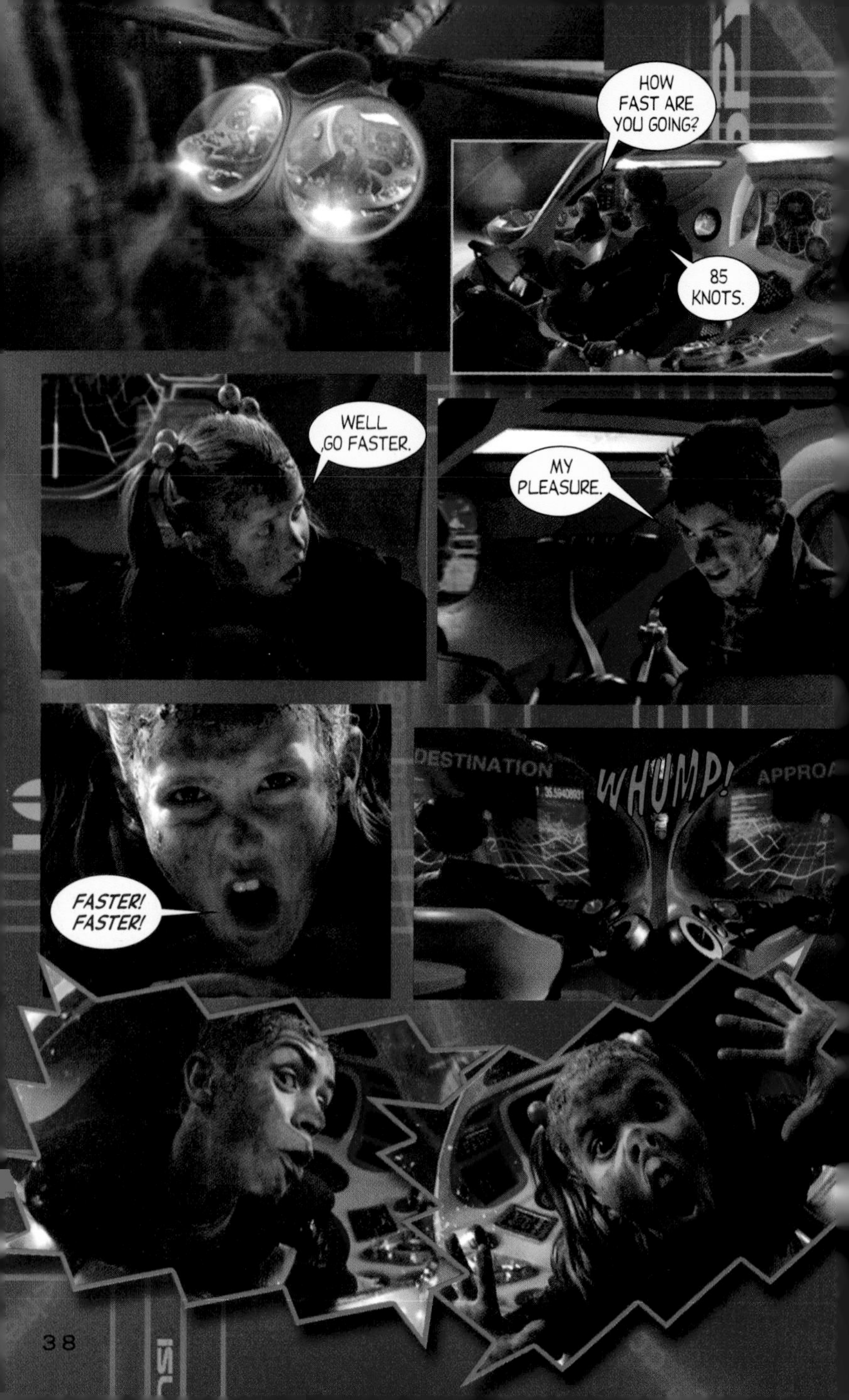
HOW FAST ARE YOU GOING?
85 KNOTS.
WELL, GO FASTER.
MY PLEASURE.
FASTER! FASTER!
DESTINATION
WHUMP!
APPROA

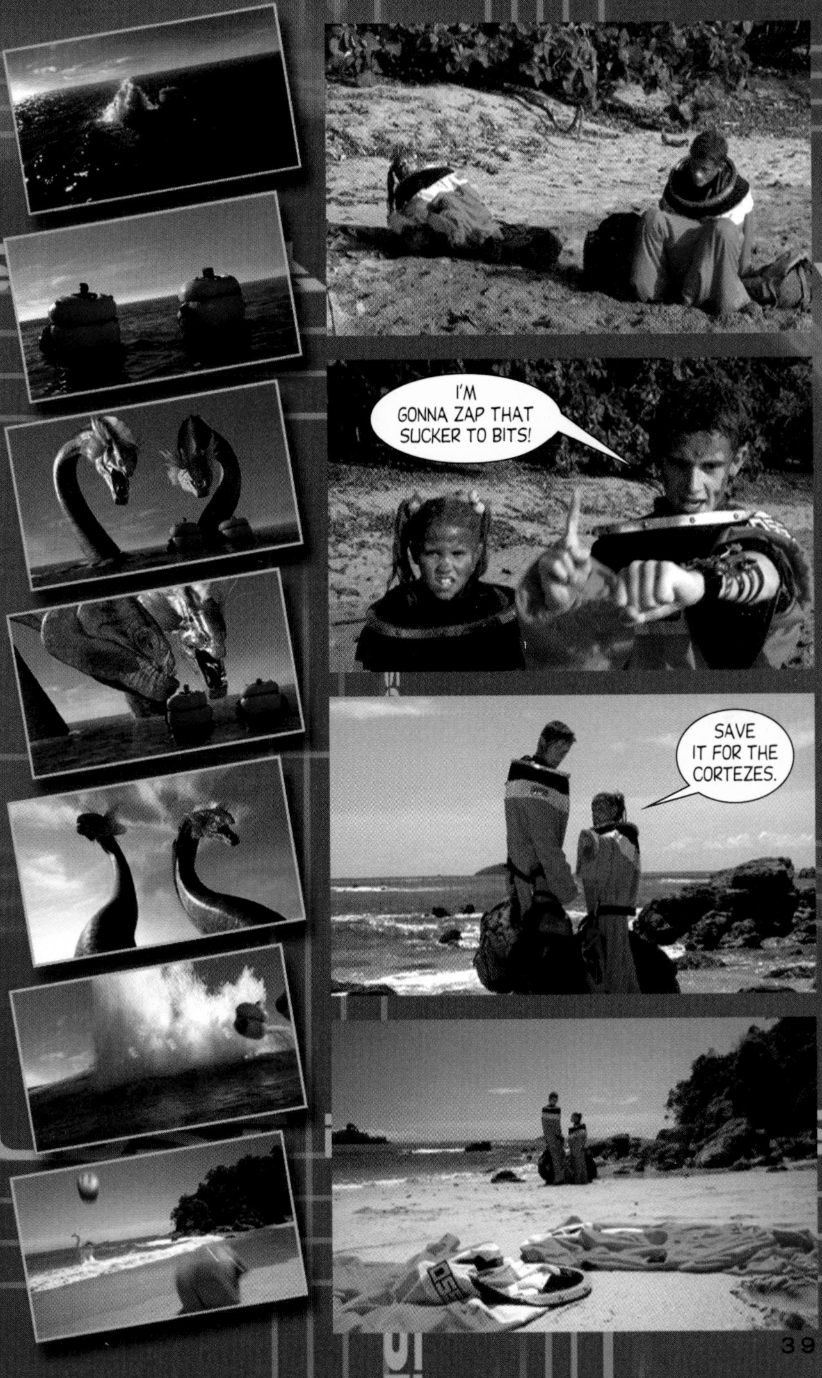
I'M GONNA ZAP THAT SUCKER TO BITS!
SAVE IT FOR THE CORTEZES.

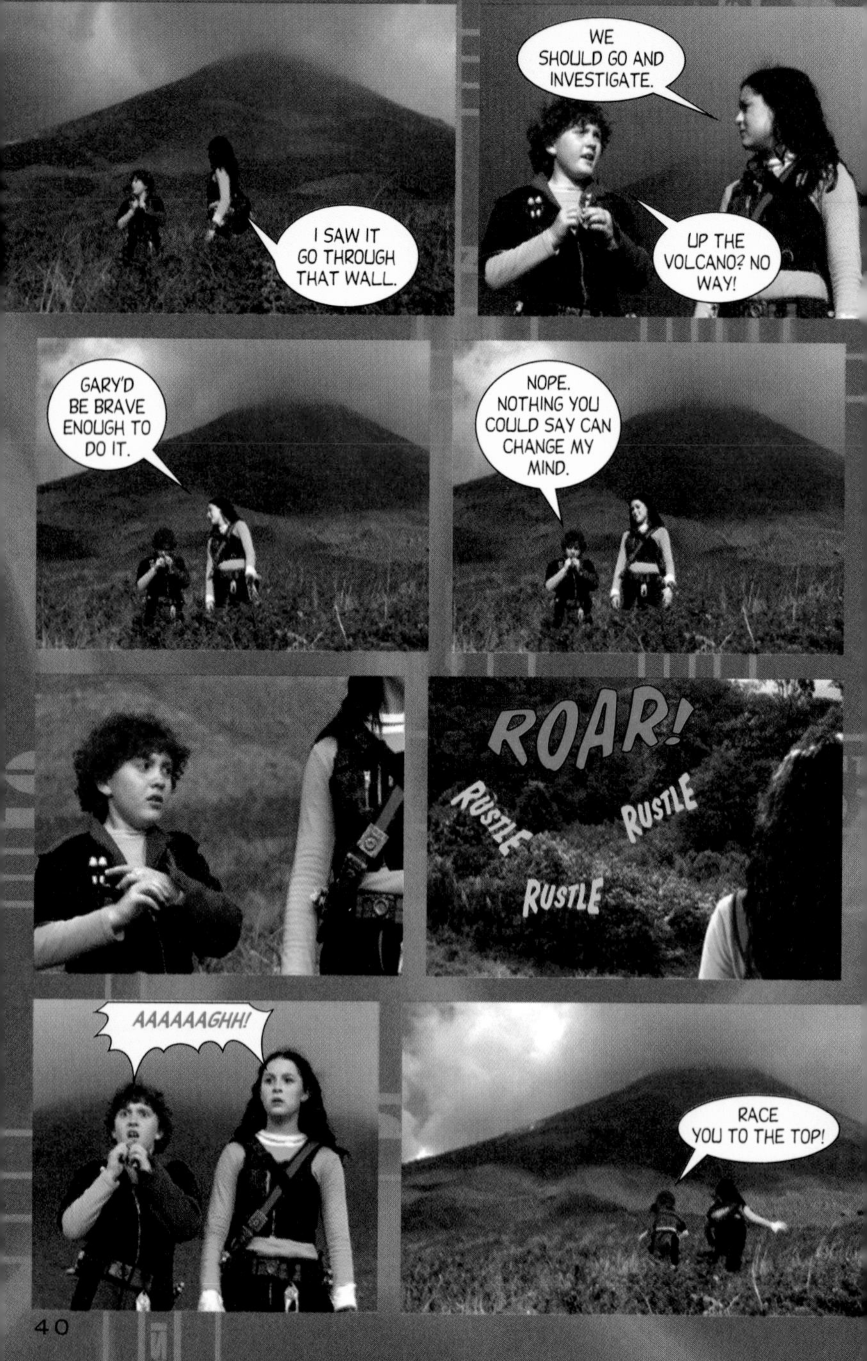
I SAW IT GO THROUGH THAT WALL.
WE SHOULD GO AND INVESTIGATE.
UP THE VOLCANO? NO WAY!
GARY'D BE BRAVE ENOUGH TO DO IT.
NOPE. NOTHING YOU COULD SAY CAN CHANGE MY MIND.
ROAR!
RUSTLE
RUSTLE
RUSTLE
AAAAAAGHH!
RACE YOU TO THE TOP!

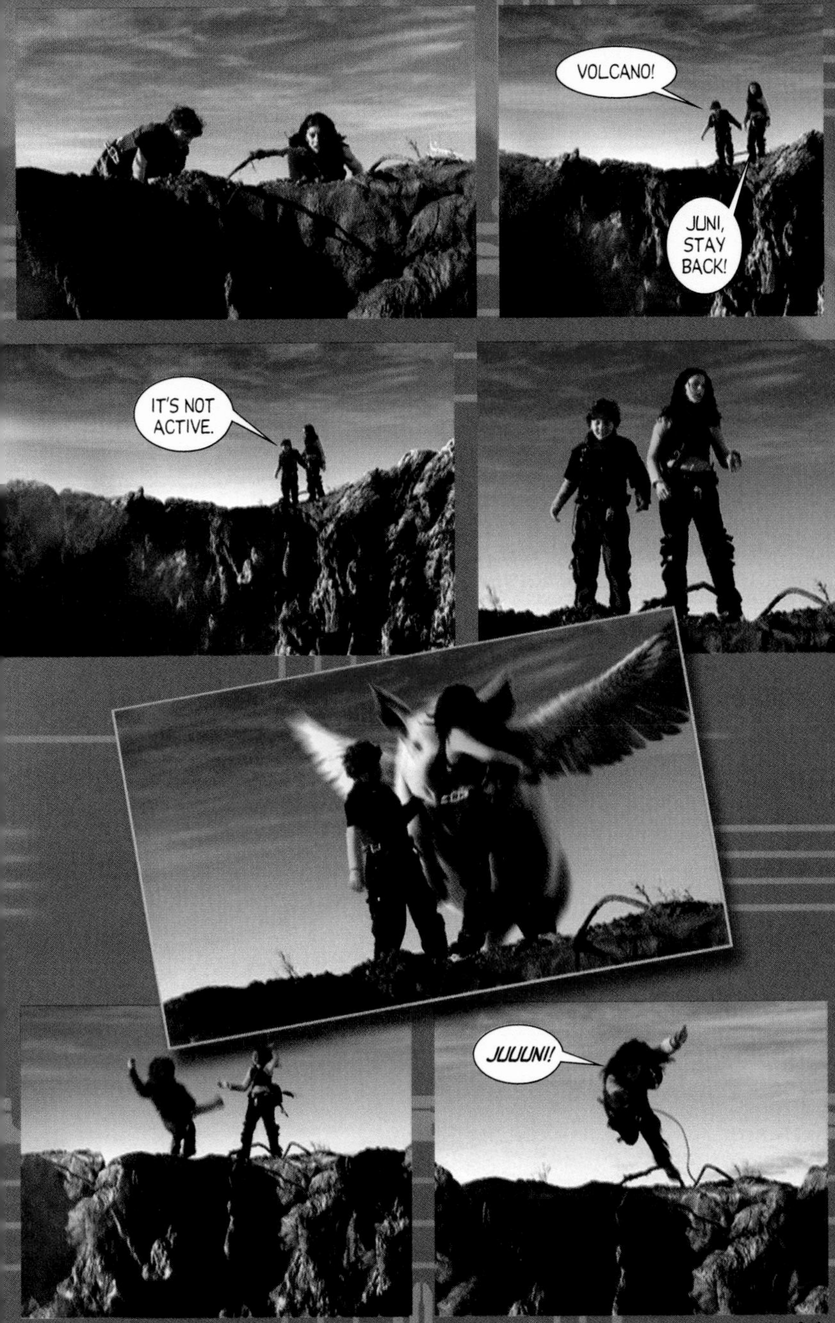
VOLCANO!
JUNI, STAY BACK!
IT'S NOT ACTIVE.
JUUUNI!

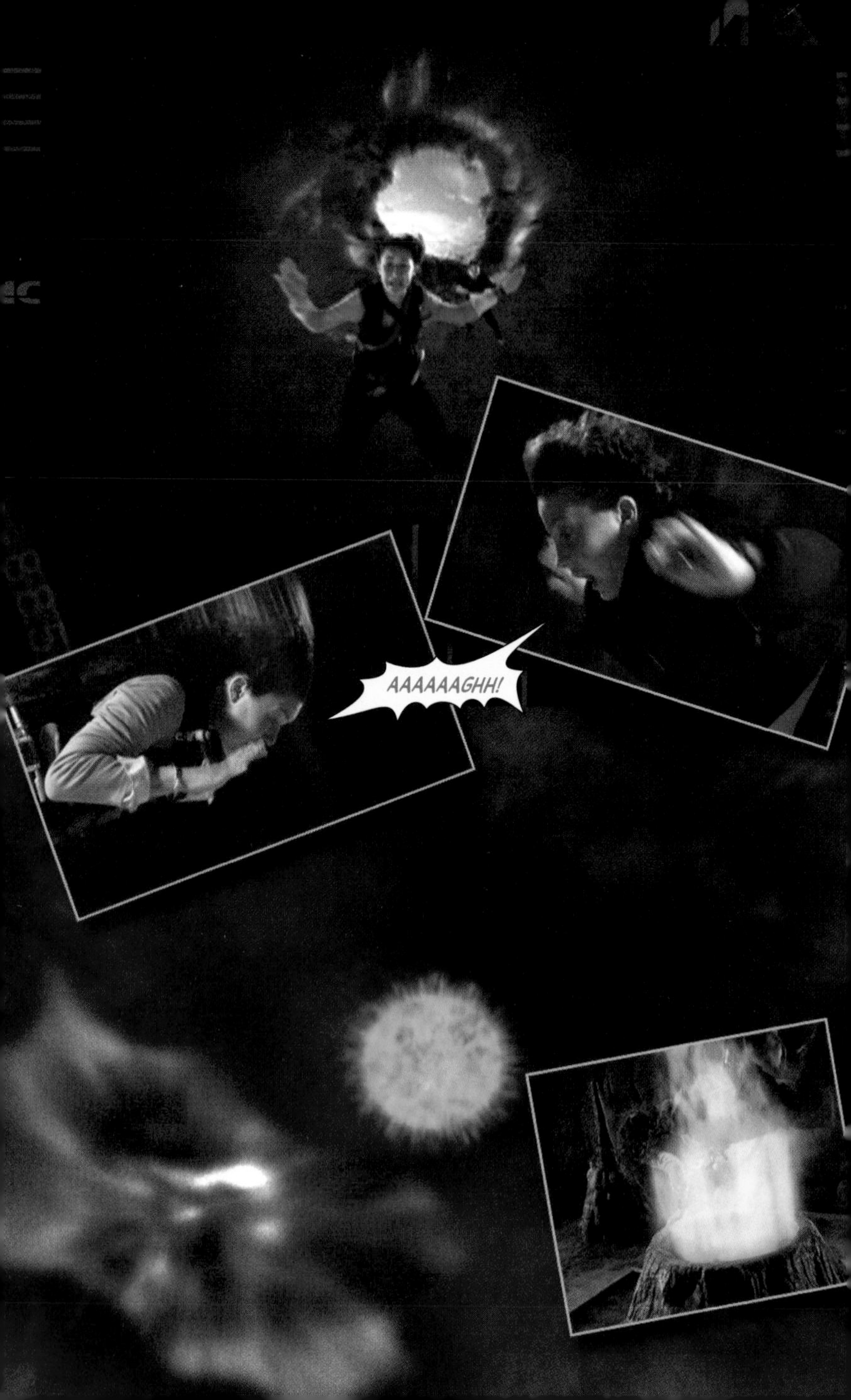
AAAAAAGHH!

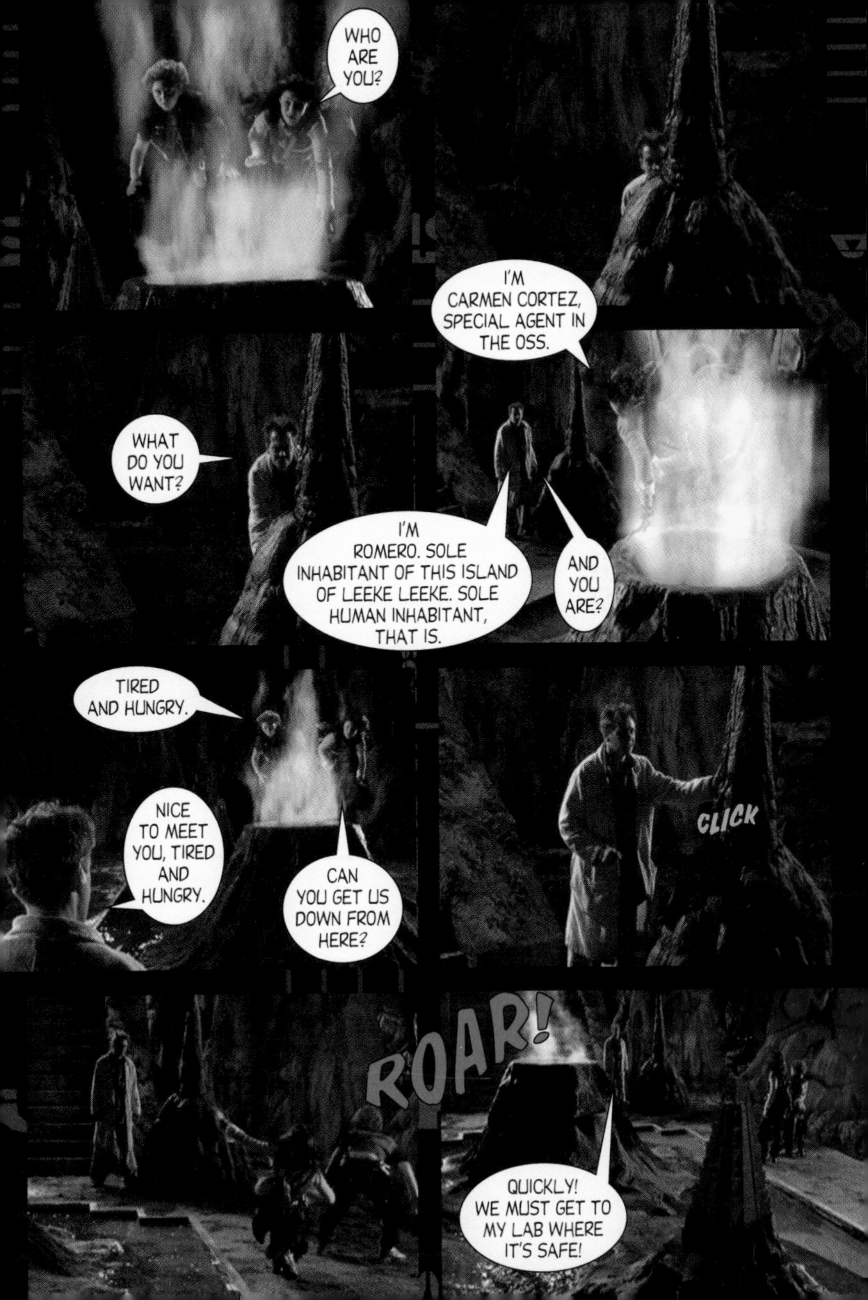
WHO ARE YOU?
I'M CARMEN CORTEZ, SPECIAL AGENT IN THE OSS.
WHAT DO YOU WANT?
I'M ROMERO. SOLE INHABITANT OF THIS ISLAND OF LEEKE LEEKE. SOLE HUMAN INHABITANT, THAT IS.
AND YOU ARE?
TIRED AND HUNGRY.
NICE TO MEET YOU, TIRED AND HUNGRY.
CAN YOU GET US DOWN FROM HERE?
CLICK
ROAR!
QUICKLY! WE MUST GET TO MY LAB WHERE IT'S SAFE!

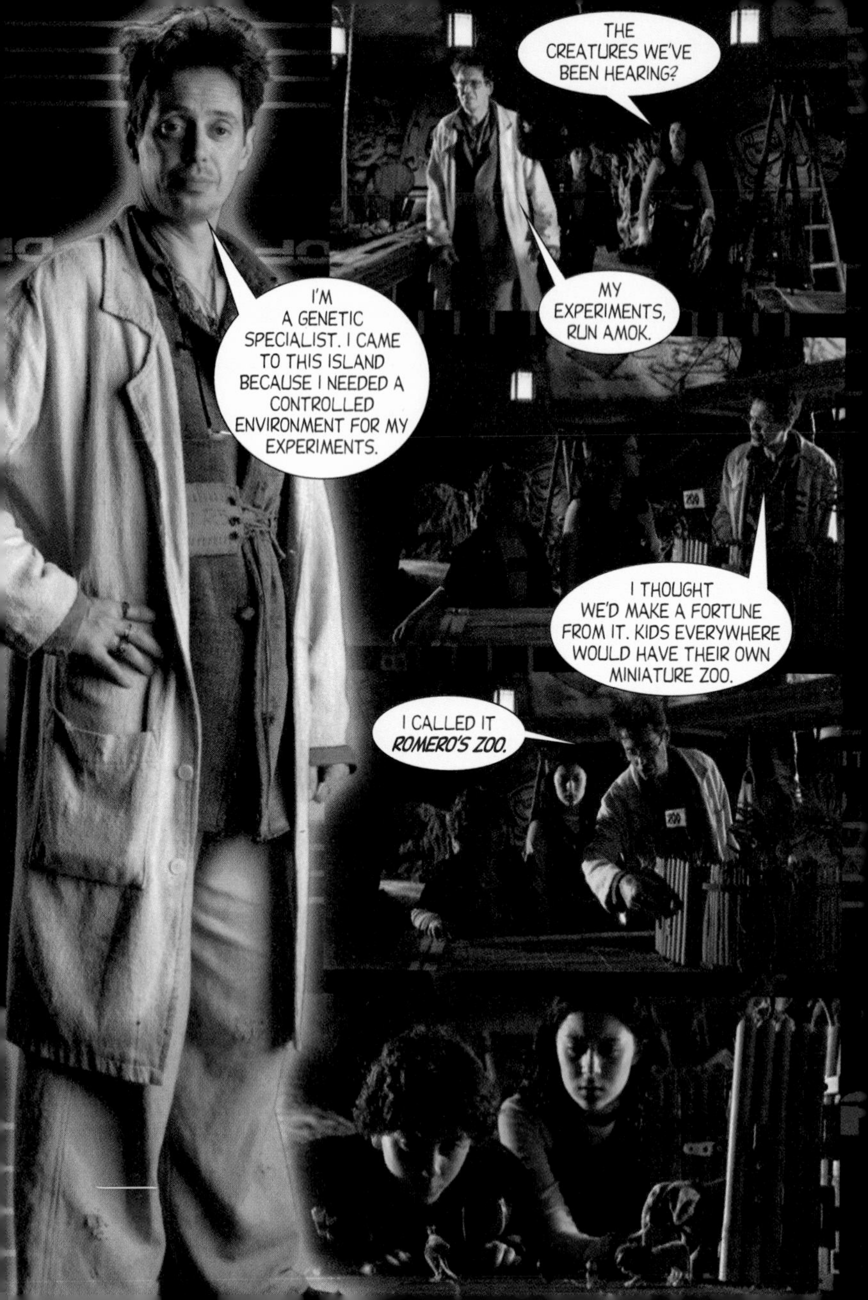
I'M A GENETIC SPECIALIST. I CAME TO THIS ISLAND BECAUSE I NEEDED A CONTROLLED ENVIRONMENT FOR MY EXPERIMENTS.
THE CREATURES WE'VE BEEN HEARING?
MY EXPERIMENTS, RUN AMOK.
I THOUGHT WE'D MAKE A FORTUNE FROM IT. KIDS EVERYWHERE WOULD HAVE THEIR OWN MINIATURE ZOO.
I CALLED IT *ROMERO'S ZOO.*

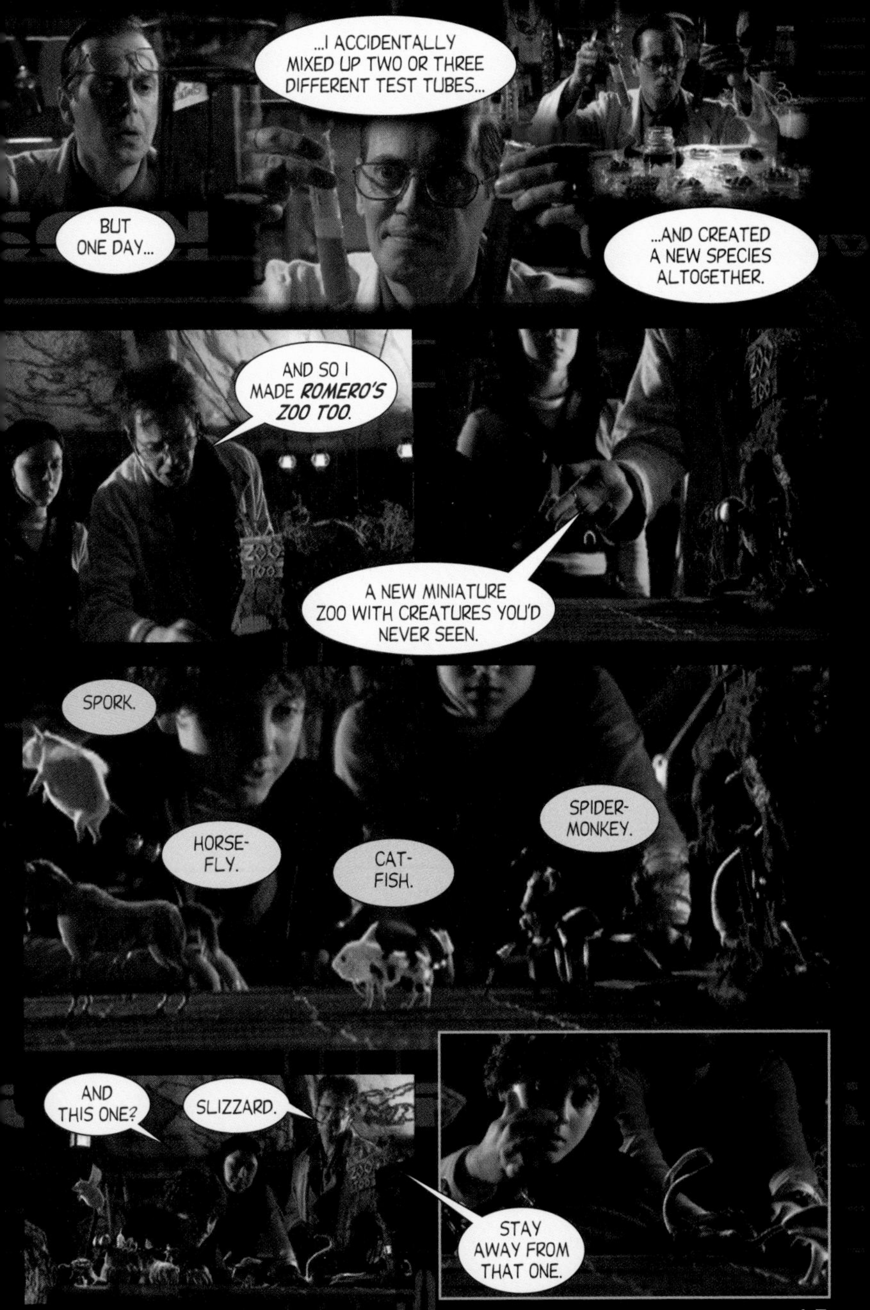
BUT ONE DAY...
...I ACCIDENTALLY MIXED UP TWO OR THREE DIFFERENT TEST TUBES...
...AND CREATED A NEW SPECIES ALTOGETHER.
AND SO I MADE *ROMERO'S ZOO TOO*.
A NEW MINIATURE ZOO WITH CREATURES YOU'D NEVER SEEN.
SPORK.
HORSE-FLY.
CAT-FISH.
SPIDER-MONKEY.
AND THIS ONE?
SLIZZARD.
STAY AWAY FROM THAT ONE.

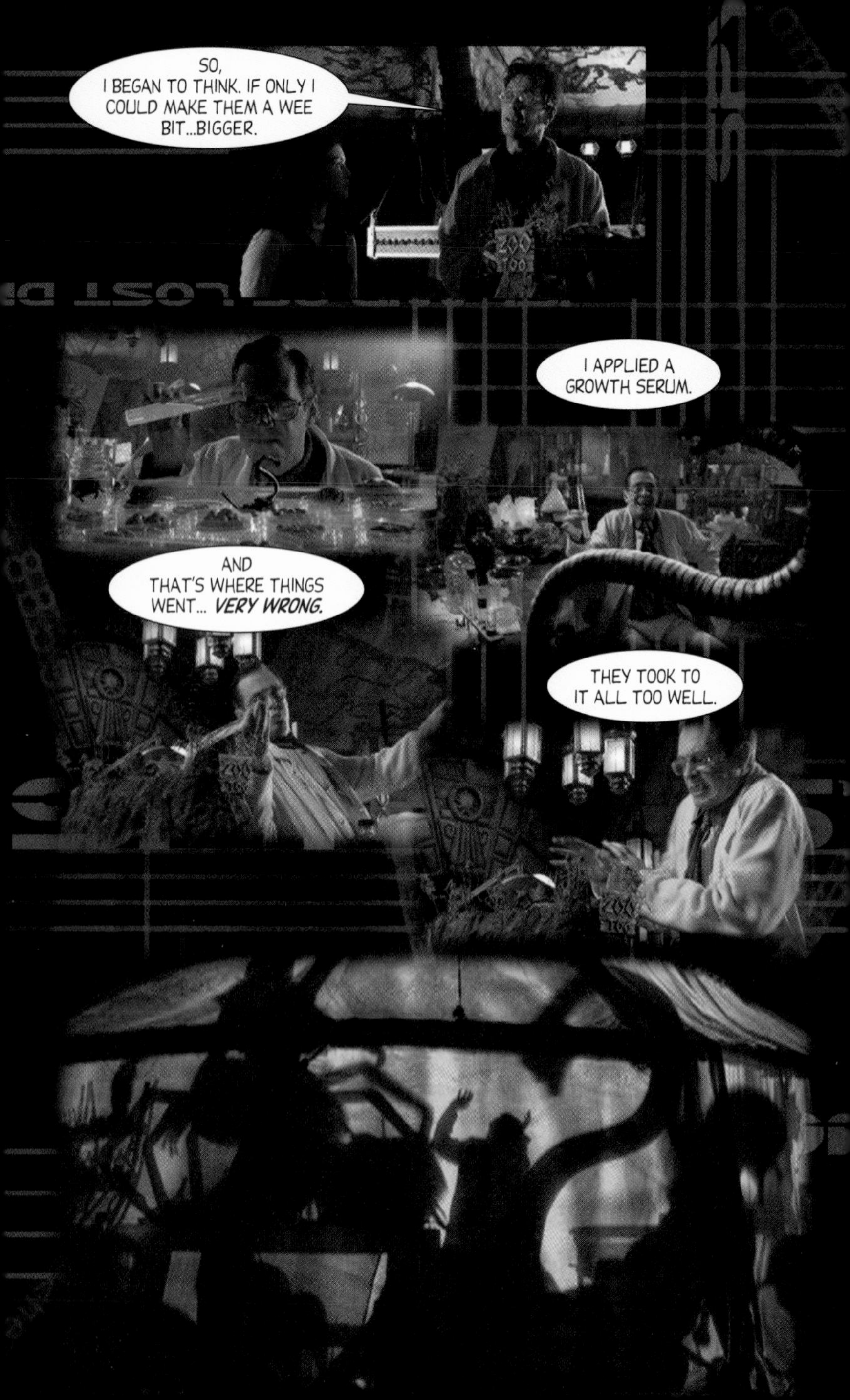
SO, I BEGAN TO THINK. IF ONLY I COULD MAKE THEM A WEE BIT...BIGGER.
I APPLIED A GROWTH SERUM.
AND THAT'S WHERE THINGS WENT... ***VERY WRONG.***
THEY TOOK TO IT ALL TOO WELL.

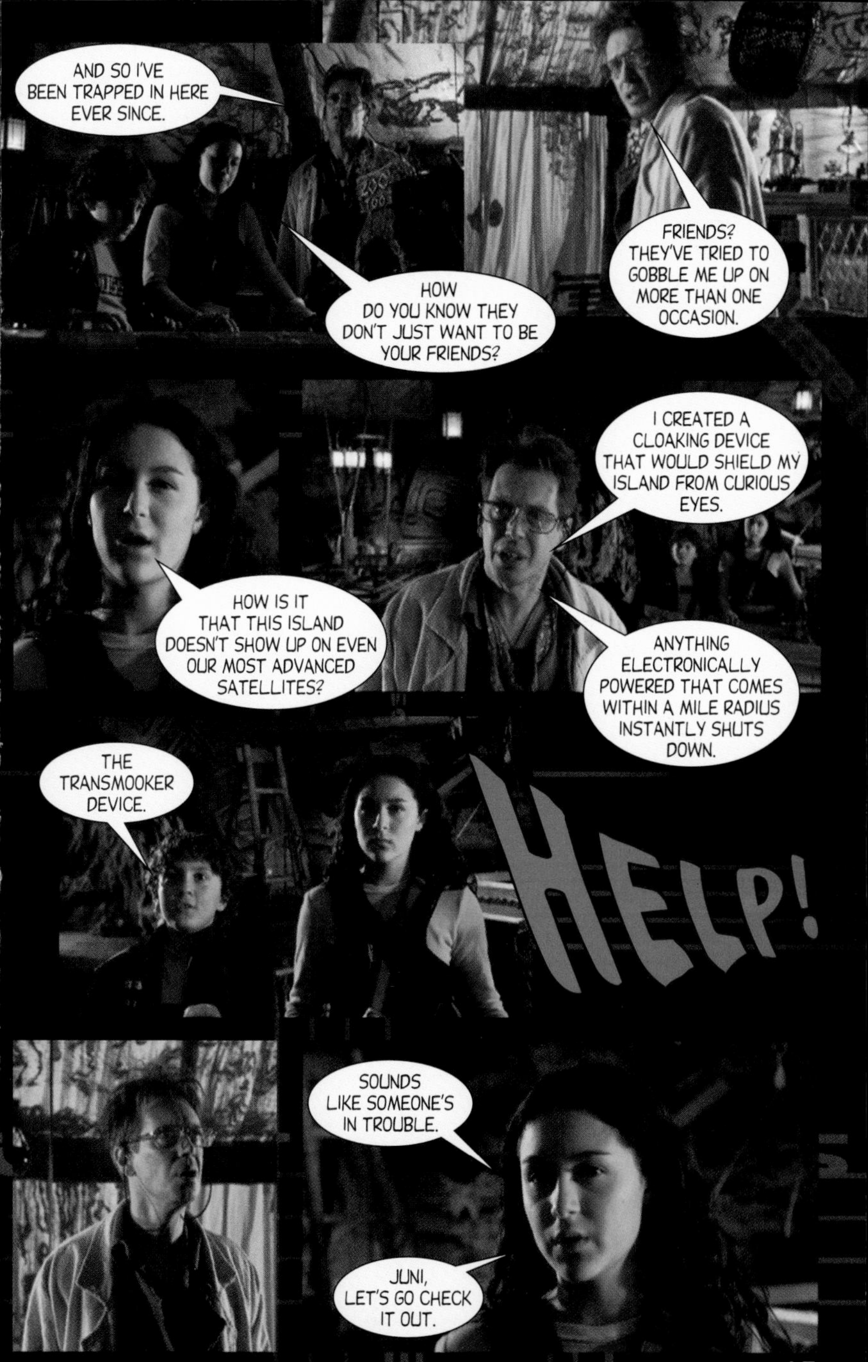
AND SO I'VE BEEN TRAPPED IN HERE EVER SINCE.
HOW DO YOU KNOW THEY DON'T JUST WANT TO BE YOUR FRIENDS?
FRIENDS? THEY'VE TRIED TO GOBBLE ME UP ON MORE THAN ONE OCCASION.
HOW IS IT THAT THIS ISLAND DOESN'T SHOW UP ON EVEN OUR MOST ADVANCED SATELLITES?
I CREATED A CLOAKING DEVICE THAT WOULD SHIELD MY ISLAND FROM CURIOUS EYES.
ANYTHING ELECTRONICALLY POWERED THAT COMES WITHIN A MILE RADIUS INSTANTLY SHUTS DOWN.
THE TRANSMOOKER DEVICE.
HELP!
SOUNDS LIKE SOMEONE'S IN TROUBLE.
JUNI, LET'S GO CHECK IT OUT.

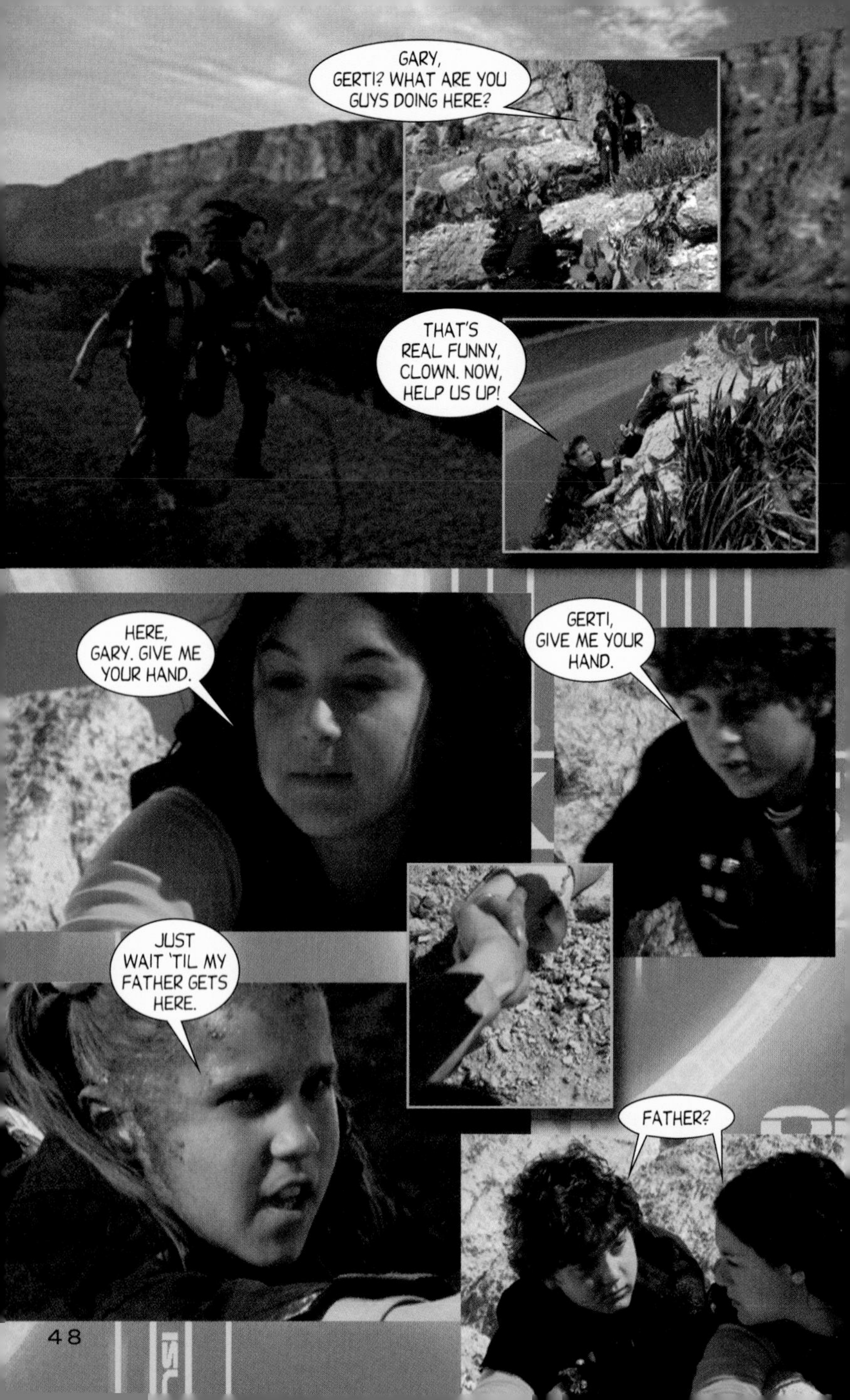
GARY, GERTI? WHAT ARE YOU GUYS DOING HERE?
THAT'S REAL FUNNY, CLOWN. NOW, HELP US UP!
HERE, GARY. GIVE ME YOUR HAND.
GERTI, GIVE ME YOUR HAND.
JUST WAIT 'TIL MY FATHER GETS HERE.
FATHER?

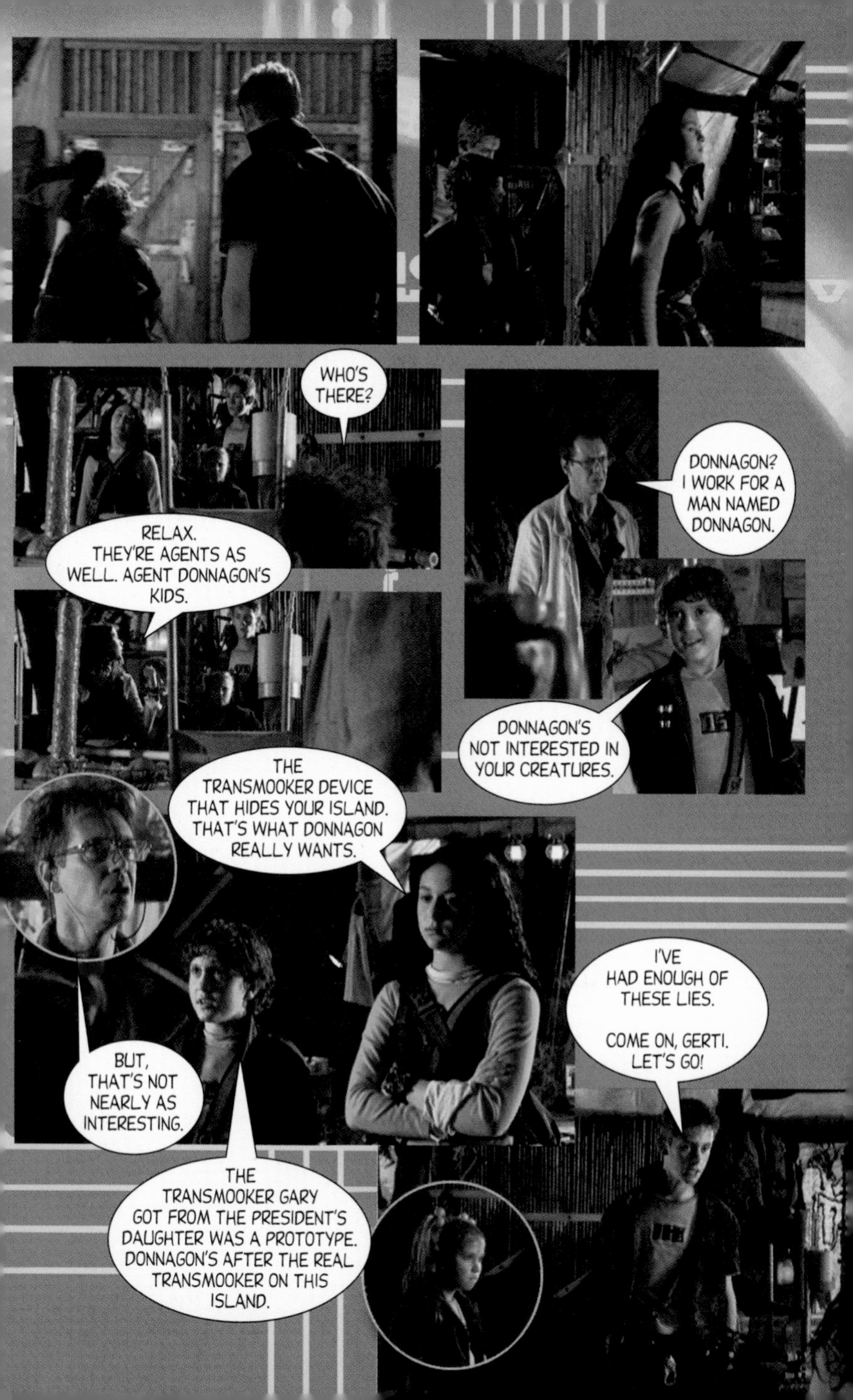
WHO'S THERE?
DONNAGON? I WORK FOR A MAN NAMED DONNAGON.
RELAX. THEY'RE AGENTS AS WELL. AGENT DONNAGON'S KIDS.
DONNAGON'S NOT INTERESTED IN YOUR CREATURES.
THE TRANSMOOKER DEVICE THAT HIDES YOUR ISLAND. THAT'S WHAT DONNAGON REALLY WANTS.
BUT, THAT'S NOT NEARLY AS INTERESTING.
THE TRANSMOOKER GARY GOT FROM THE PRESIDENT'S DAUGHTER WAS A PROTOTYPE. DONNAGON'S AFTER THE REAL TRANSMOOKER ON THIS ISLAND.
I'VE HAD ENOUGH OF THESE LIES.
COME ON, GERTI. LET'S GO!

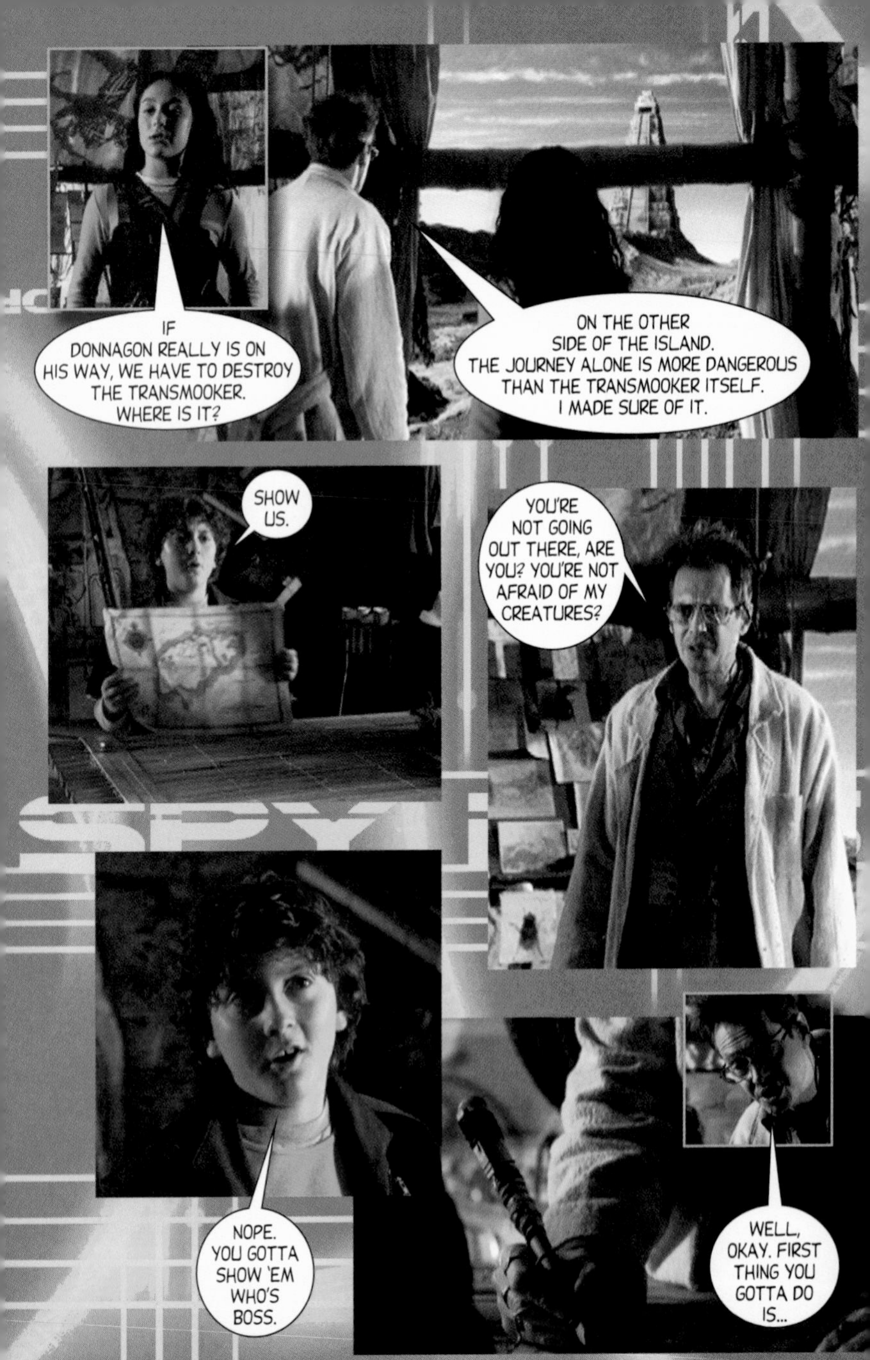
IF DONNAGON REALLY IS ON HIS WAY, WE HAVE TO DESTROY THE TRANSMOOKER. WHERE IS IT?
ON THE OTHER SIDE OF THE ISLAND. THE JOURNEY ALONE IS MORE DANGEROUS THAN THE TRANSMOOKER ITSELF. I MADE SURE OF IT.
SHOW US.
YOU'RE NOT GOING OUT THERE, ARE YOU? YOU'RE NOT AFRAID OF MY CREATURES?
NOPE. YOU GOTTA SHOW 'EM WHO'S BOSS.
WELL, OKAY. FIRST THING YOU GOTTA DO IS...

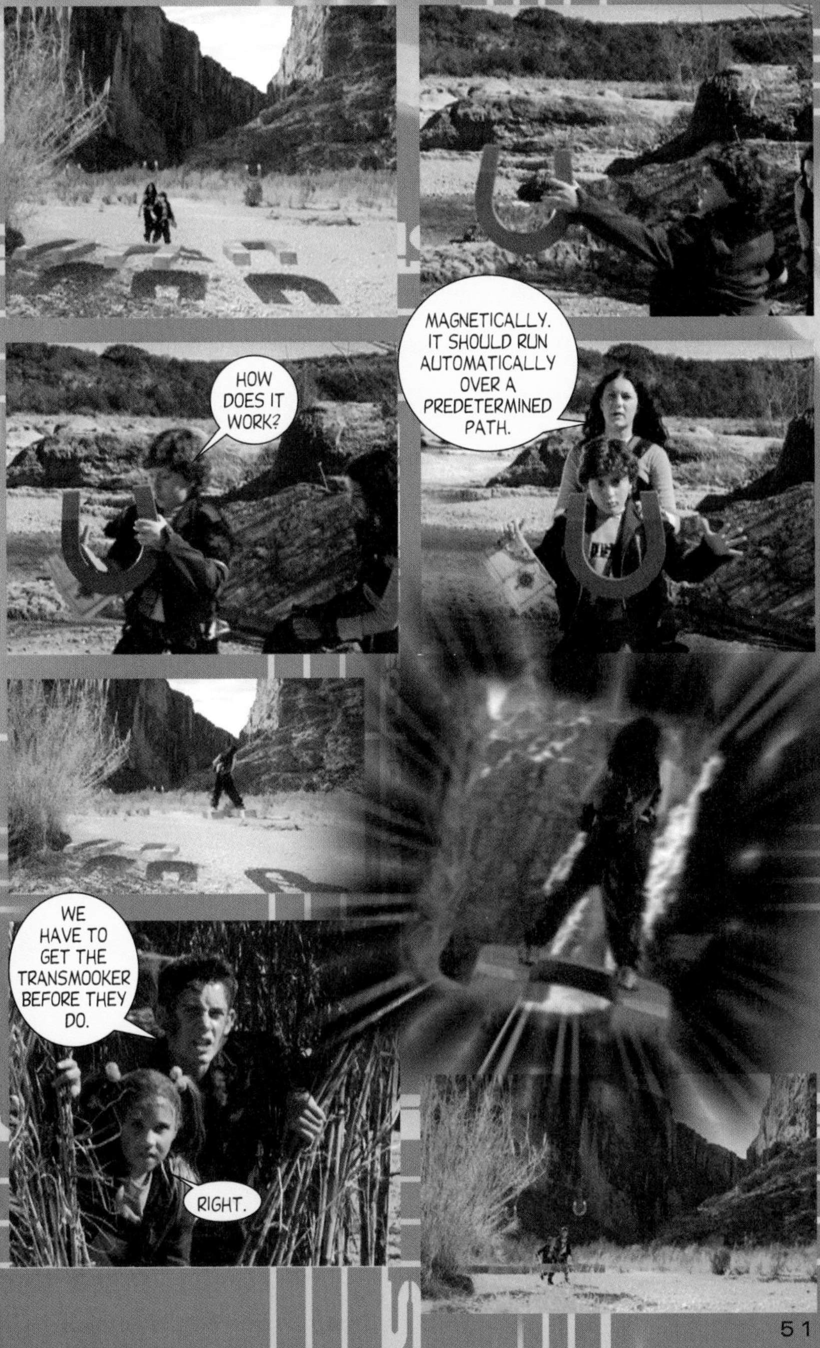
HOW DOES IT WORK?
MAGNETICALLY. IT SHOULD RUN AUTOMATICALLY OVER A PREDETERMINED PATH.
WE HAVE TO GET THE TRANSMOOKER BEFORE THEY DO.
RIGHT.

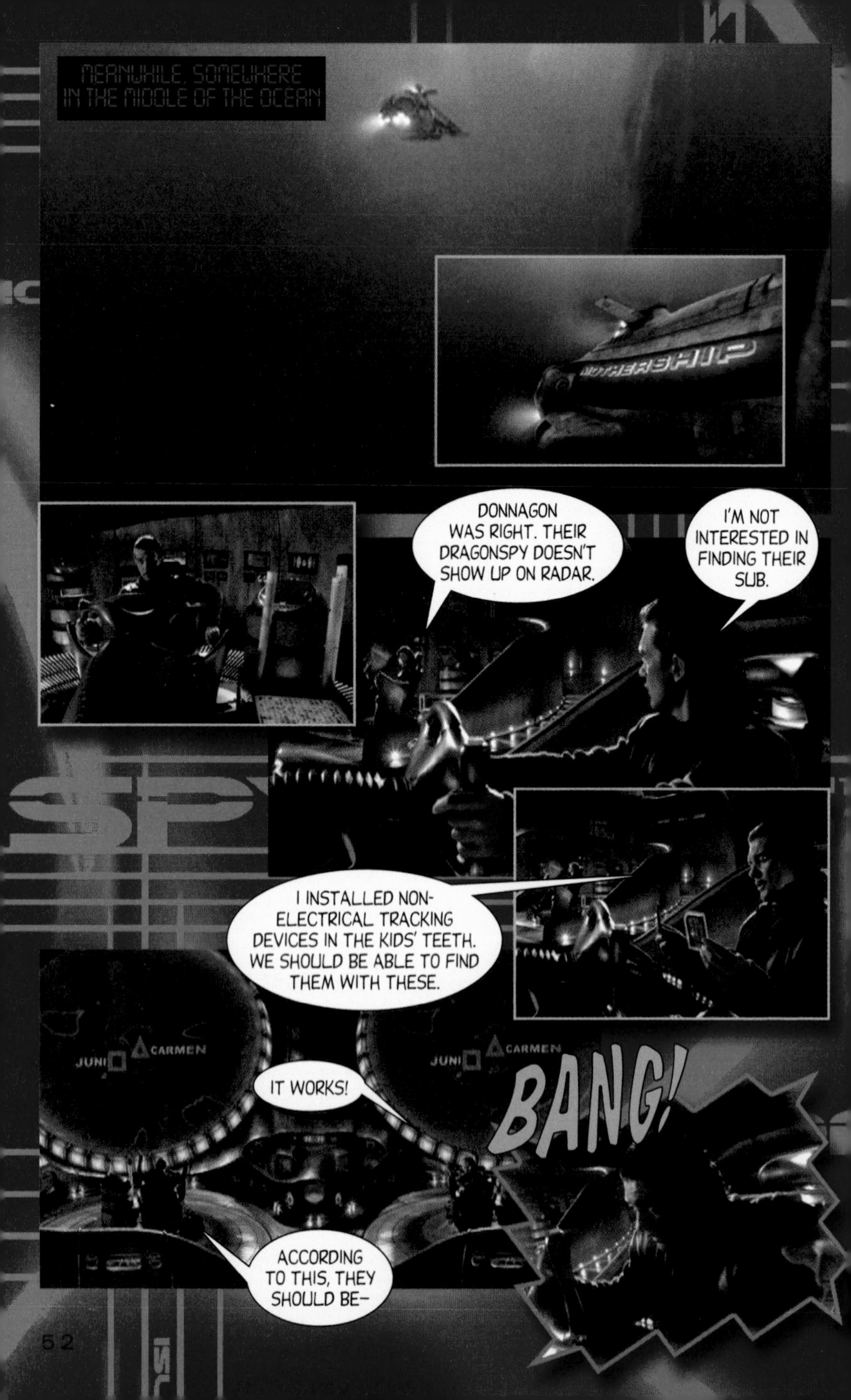
MEANWHILE, SOMEWHERE IN THE MIDDLE OF THE OCEAN
MOTHERSHIP
DONNAGON WAS RIGHT. THEIR DRAGONSPY DOESN'T SHOW UP ON RADAR.
I'M NOT INTERESTED IN FINDING THEIR SUB.
I INSTALLED NON-ELECTRICAL TRACKING DEVICES IN THE KIDS' TEETH. WE SHOULD BE ABLE TO FIND THEM WITH THESE.
JUNI CARMEN
JUNI CARMEN
IT WORKS!
ACCORDING TO THIS, THEY SHOULD BE—
BANG!

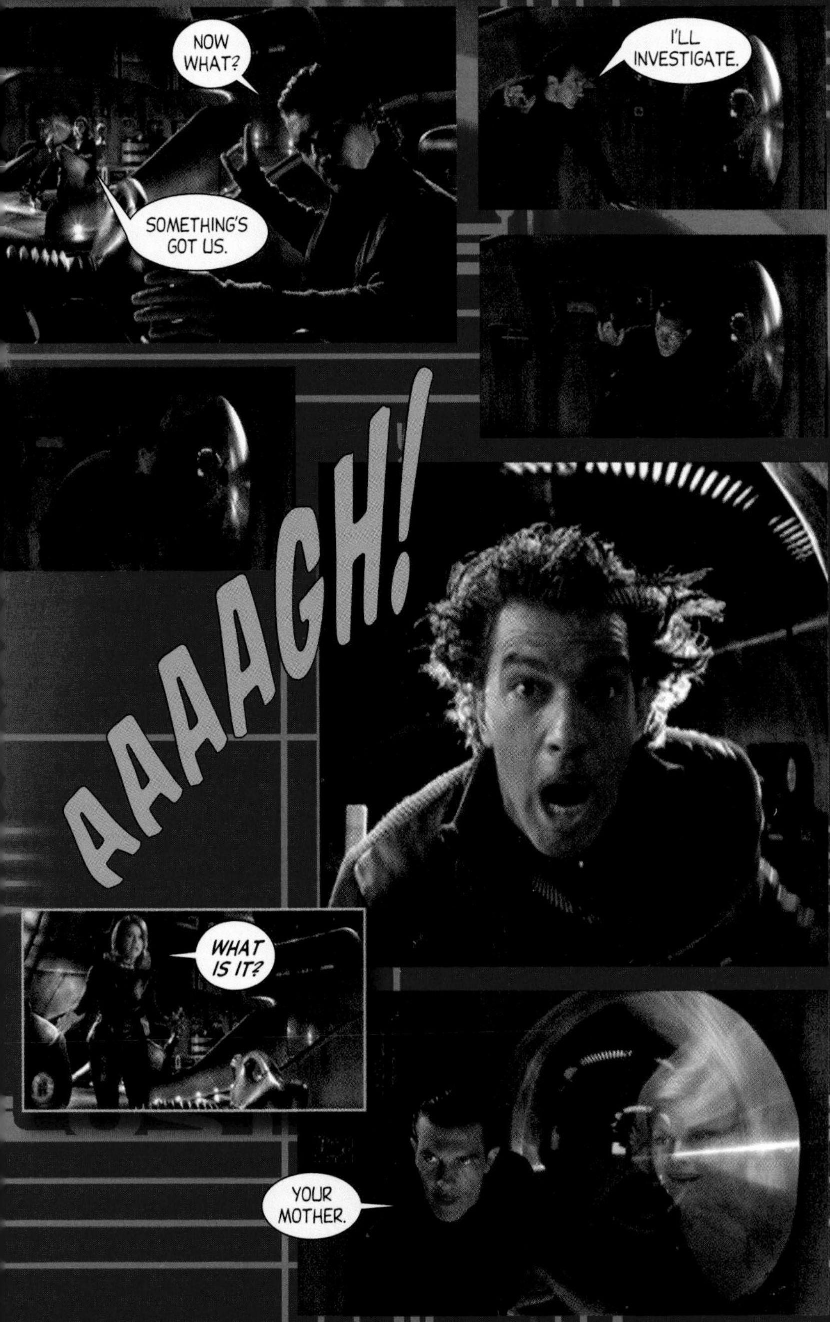
NOW WHAT?
SOMETHING'S GOT US.
I'LL INVESTIGATE.
AAAAGH!
WHAT IS IT?
YOUR MOTHER.

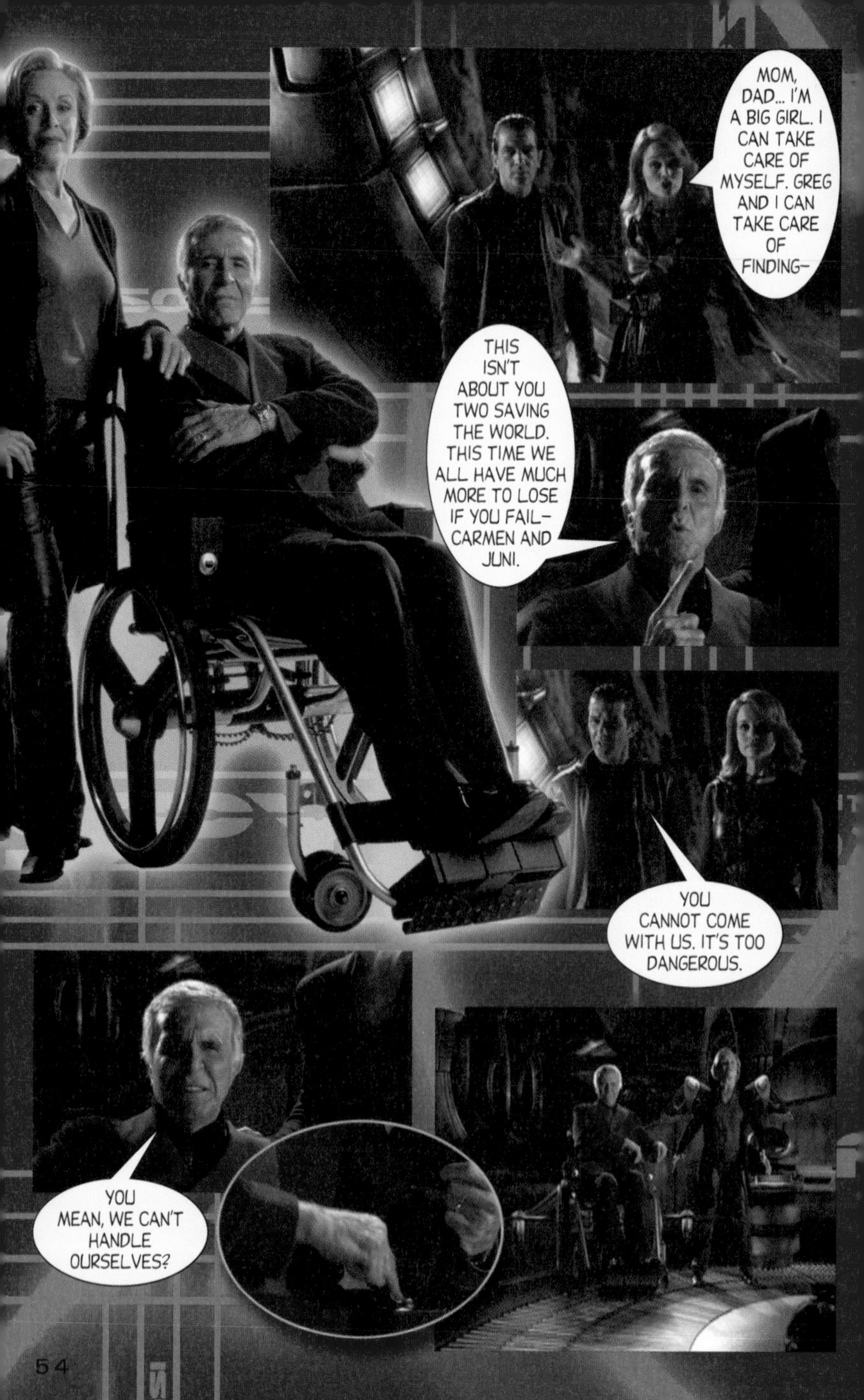
MOM, DAD... I'M A BIG GIRL. I CAN TAKE CARE OF MYSELF. GREG AND I CAN TAKE CARE OF FINDING—
THIS ISN'T ABOUT YOU TWO SAVING THE WORLD. THIS TIME WE ALL HAVE MUCH MORE TO LOSE IF YOU FAIL—CARMEN AND JUNI.
YOU CANNOT COME WITH US. IT'S TOO DANGEROUS.
YOU MEAN, WE CAN'T HANDLE OURSELVES?

CHAPTER 3

SPY KIDS™

ISLAND OF LOST DREAMS

RACE FOR THE TRANSMOOKER

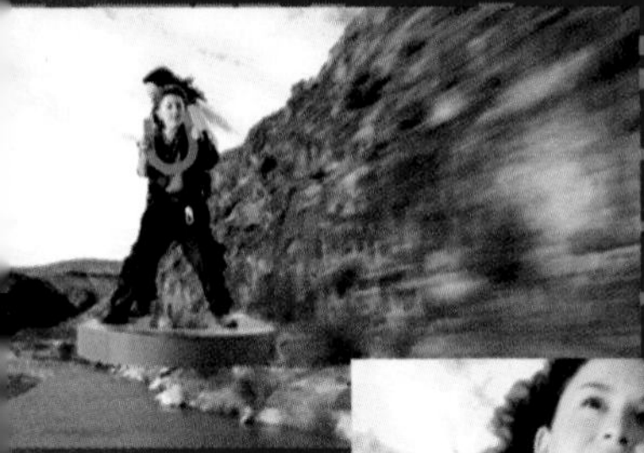

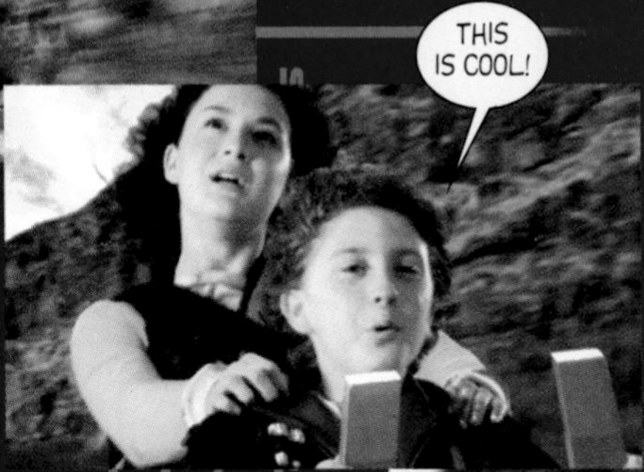
THIS IS COOL!

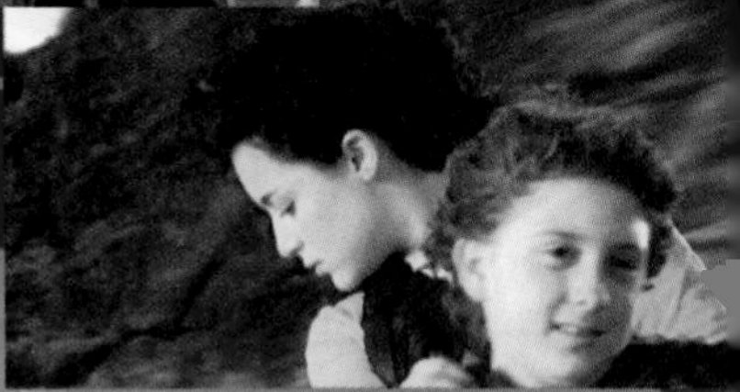

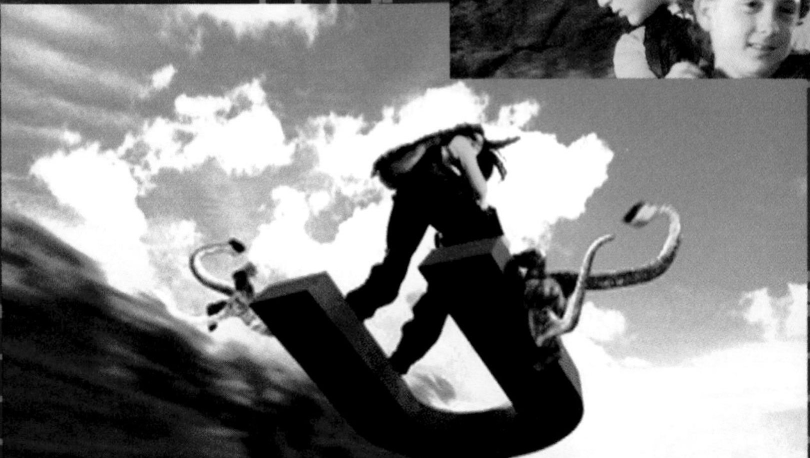

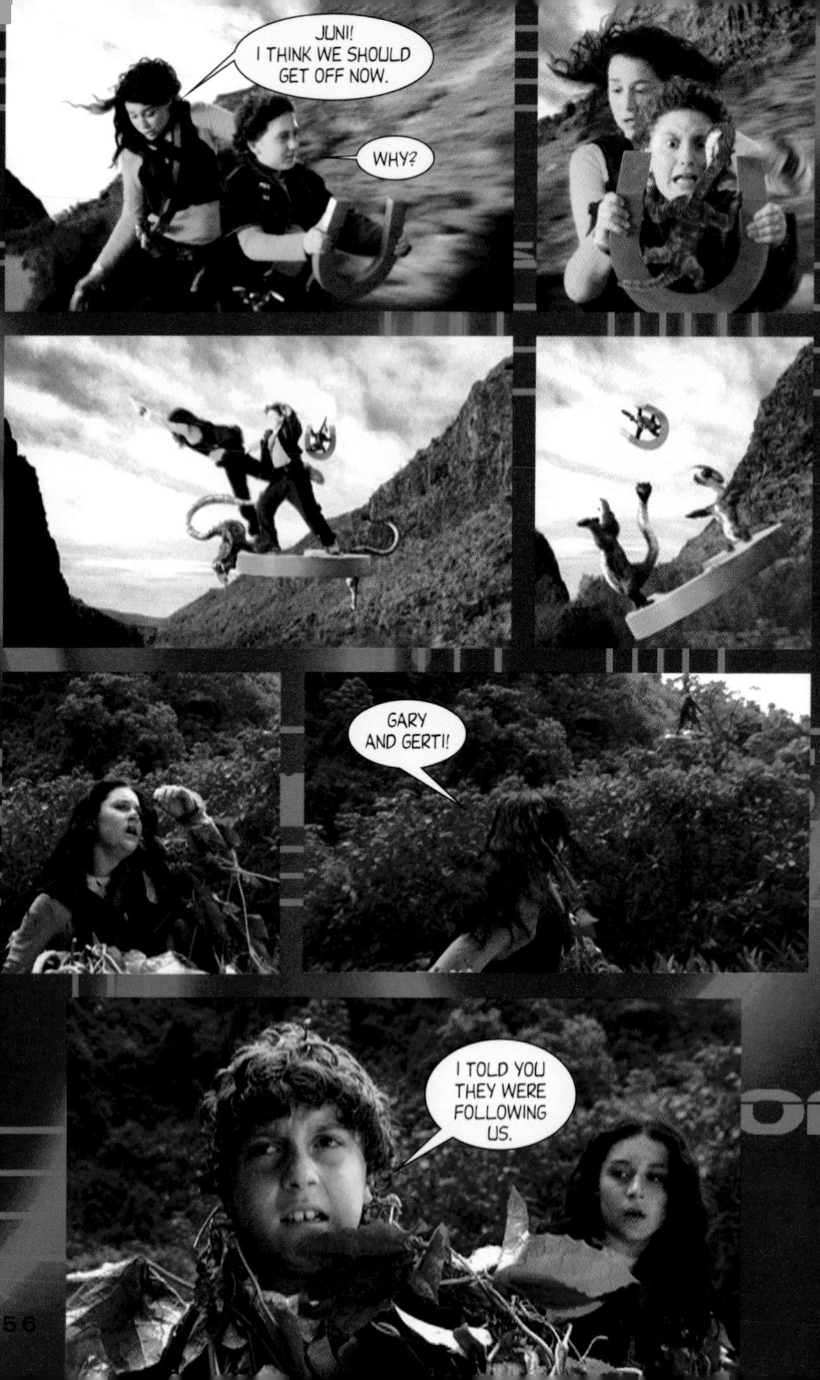
JUNI!
I THINK WE SHOULD
GET OFF NOW.
WHY?
GARY
AND GERTI!
I TOLD YOU
THEY WERE
FOLLOWING
US.

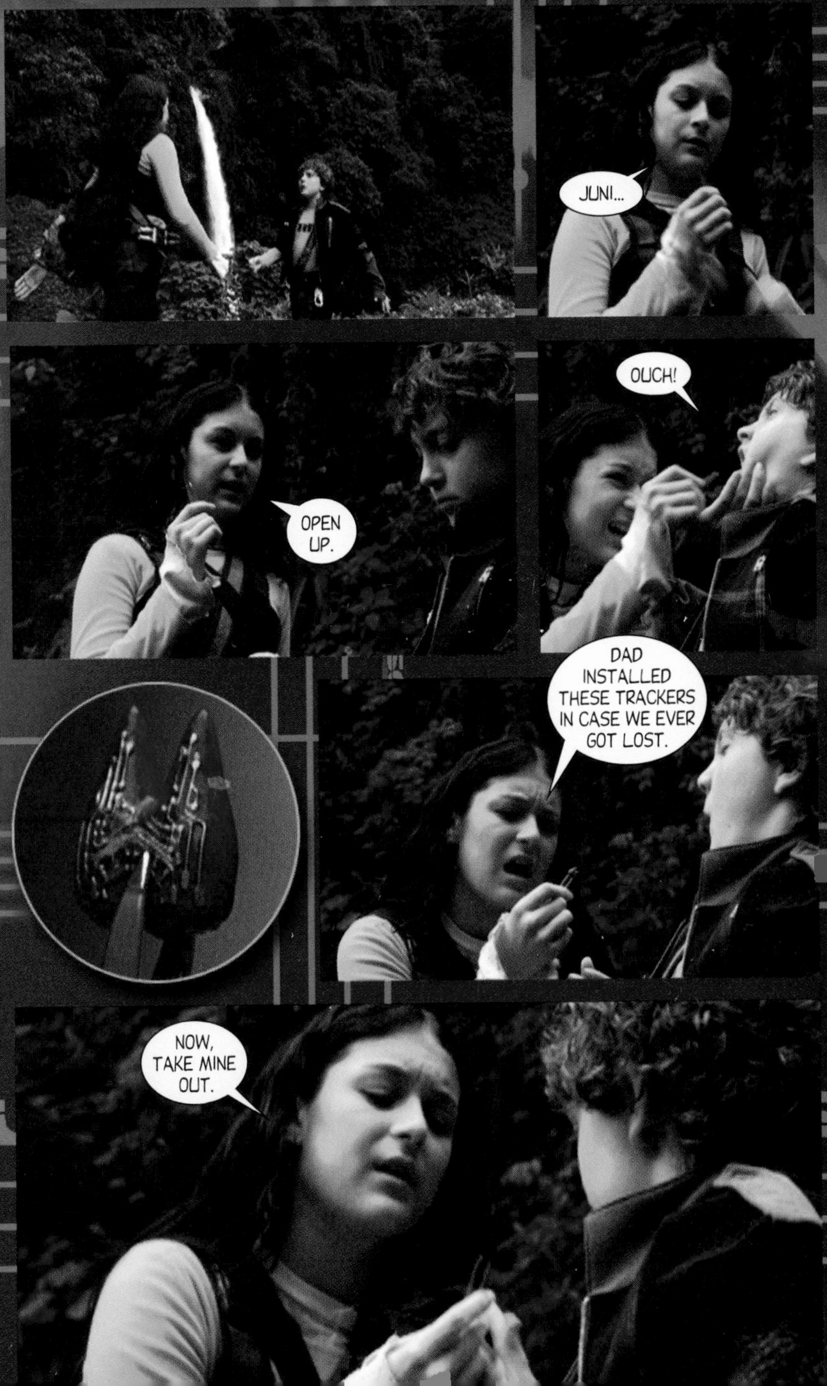
JUNI...
OPEN UP.
OUCH!
DAD INSTALLED THESE TRACKERS IN CASE WE EVER GOT LOST.
NOW, TAKE MINE OUT.

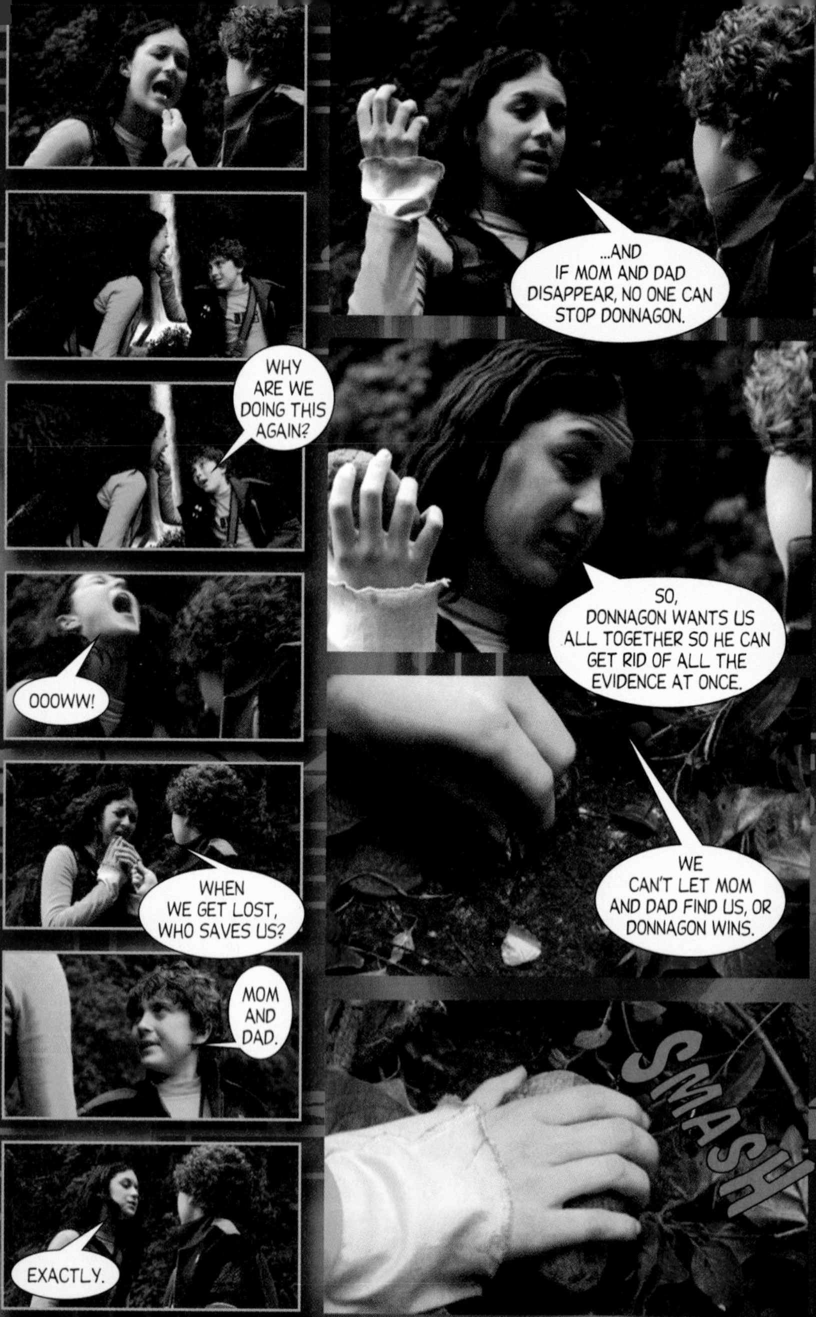
WHY ARE WE DOING THIS AGAIN?
OOOWW!
WHEN WE GET LOST, WHO SAVES US?
MOM AND DAD.
EXACTLY.
...AND IF MOM AND DAD DISAPPEAR, NO ONE CAN STOP DONNAGON.
SO, DONNAGON WANTS US ALL TOGETHER SO HE CAN GET RID OF ALL THE EVIDENCE AT ONCE.
WE CAN'T LET MOM AND DAD FIND US, OR DONNAGON WINS.
SMASH

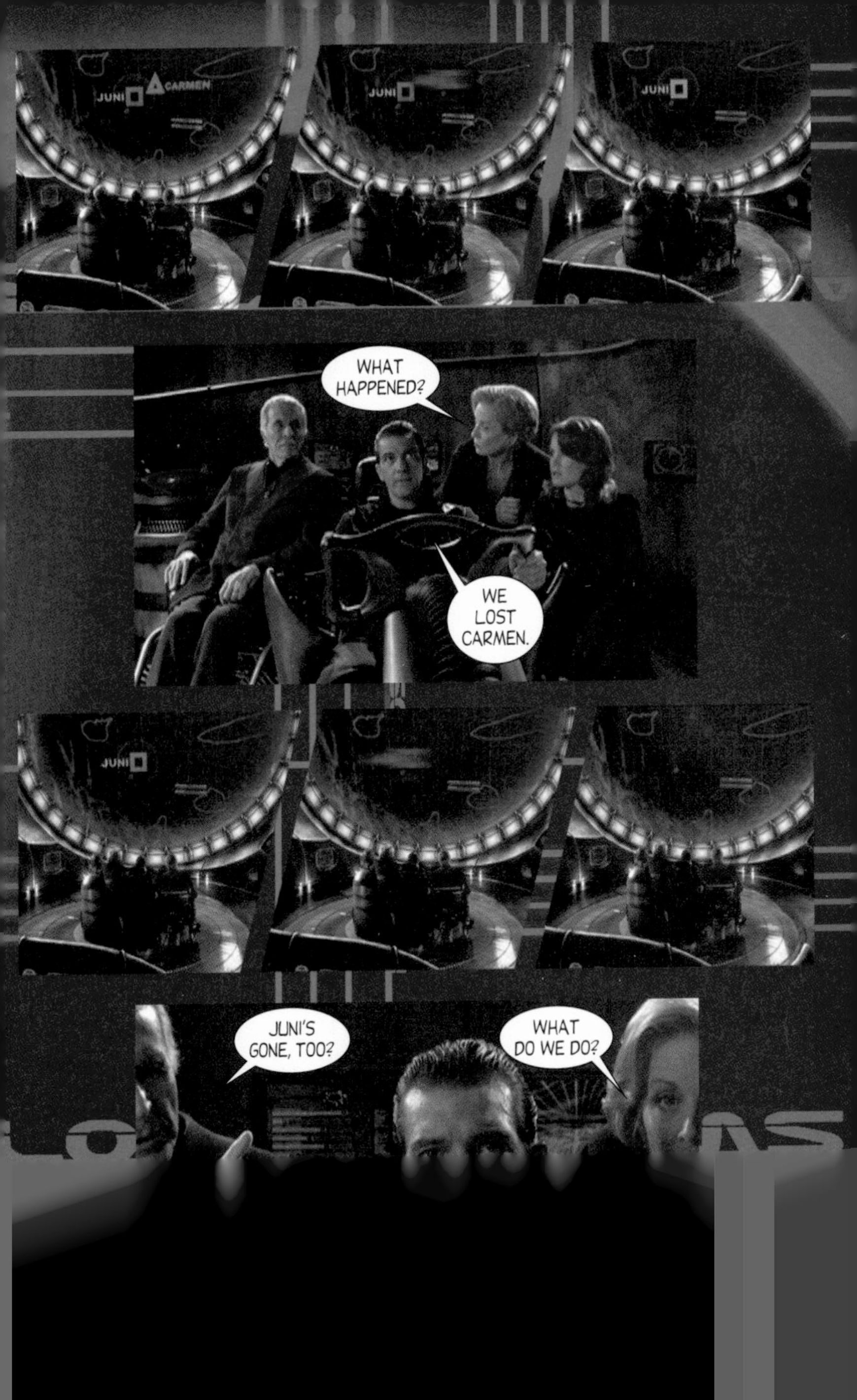
JUNI
CARMEN
JUNI
JUNI
WHAT HAPPENED?
WE LOST CARMEN.
JUNI
JUNI'S GONE, TOO?
WHAT DO WE DO?

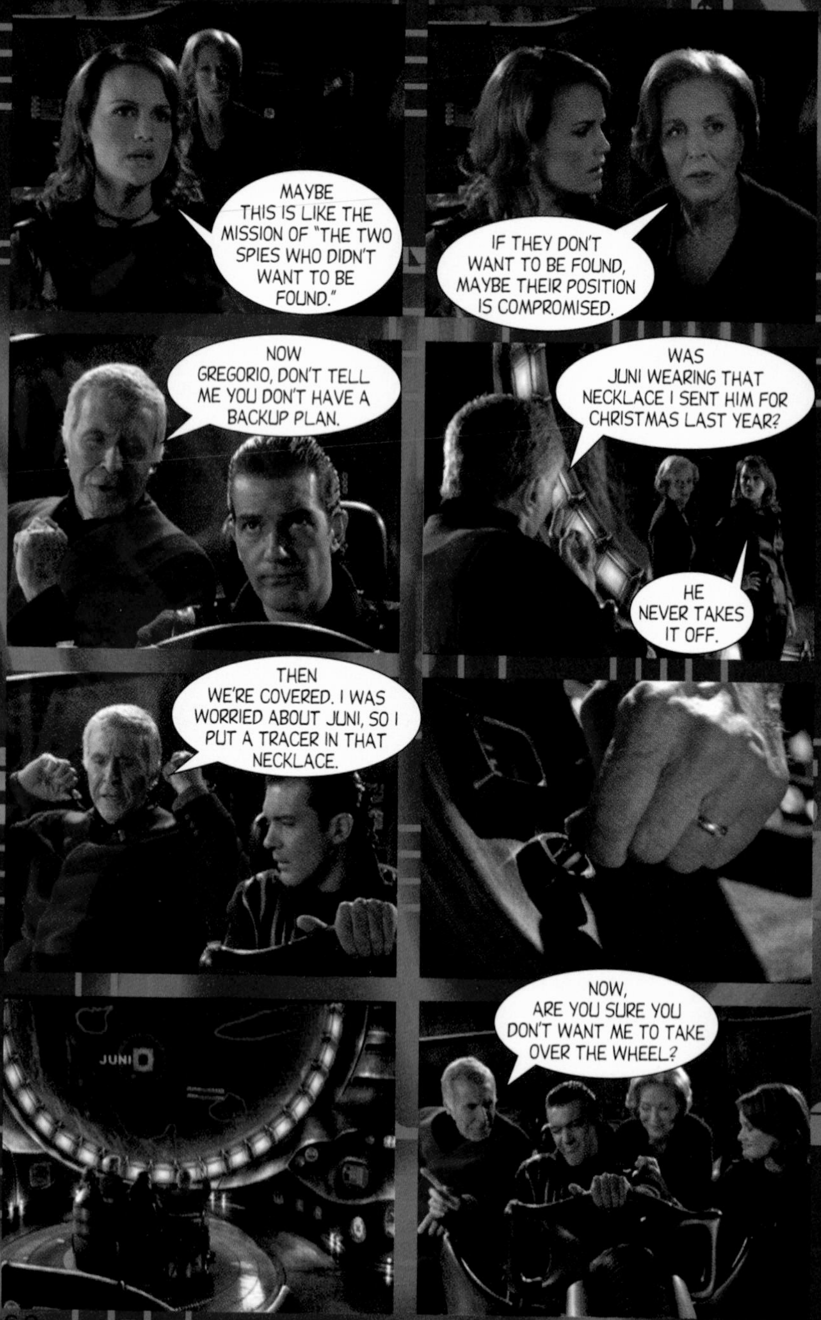
MAYBE THIS IS LIKE THE MISSION OF "THE TWO SPIES WHO DIDN'T WANT TO BE FOUND."
IF THEY DON'T WANT TO BE FOUND, MAYBE THEIR POSITION IS COMPROMISED.
NOW GREGORIO, DON'T TELL ME YOU DON'T HAVE A BACKUP PLAN.
WAS JUNI WEARING THAT NECKLACE I SENT HIM FOR CHRISTMAS LAST YEAR?
HE NEVER TAKES IT OFF.
THEN WE'RE COVERED. I WAS WORRIED ABOUT JUNI, SO I PUT A TRACER IN THAT NECKLACE.
JUNI
NOW, ARE YOU SURE YOU DON'T WANT ME TO TAKE OVER THE WHEEL?

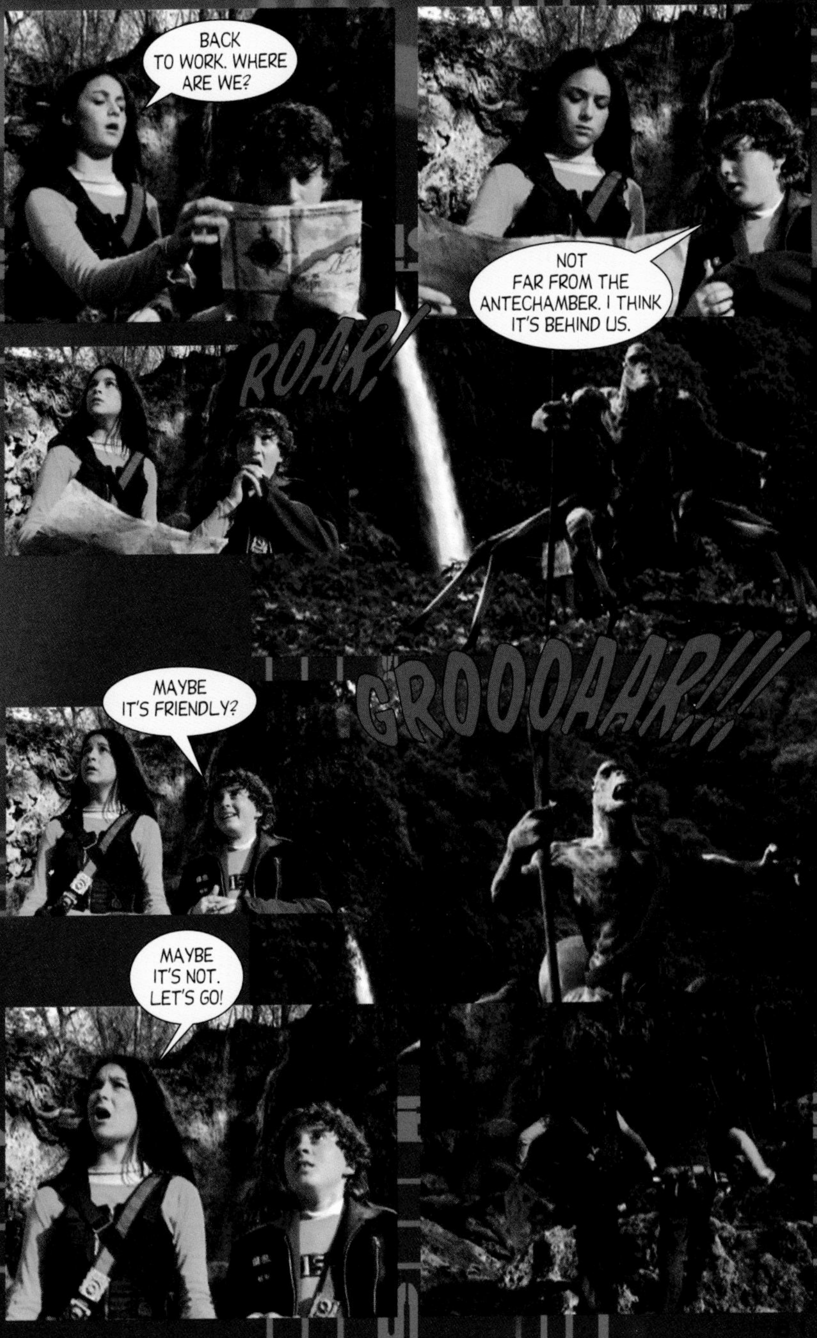
BACK TO WORK. WHERE ARE WE?
NOT FAR FROM THE ANTECHAMBER. I THINK IT'S BEHIND US.
ROAR!
GROOOAAR!!!
MAYBE IT'S FRIENDLY?
MAYBE IT'S NOT. LET'S GO!

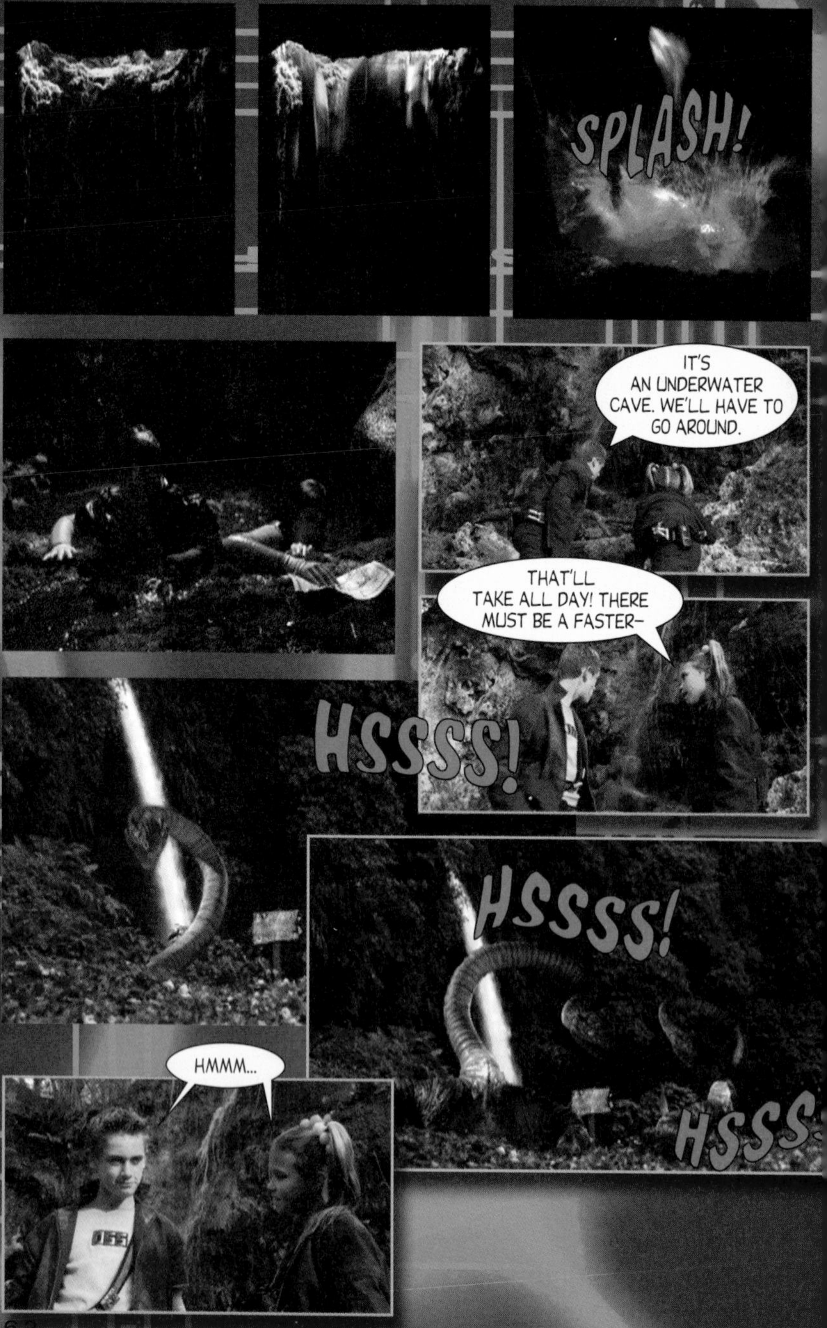
SPLASH!
IT'S AN UNDERWATER CAVE. WE'LL HAVE TO GO AROUND.
THAT'LL TAKE ALL DAY! THERE MUST BE A FASTER–
HSSSS!
HSSSS!
HSSS
HMMM...

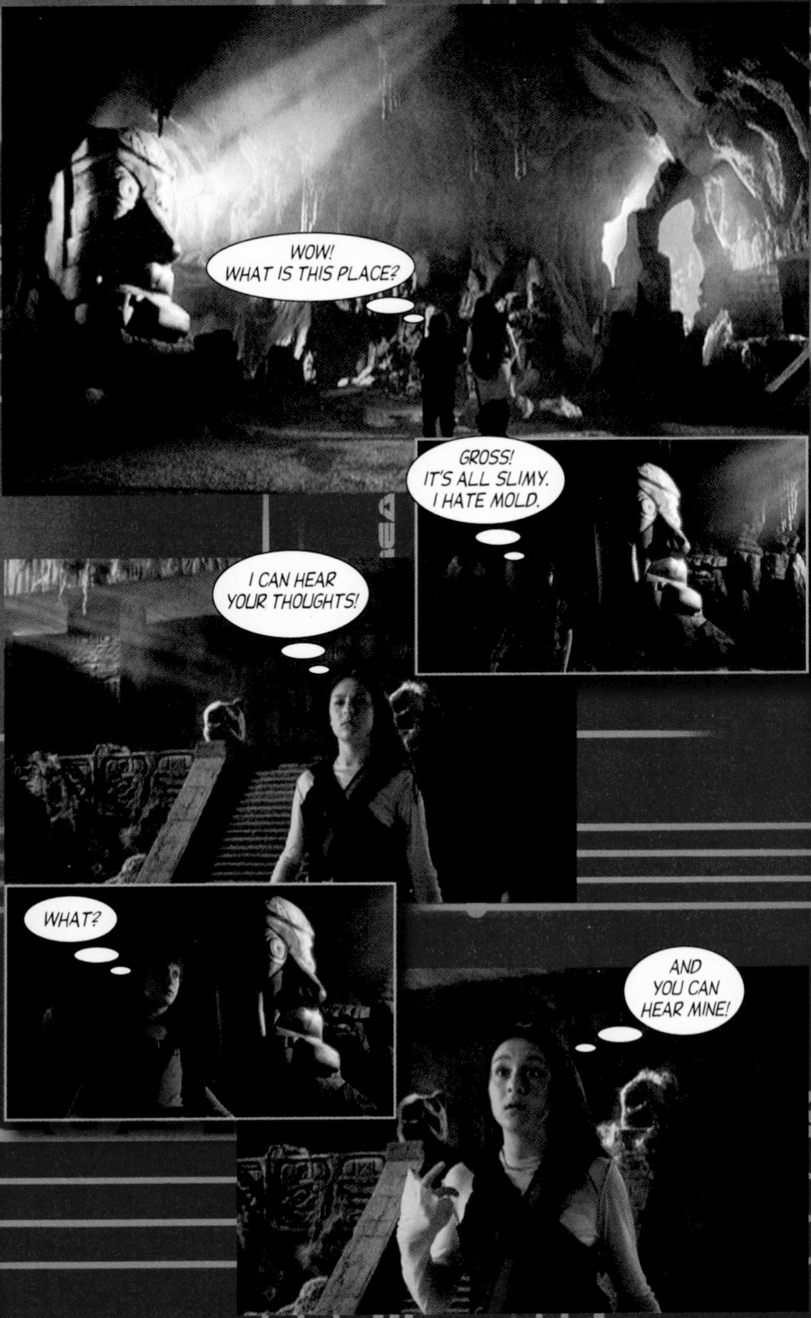
WOW!
WHAT IS THIS PLACE?
GROSS!
IT'S ALL SLIMY.
I HATE MOLD.
I CAN HEAR
YOUR THOUGHTS!
WHAT?
AND
YOU CAN
HEAR MINE!

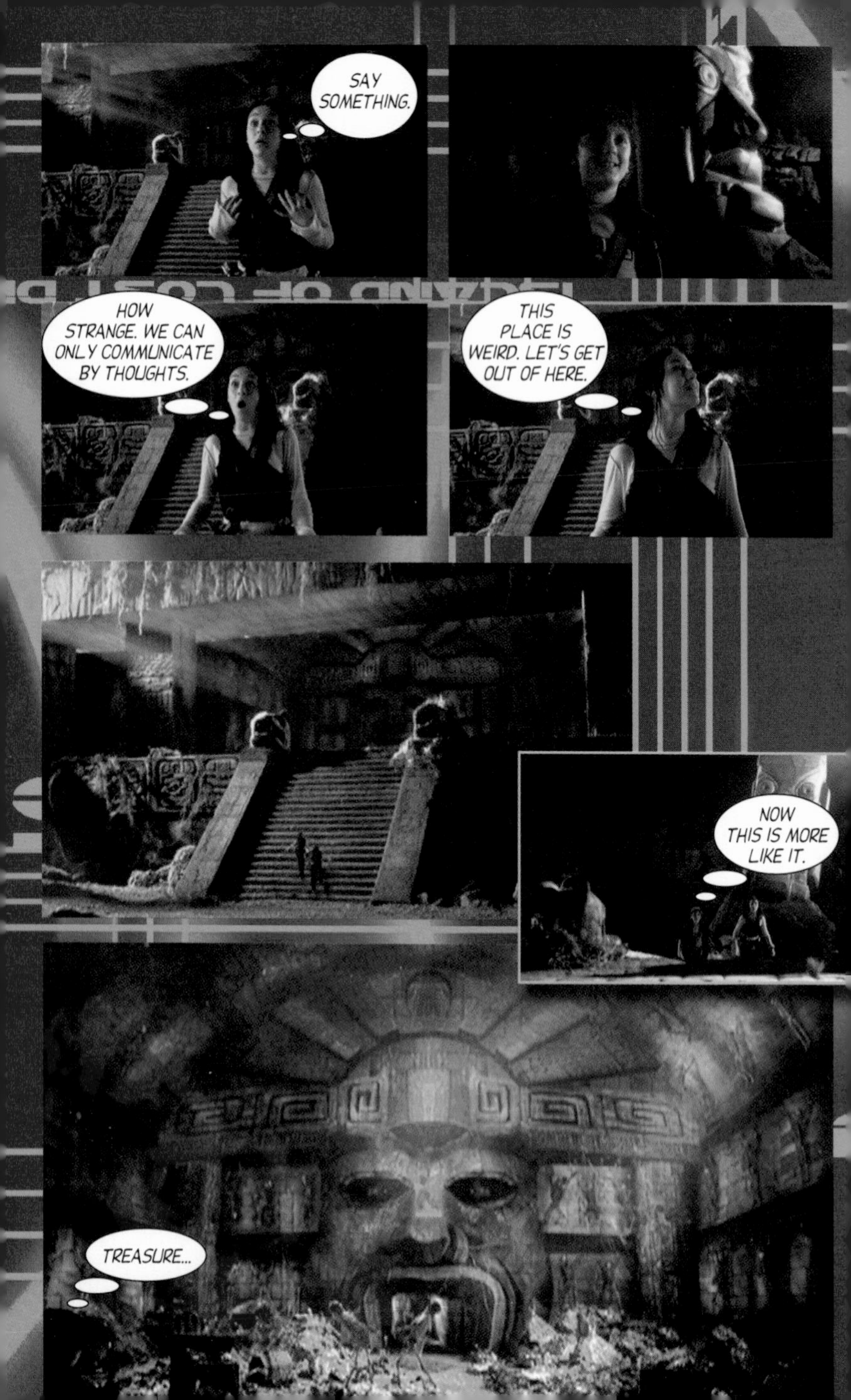
SAY SOMETHING.
HOW STRANGE. WE CAN ONLY COMMUNICATE BY THOUGHTS.
THIS PLACE IS WEIRD. LET'S GET OUT OF HERE.
NOW THIS IS MORE LIKE IT.
TREASURE...

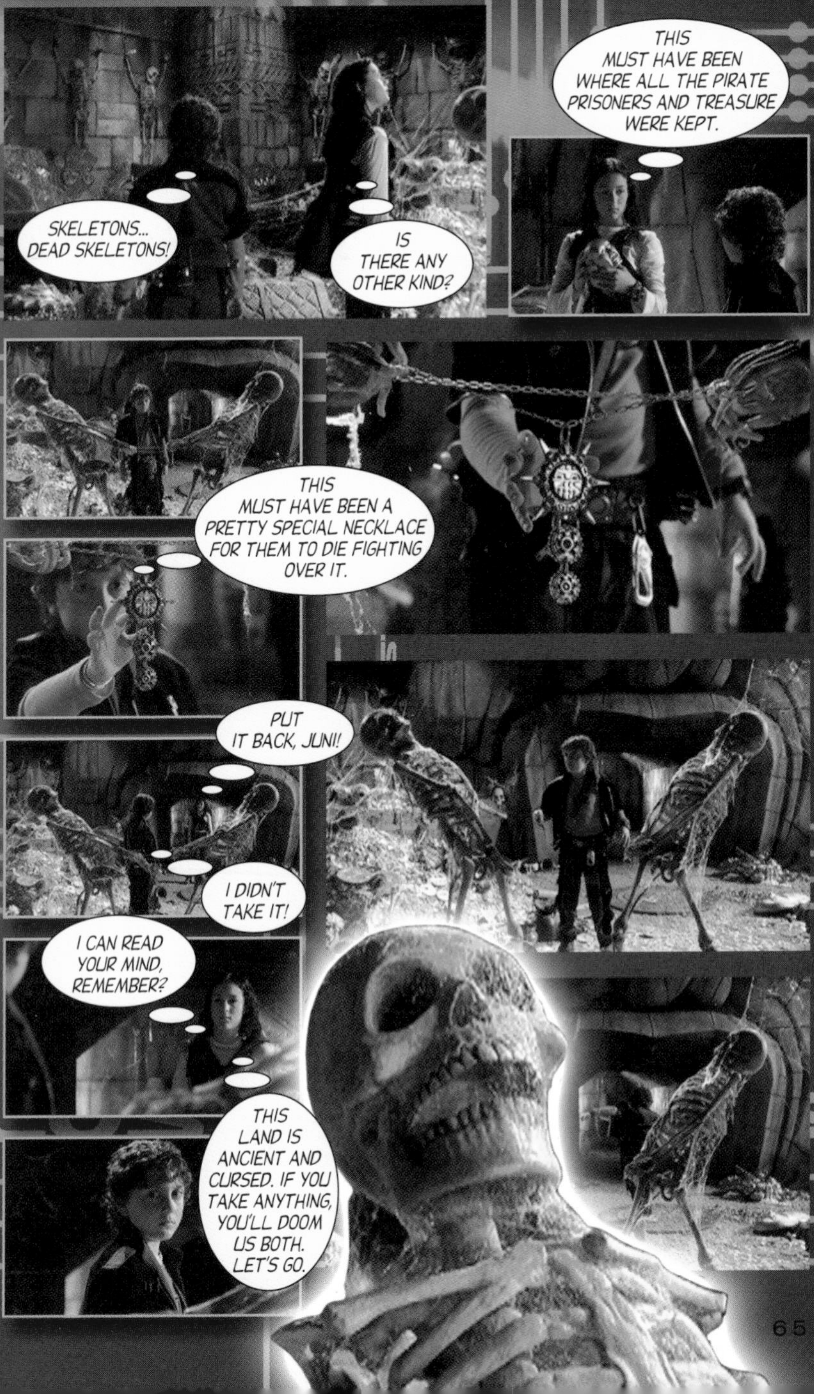
SKELETONS... DEAD SKELETONS!
IS THERE ANY OTHER KIND?
THIS MUST HAVE BEEN WHERE ALL THE PIRATE PRISONERS AND TREASURE WERE KEPT.
THIS MUST HAVE BEEN A PRETTY SPECIAL NECKLACE FOR THEM TO DIE FIGHTING OVER IT.
PUT IT BACK, JUNI!
I DIDN'T TAKE IT!
I CAN READ YOUR MIND, REMEMBER?
THIS LAND IS ANCIENT AND CURSED. IF YOU TAKE ANYTHING, YOU'LL DOOM US BOTH. LET'S GO.

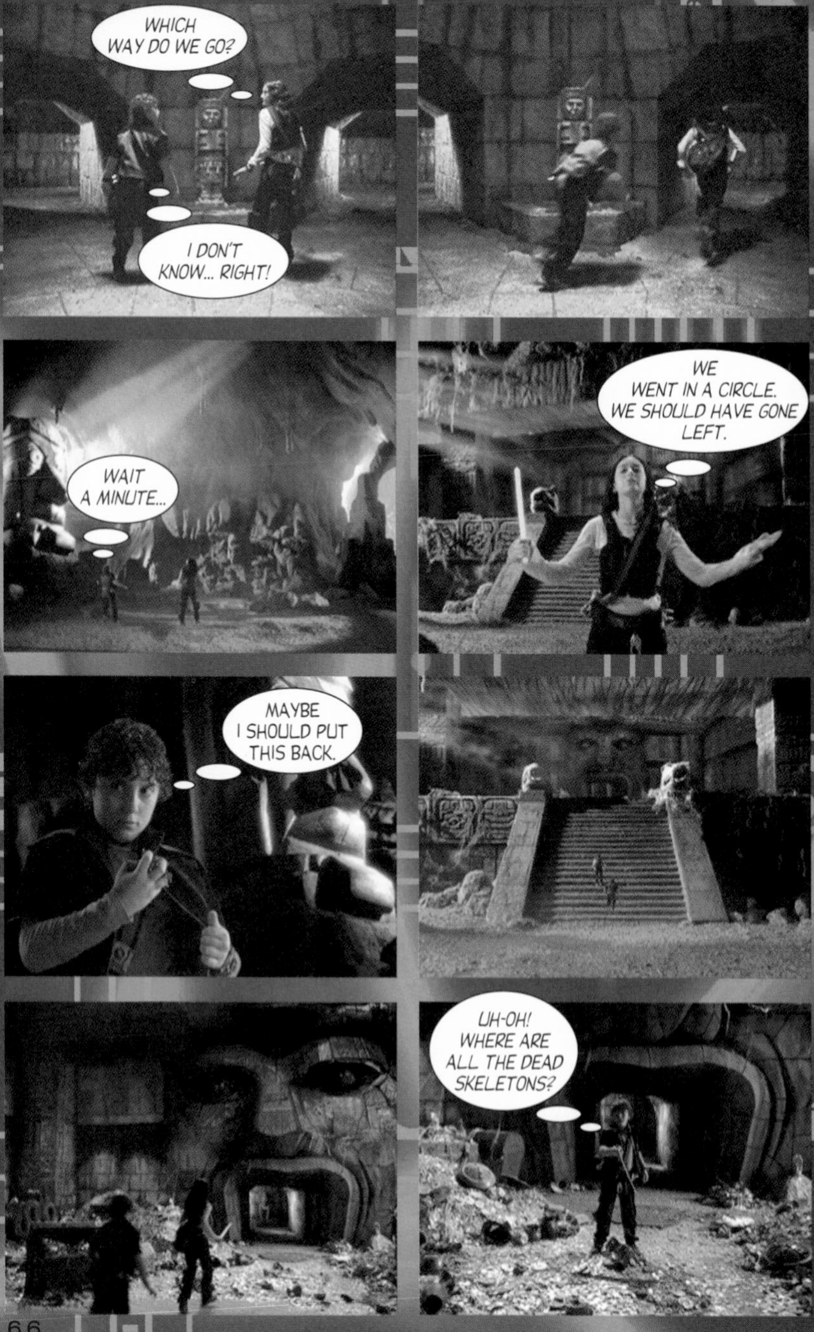
WHICH WAY DO WE GO?
I DON'T KNOW... RIGHT!
WAIT A MINUTE...
WE WENT IN A CIRCLE. WE SHOULD HAVE GONE LEFT.
MAYBE I SHOULD PUT THIS BACK.
UH-OH! WHERE ARE ALL THE DEAD SKELETONS?

EEEEEEEEK!!!!!

JUNI!!!

67

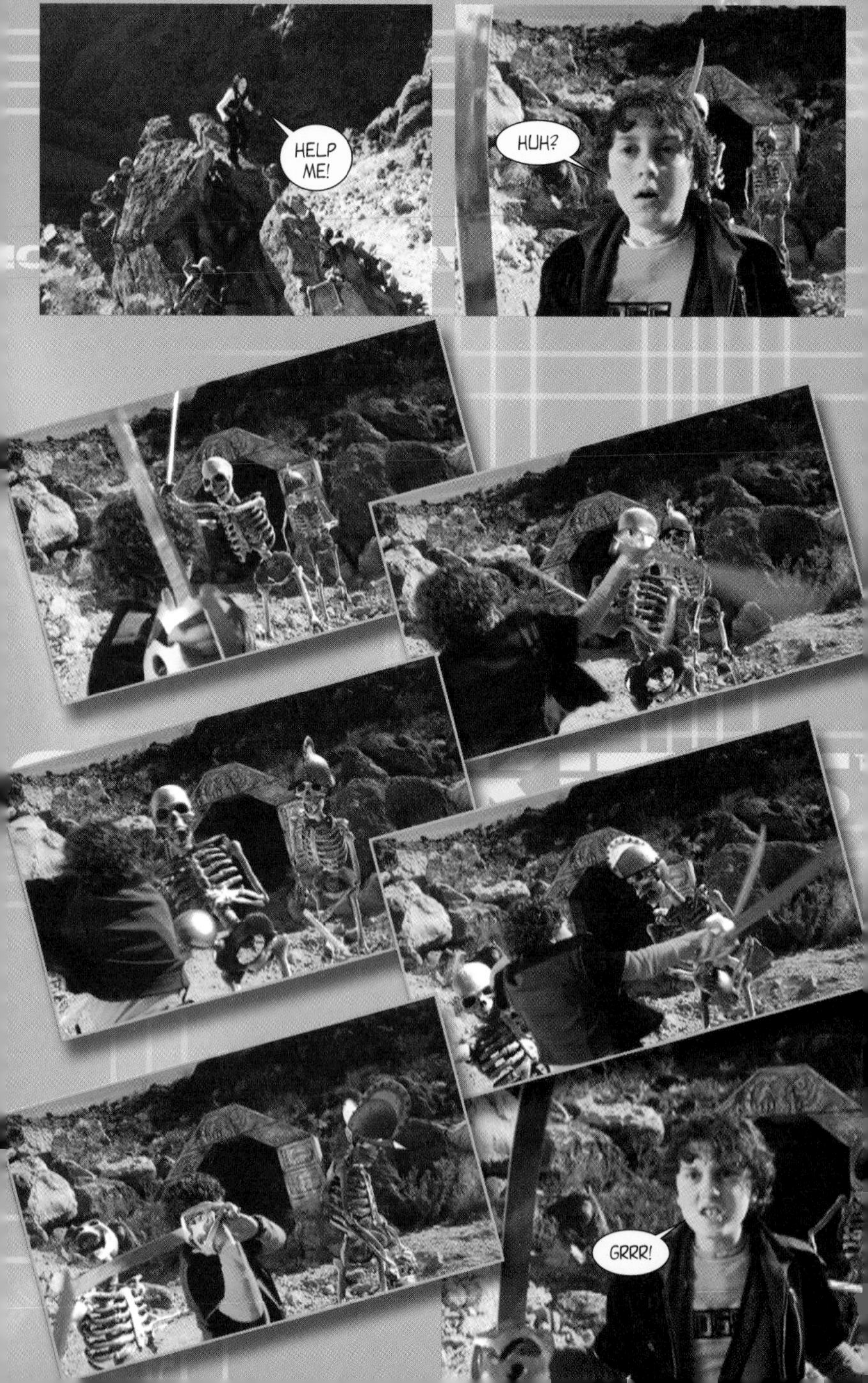
HELP ME!
HUH?
GRRR!

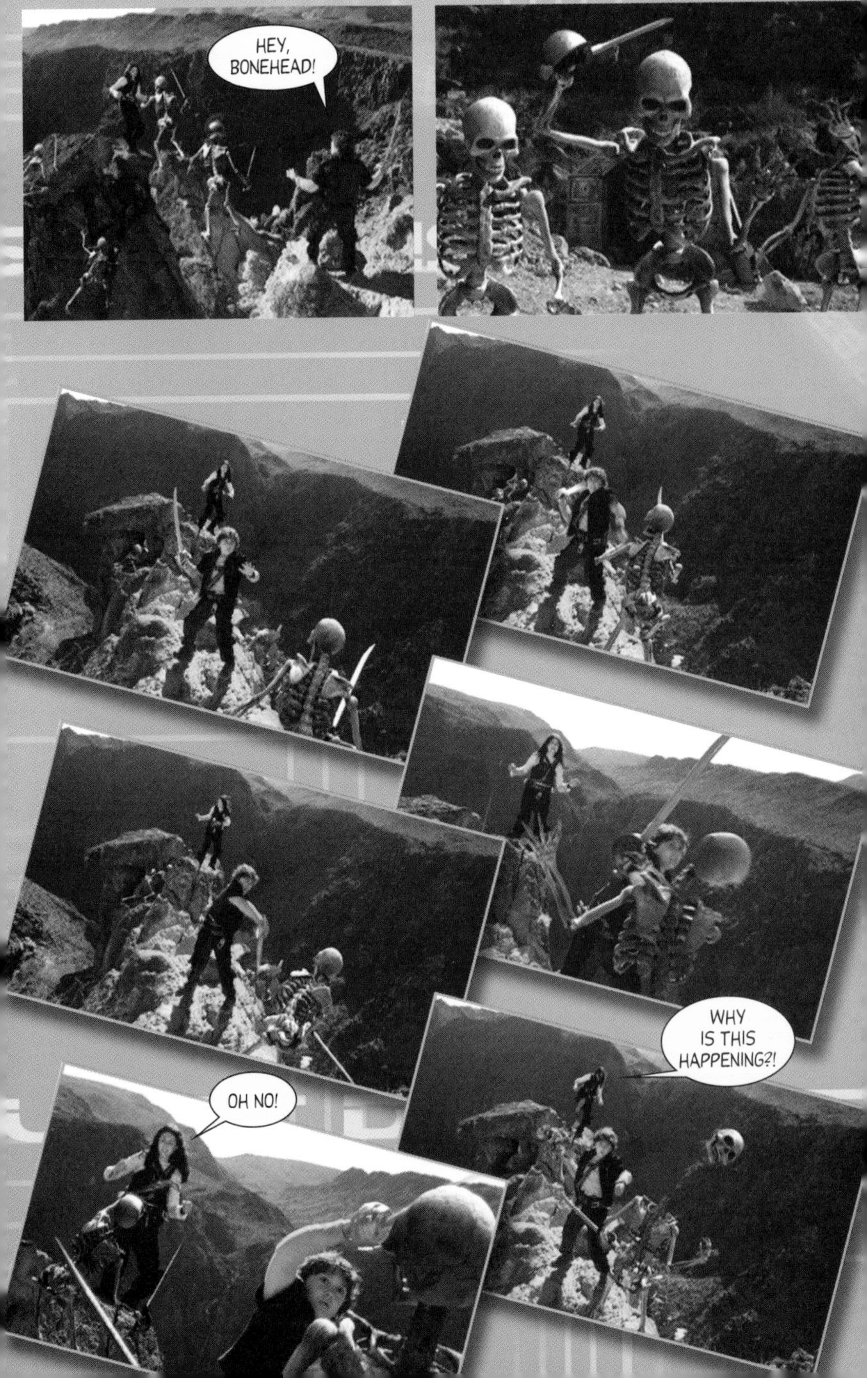
HEY, BONEHEAD!
OH NO!
WHY IS THIS HAPPENING?!

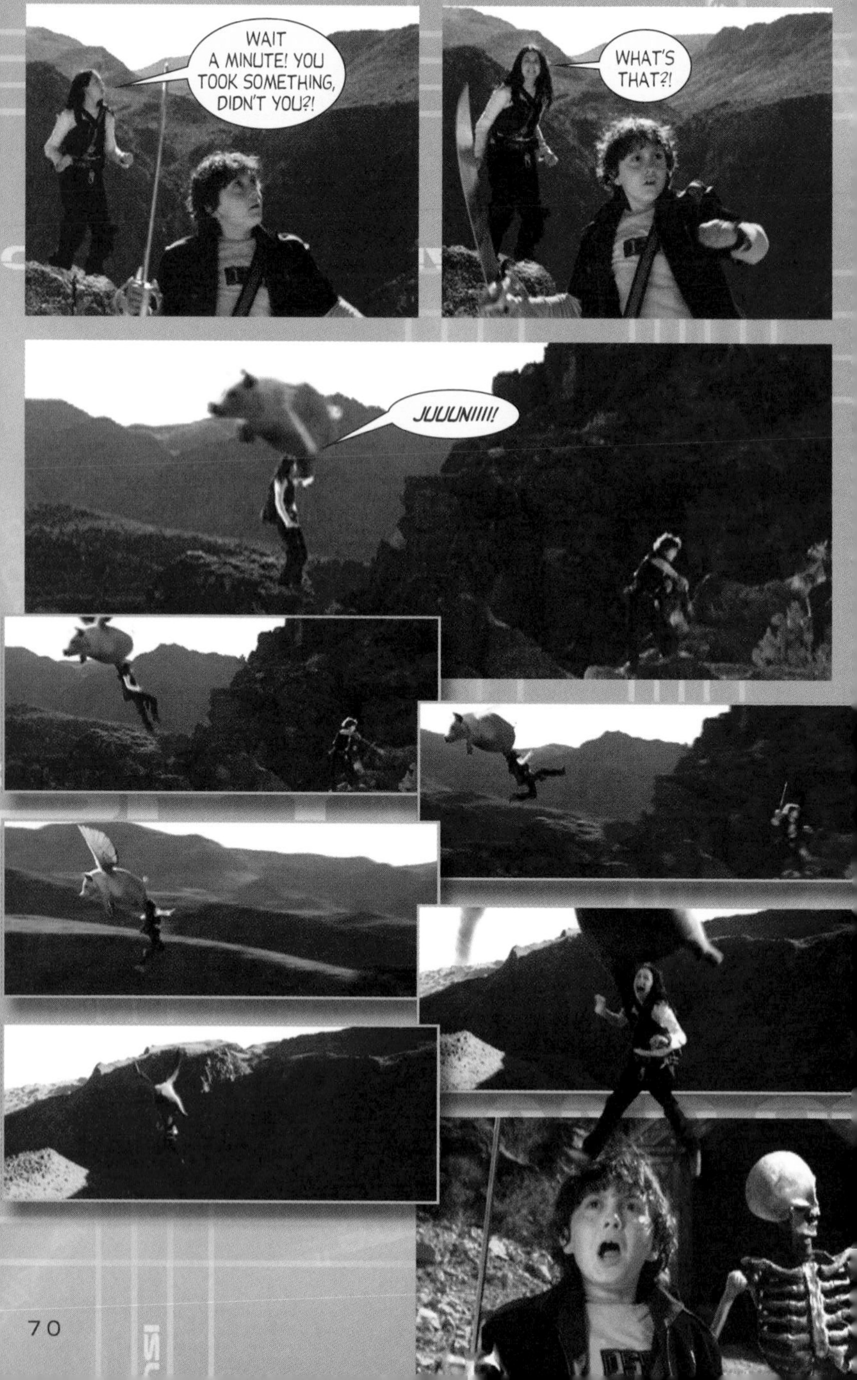
WAIT A MINUTE! YOU TOOK SOMETHING, DIDN'T YOU?!
WHAT'S THAT?!
JUUUNIIII!

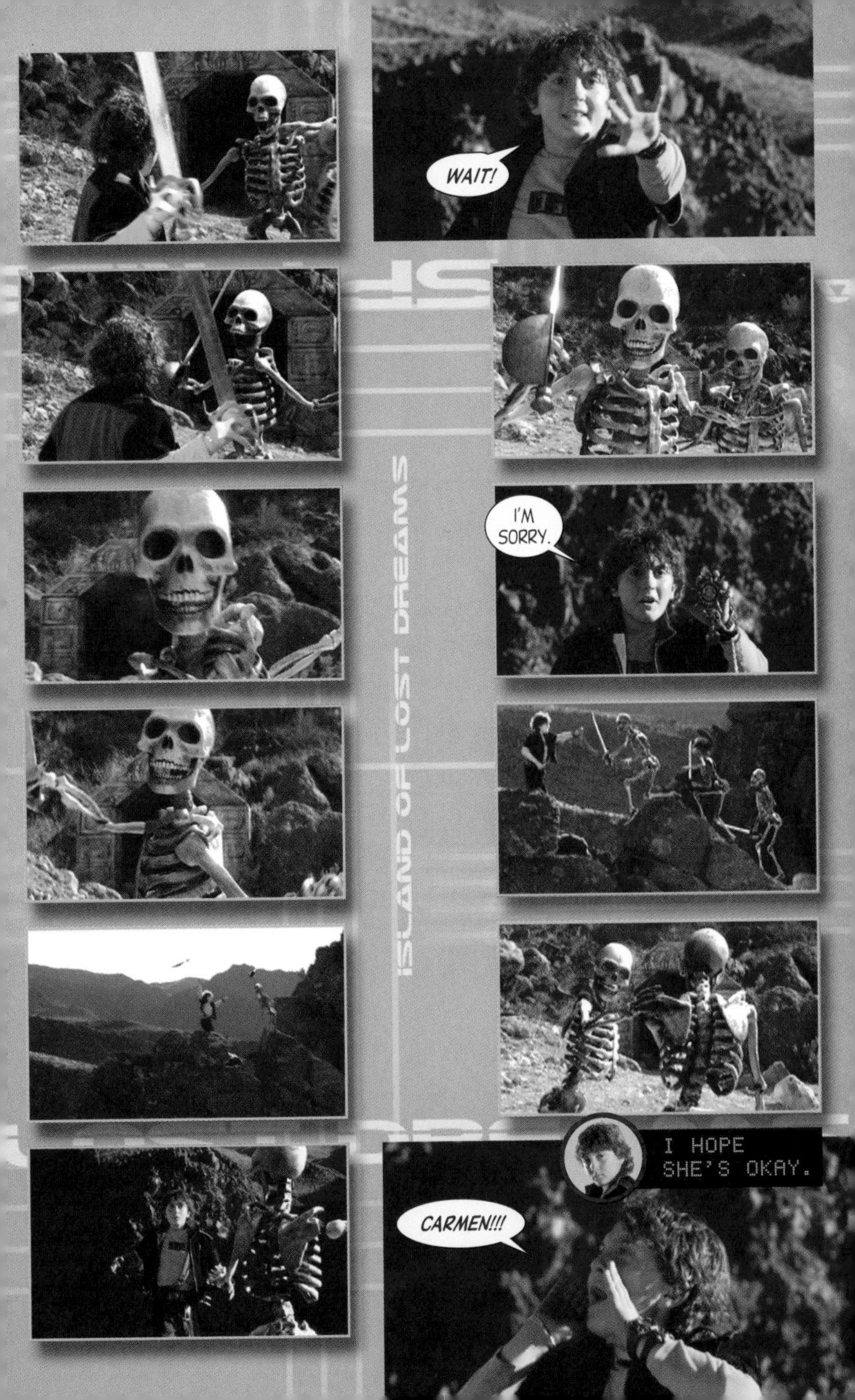
ISLAND OF LOST DREAMS
WAIT!
I'M SORRY.
I HOPE SHE'S OKAY.
CARMEN!!!

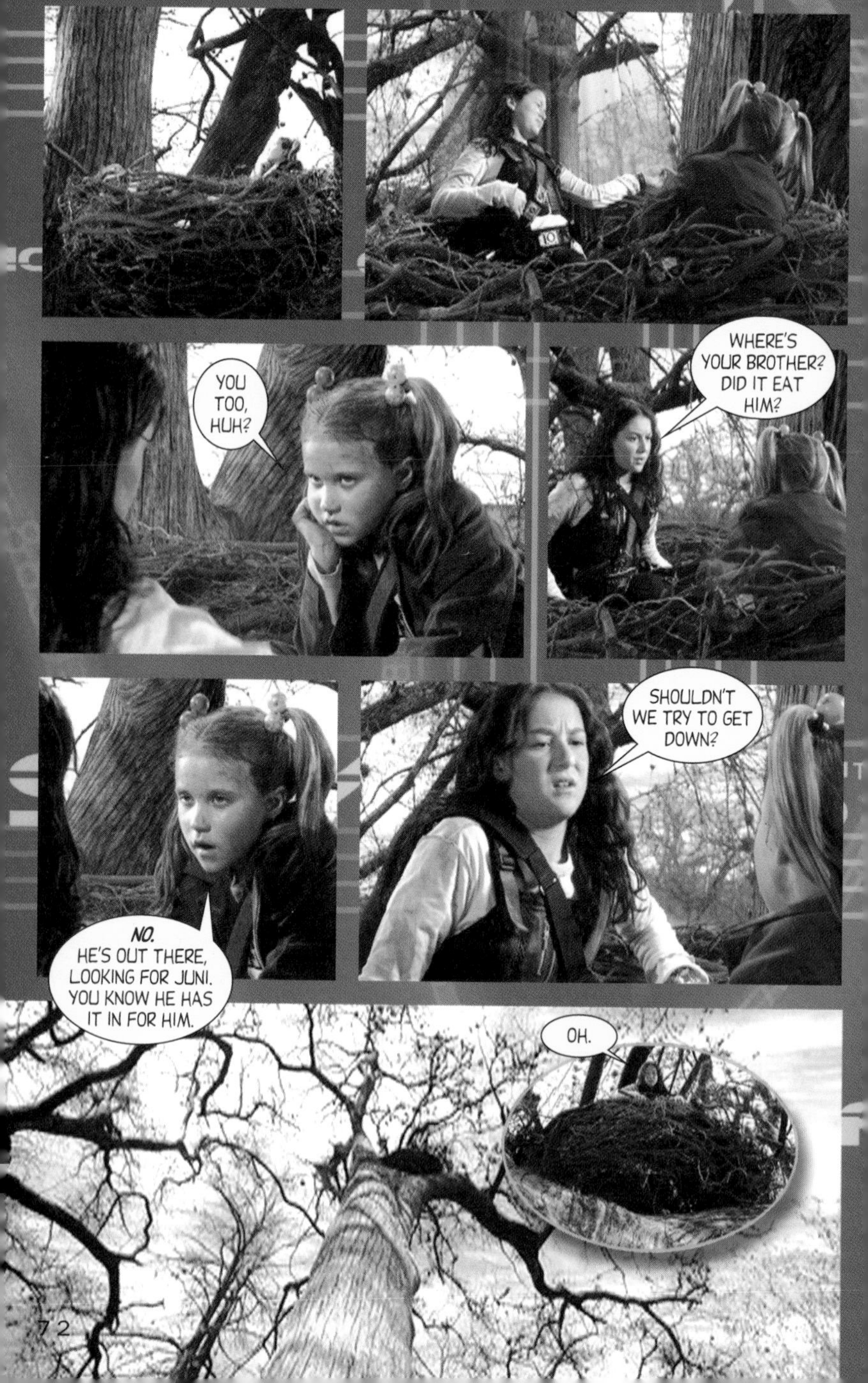
YOU TOO, HUH?
WHERE'S YOUR BROTHER? DID IT EAT HIM?
NO. HE'S OUT THERE, LOOKING FOR JUNI. YOU KNOW HE HAS IT IN FOR HIM.
SHOULDN'T WE TRY TO GET DOWN?
OH.

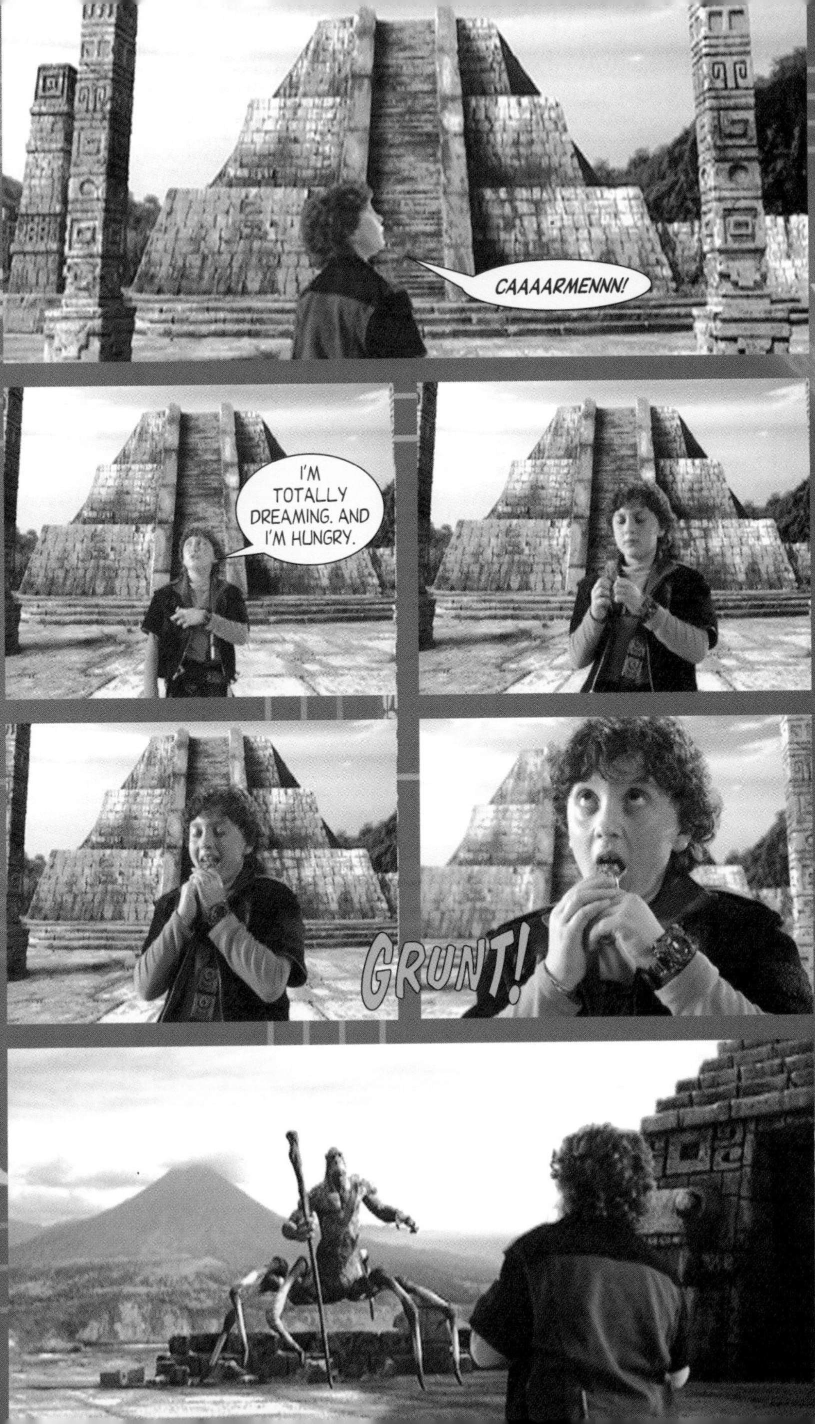
CAAAARMENNN!
I'M TOTALLY DREAMING. AND I'M HUNGRY.
GRUNT!

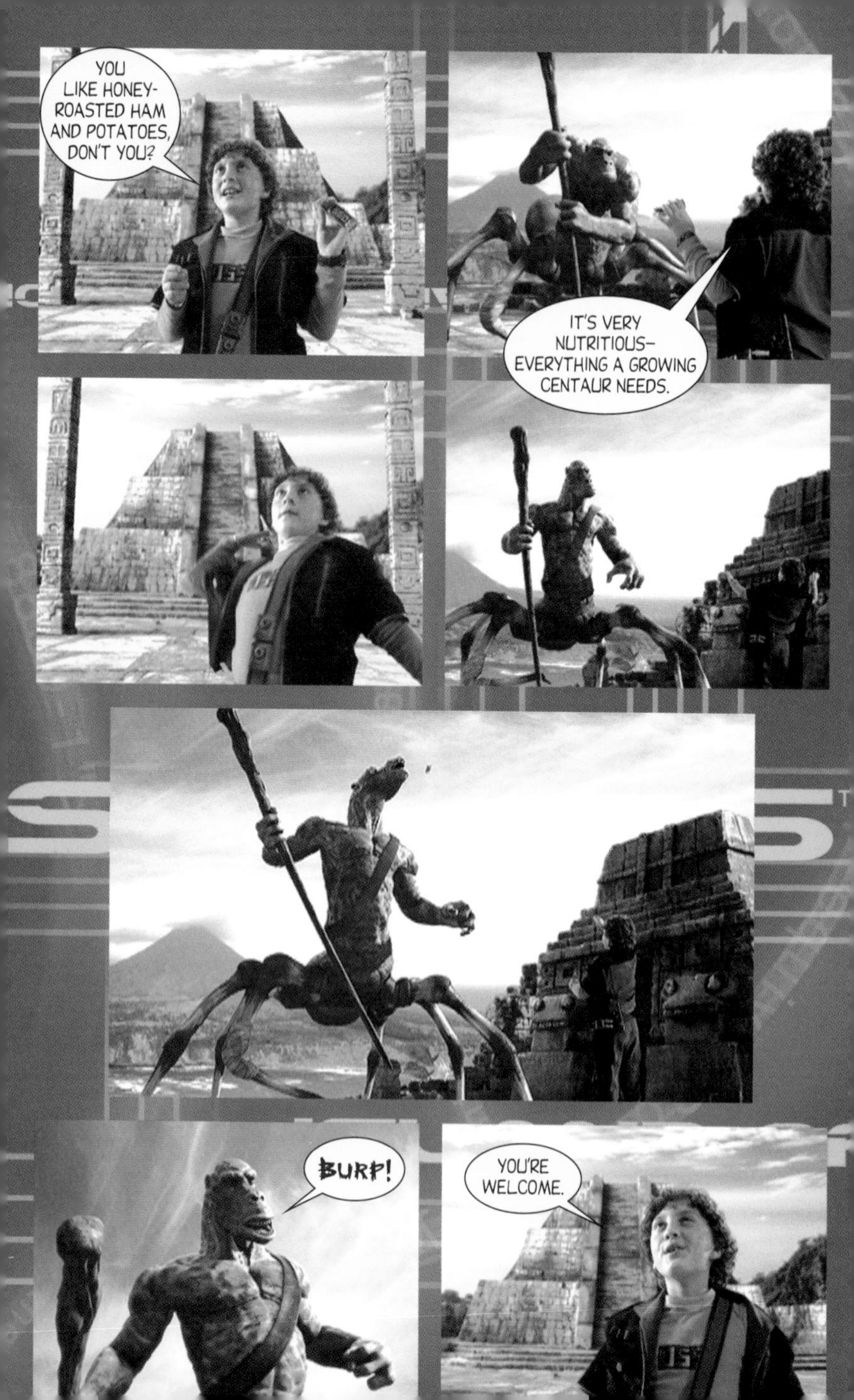
YOU LIKE HONEY-ROASTED HAM AND POTATOES, DON'T YOU?
IT'S VERY NUTRITIOUS— EVERYTHING A GROWING CENTAUR NEEDS.
BURP!
YOU'RE WELCOME.

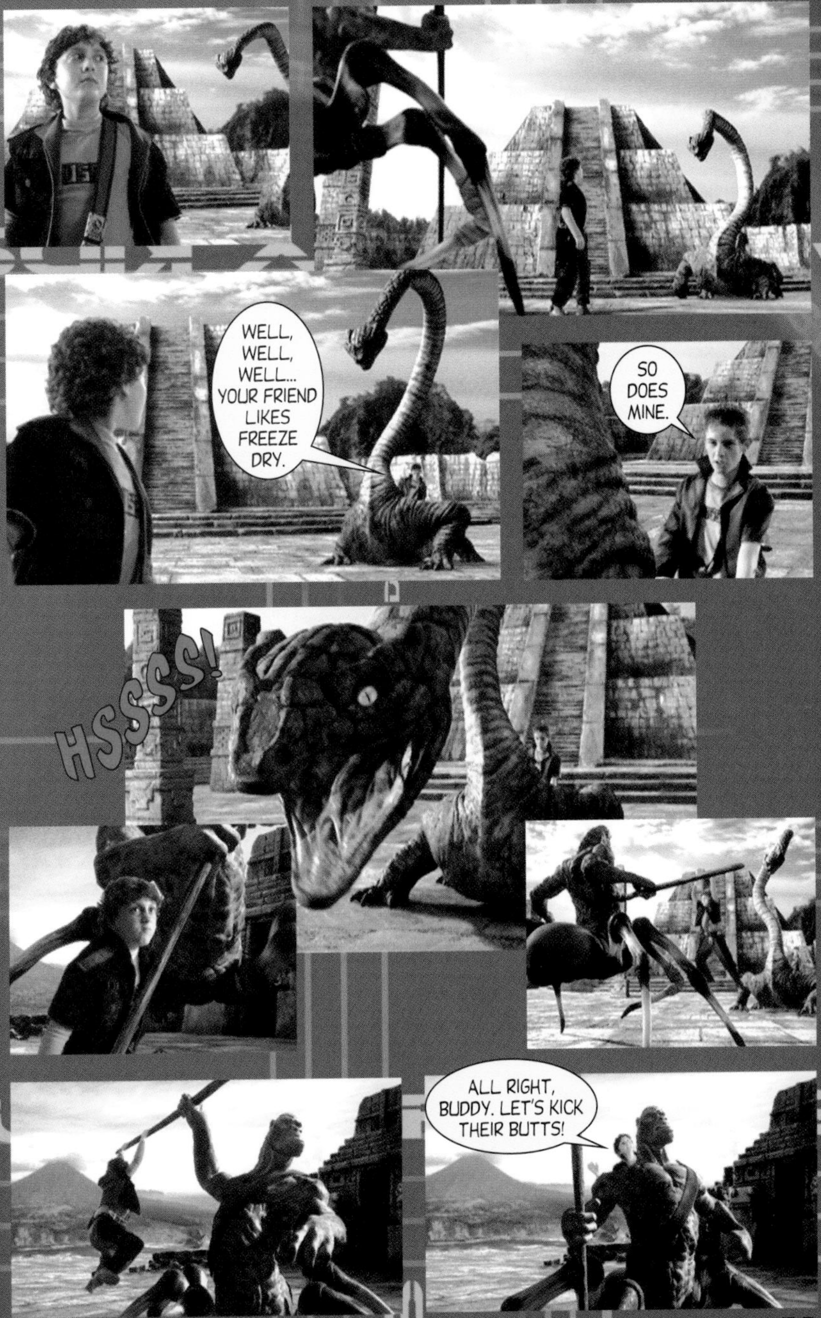
WELL, WELL, WELL... YOUR FRIEND LIKES FREEZE DRY.
SO DOES MINE.
HSSSSS!
ALL RIGHT, BUDDY. LET'S KICK THEIR BUTTS!

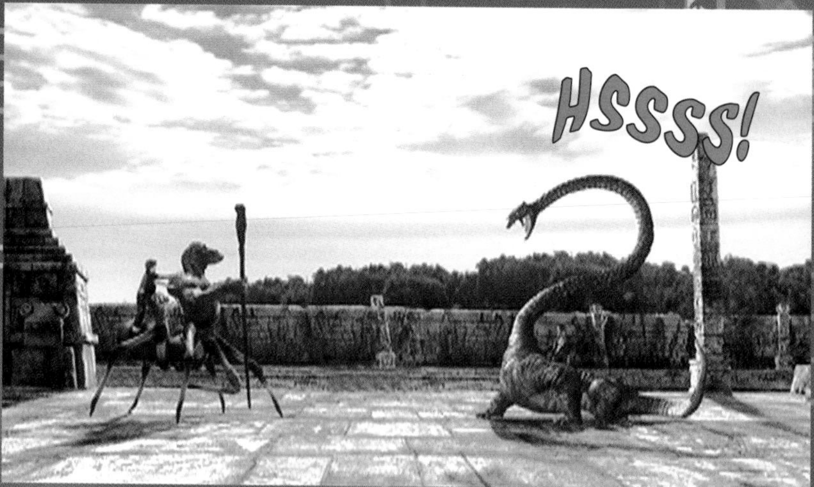
HSSSS!

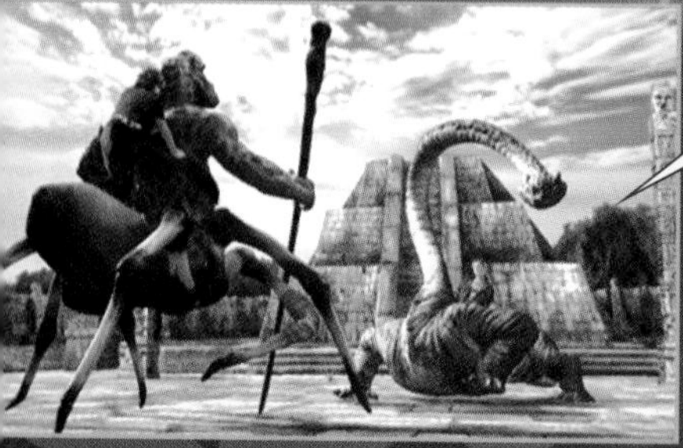
I CAN'T LET YOU BUST UP MY DAD'S MACHINE.

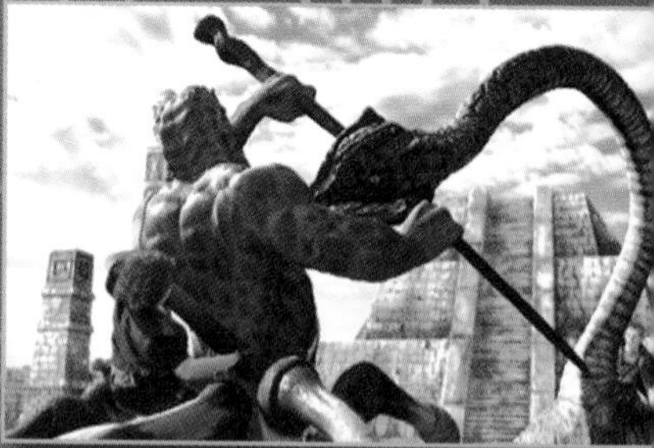

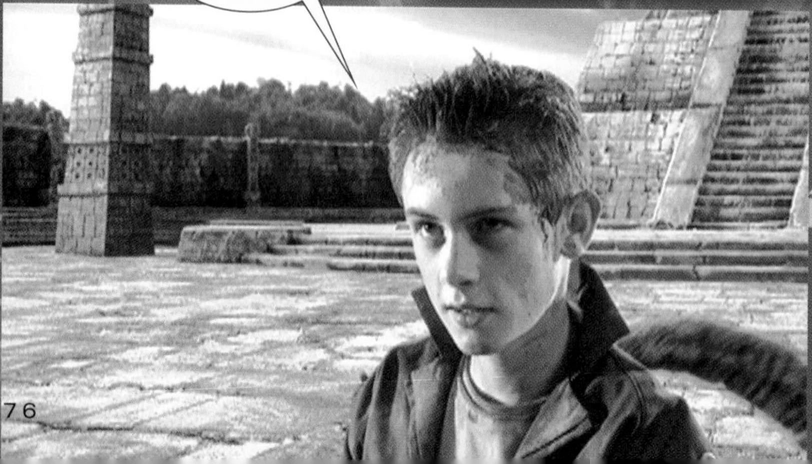
SO I GUESS I'LL JUST HAVE TO BUST YOU UP.

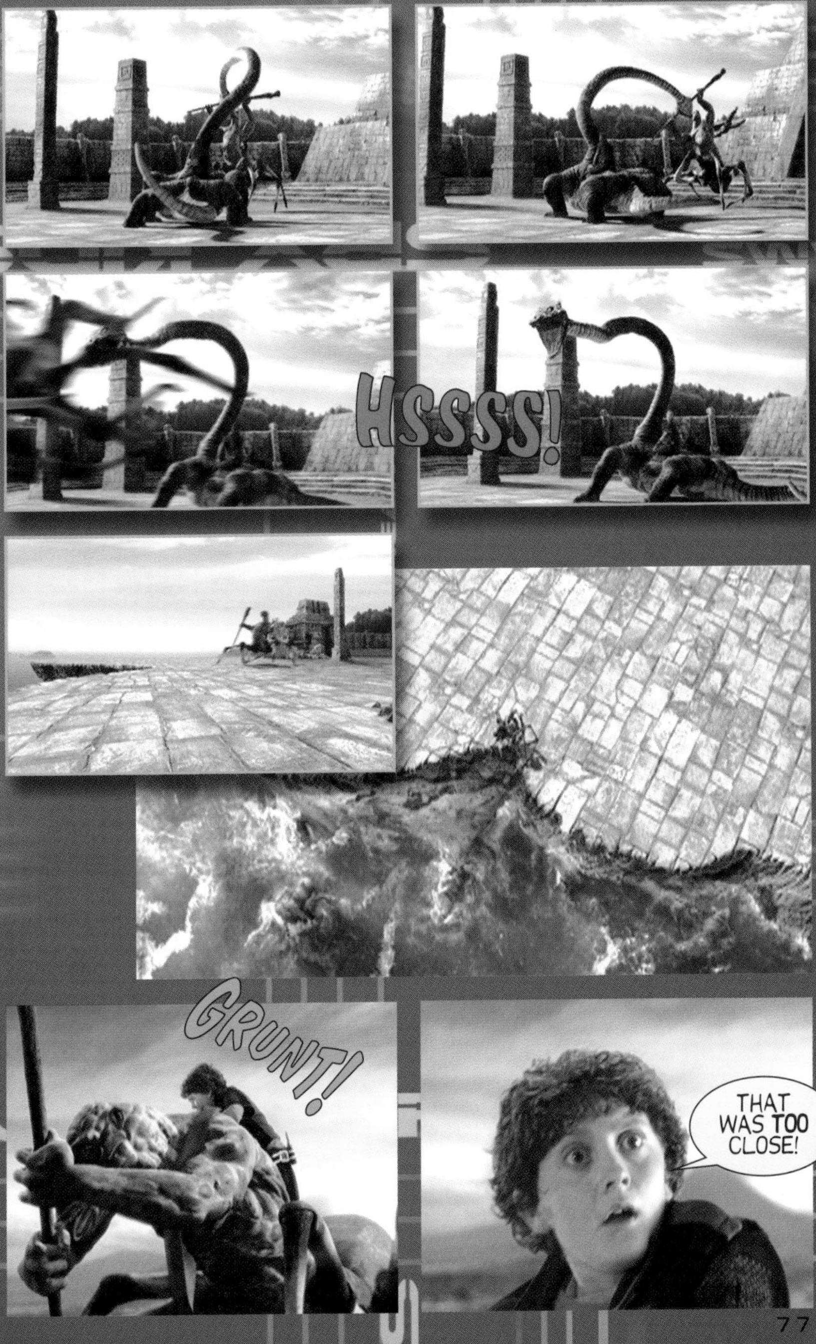
HSSSS!
GRUNT!
THAT WAS TOO CLOSE!

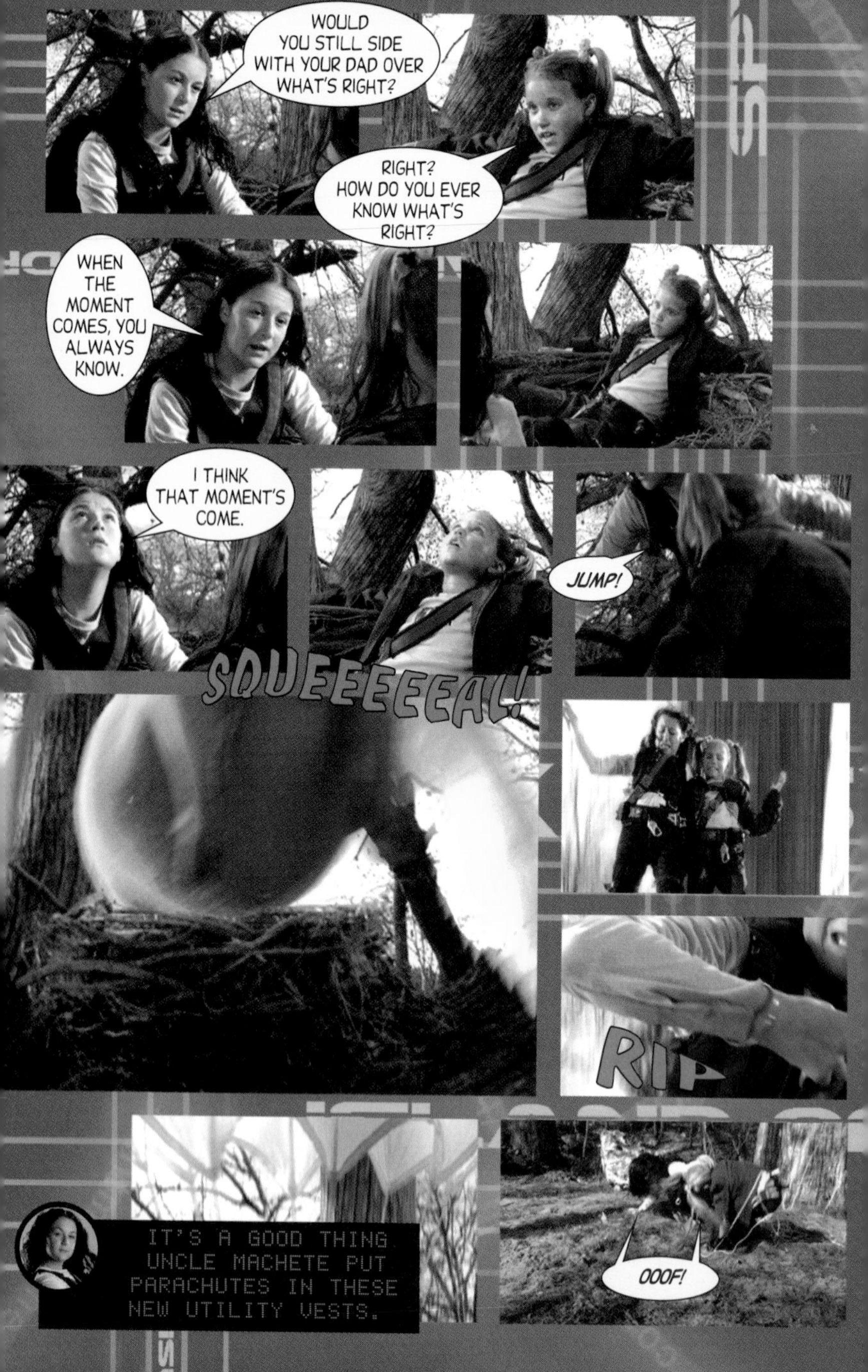
WOULD YOU STILL SIDE WITH YOUR DAD OVER WHAT'S RIGHT?
RIGHT? HOW DO YOU EVER KNOW WHAT'S RIGHT?
WHEN THE MOMENT COMES, YOU ALWAYS KNOW.
I THINK THAT MOMENT'S COME.
JUMP!
SQUEEEEEEAL!
RIP
IT'S A GOOD THING UNCLE MACHETE PUT PARACHUTES IN THESE NEW UTILITY VESTS.
OOOF!

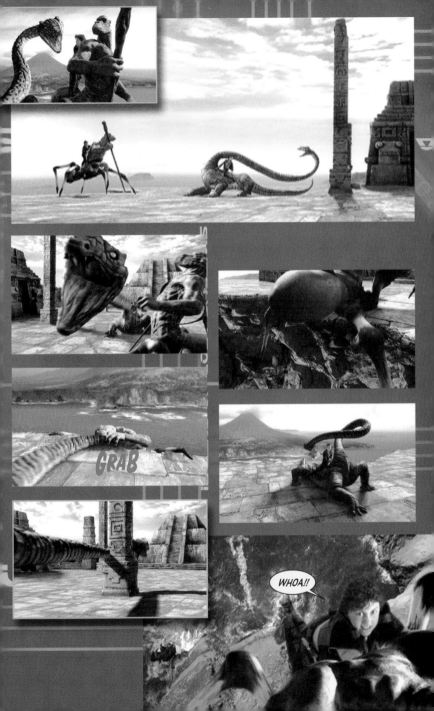

GRAB

WHOA!!

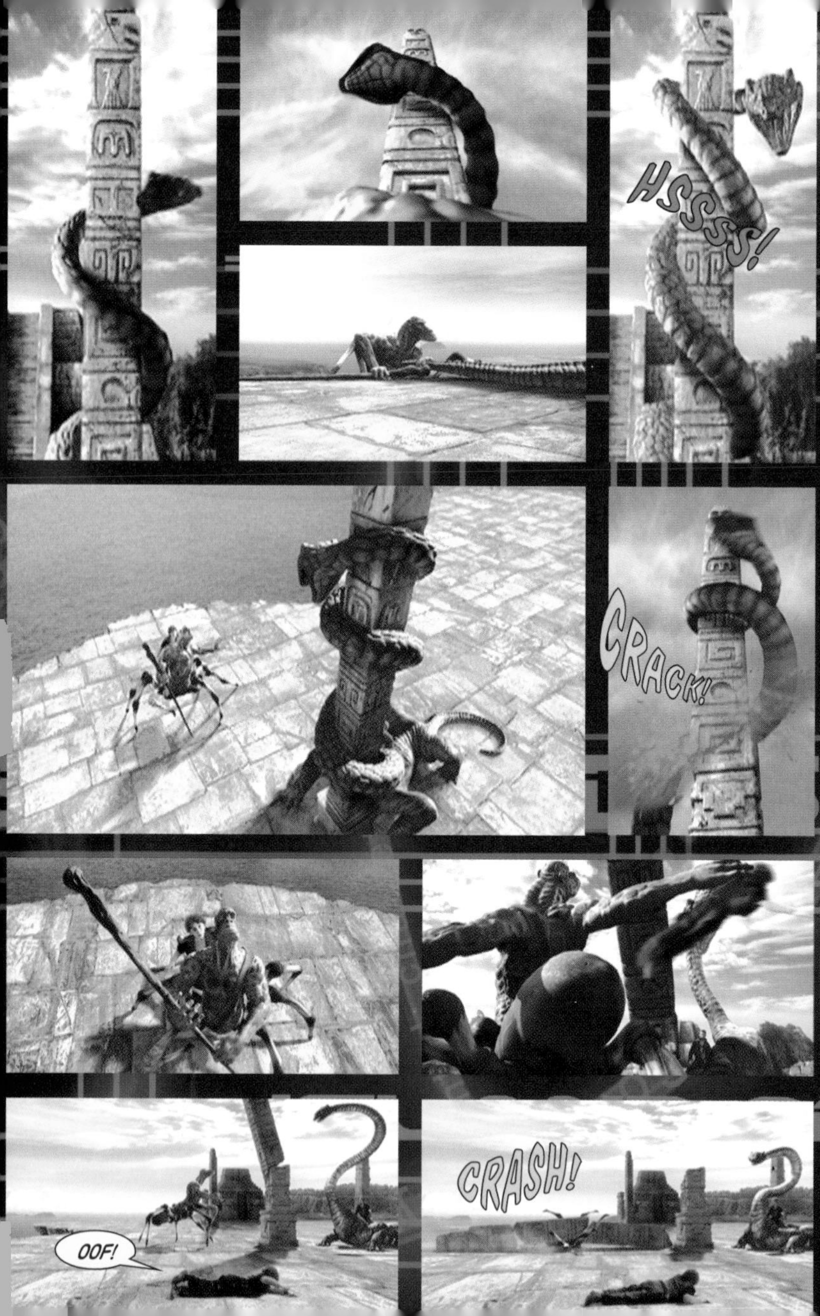
HSSSS!
CRACK!
OOF!
CRASH!

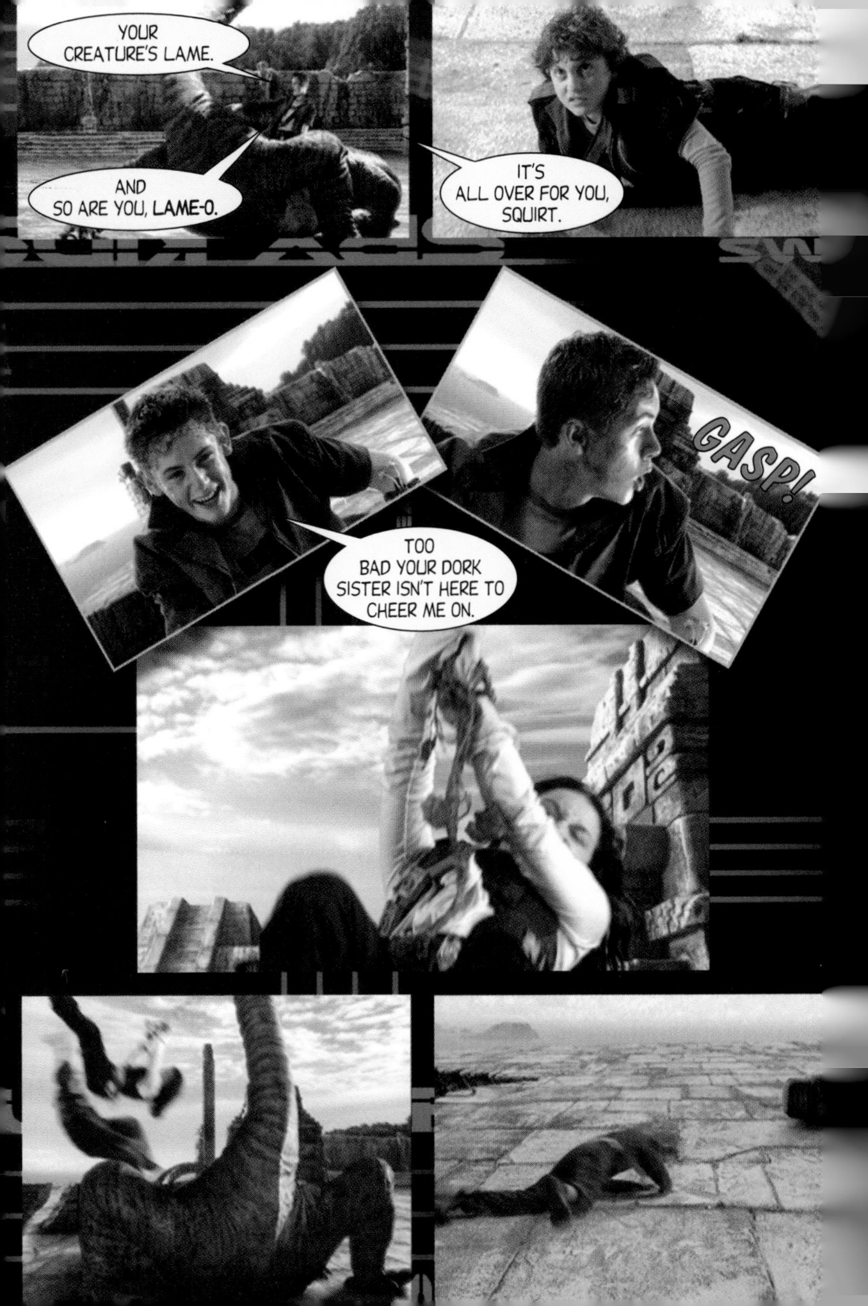
YOUR CREATURE'S LAME.
AND SO ARE YOU, LAME-O.
IT'S ALL OVER FOR YOU, SQUIRT.
TOO BAD YOUR DORK SISTER ISN'T HERE TO CHEER ME ON.
GASP!

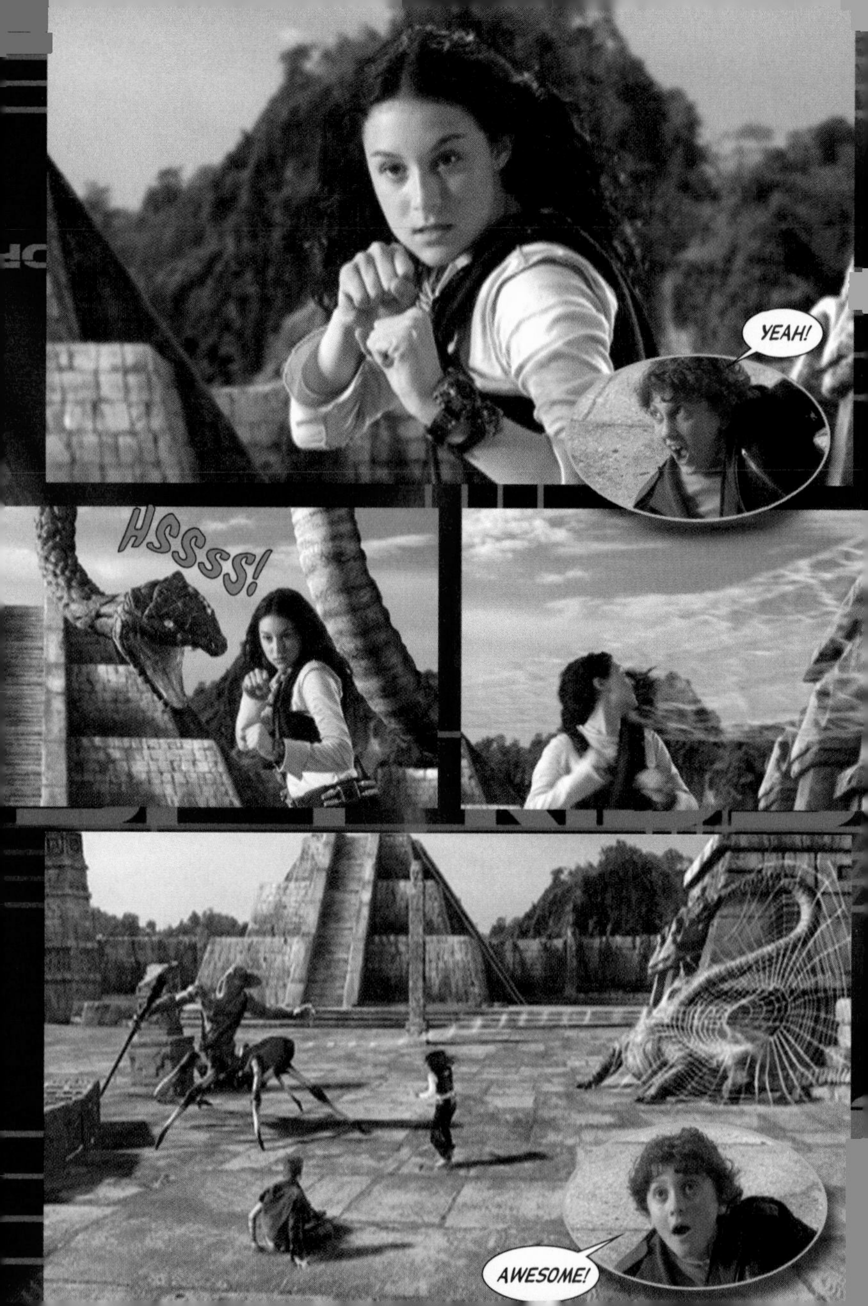
YEAH!
HSSSS!
AWESOME!

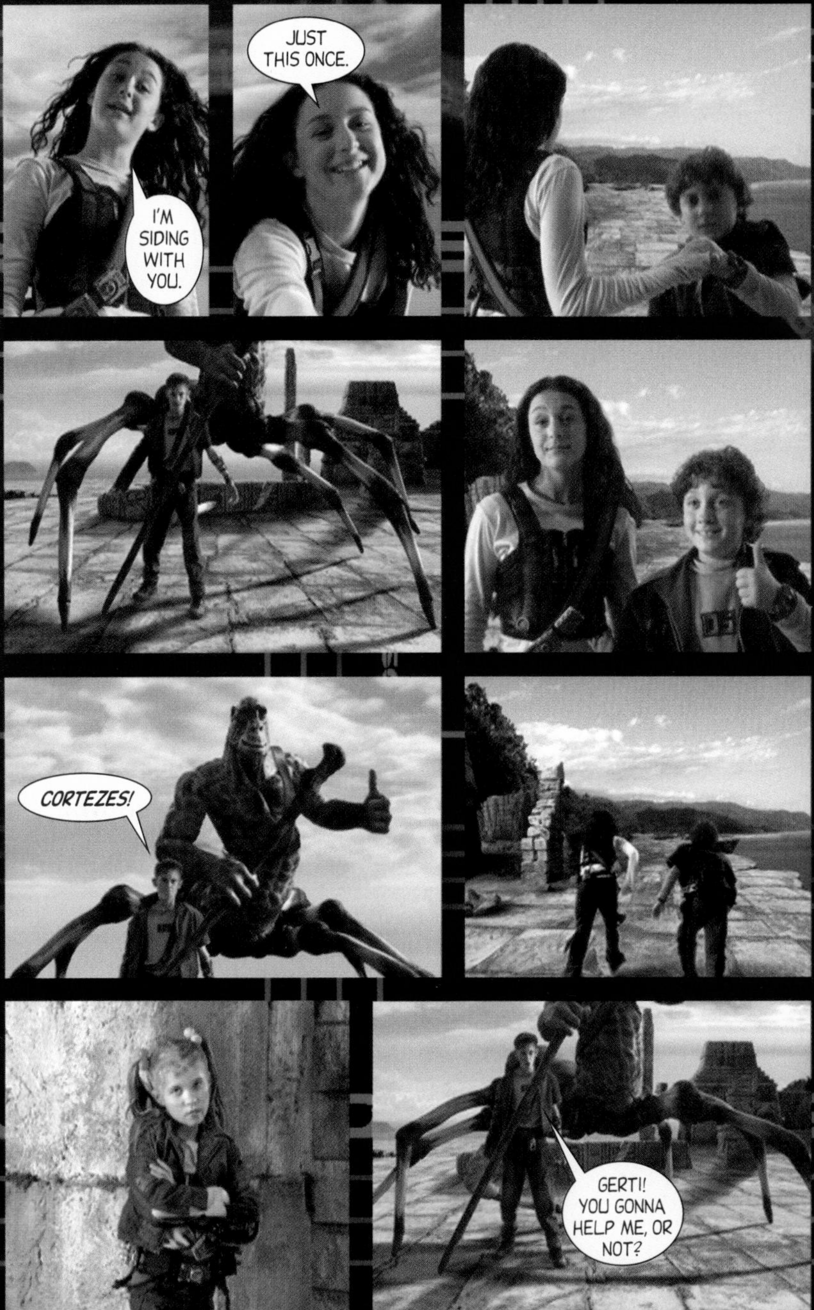
I'M SIDING WITH YOU.
JUST THIS ONCE.
CORTEZES!
GERTI! YOU GONNA HELP ME, OR NOT?

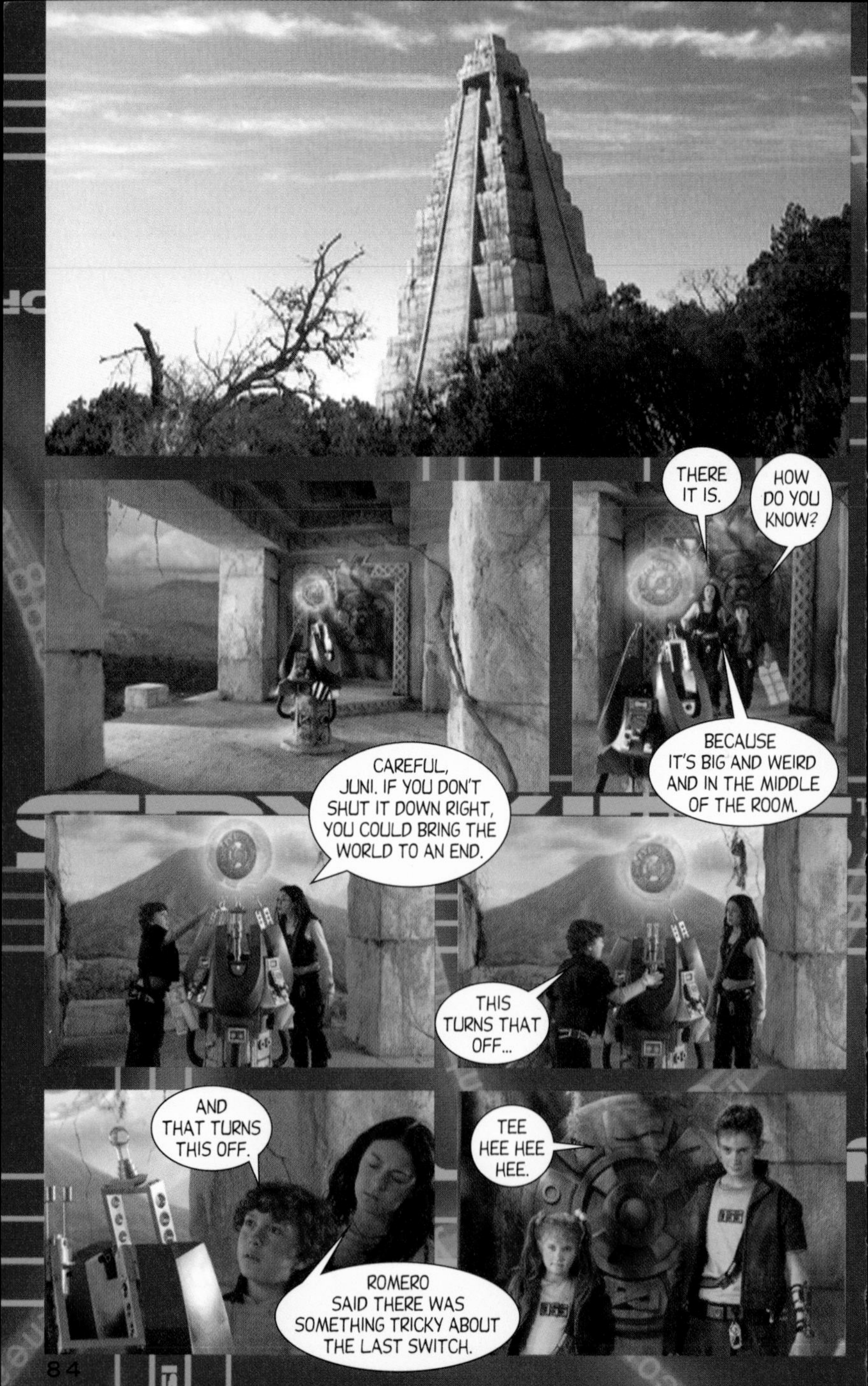
THERE IT IS.
HOW DO YOU KNOW?
BECAUSE IT'S BIG AND WEIRD AND IN THE MIDDLE OF THE ROOM.
CAREFUL, JUNI. IF YOU DON'T SHUT IT DOWN RIGHT, YOU COULD BRING THE WORLD TO AN END.
THIS TURNS THAT OFF...
AND THAT TURNS THIS OFF.
ROMERO SAID THERE WAS SOMETHING TRICKY ABOUT THE LAST SWITCH.
TEE HEE HEE HEE.

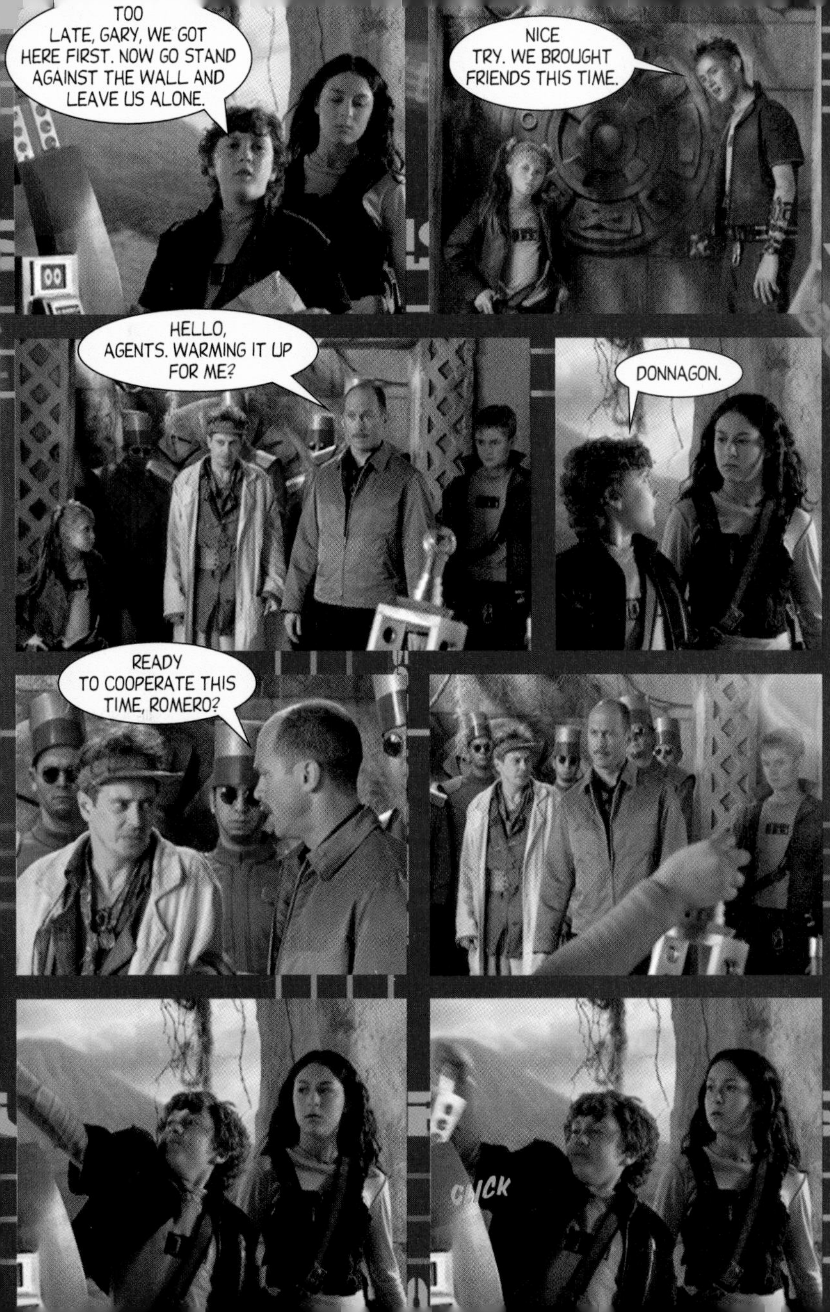
TOO LATE, GARY, WE GOT HERE FIRST. NOW GO STAND AGAINST THE WALL AND LEAVE US ALONE.
NICE TRY. WE BROUGHT FRIENDS THIS TIME.
HELLO, AGENTS. WARMING IT UP FOR ME?
DONNAGON.
READY TO COOPERATE THIS TIME, ROMERO?
CLICK

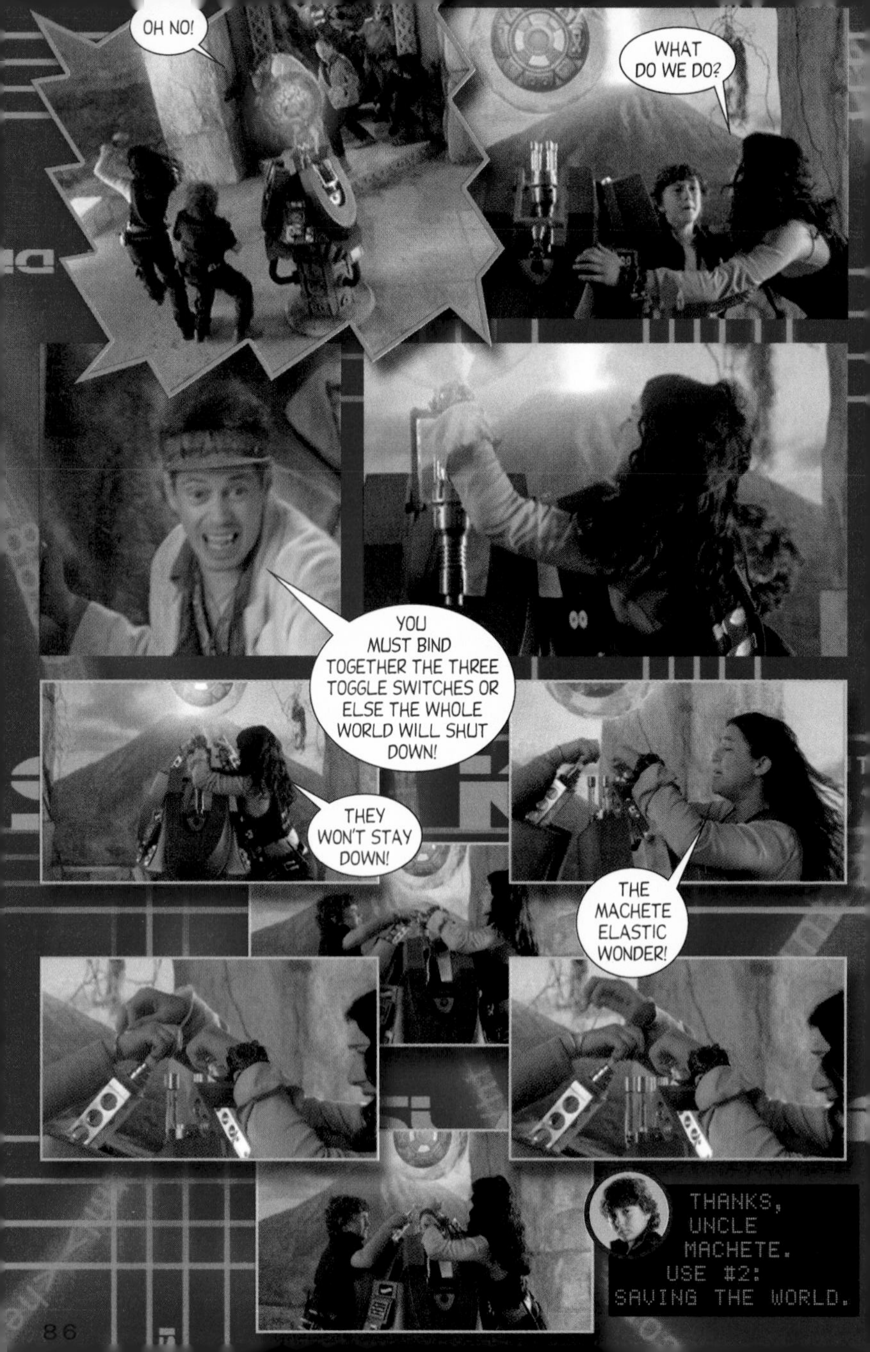
OH NO!
WHAT DO WE DO?
YOU MUST BIND TOGETHER THE THREE TOGGLE SWITCHES OR ELSE THE WHOLE WORLD WILL SHUT DOWN!
THEY WON'T STAY DOWN!
THE MACHETE ELASTIC WONDER!
THANKS, UNCLE MACHETE. USE #2: SAVING THE WORLD.

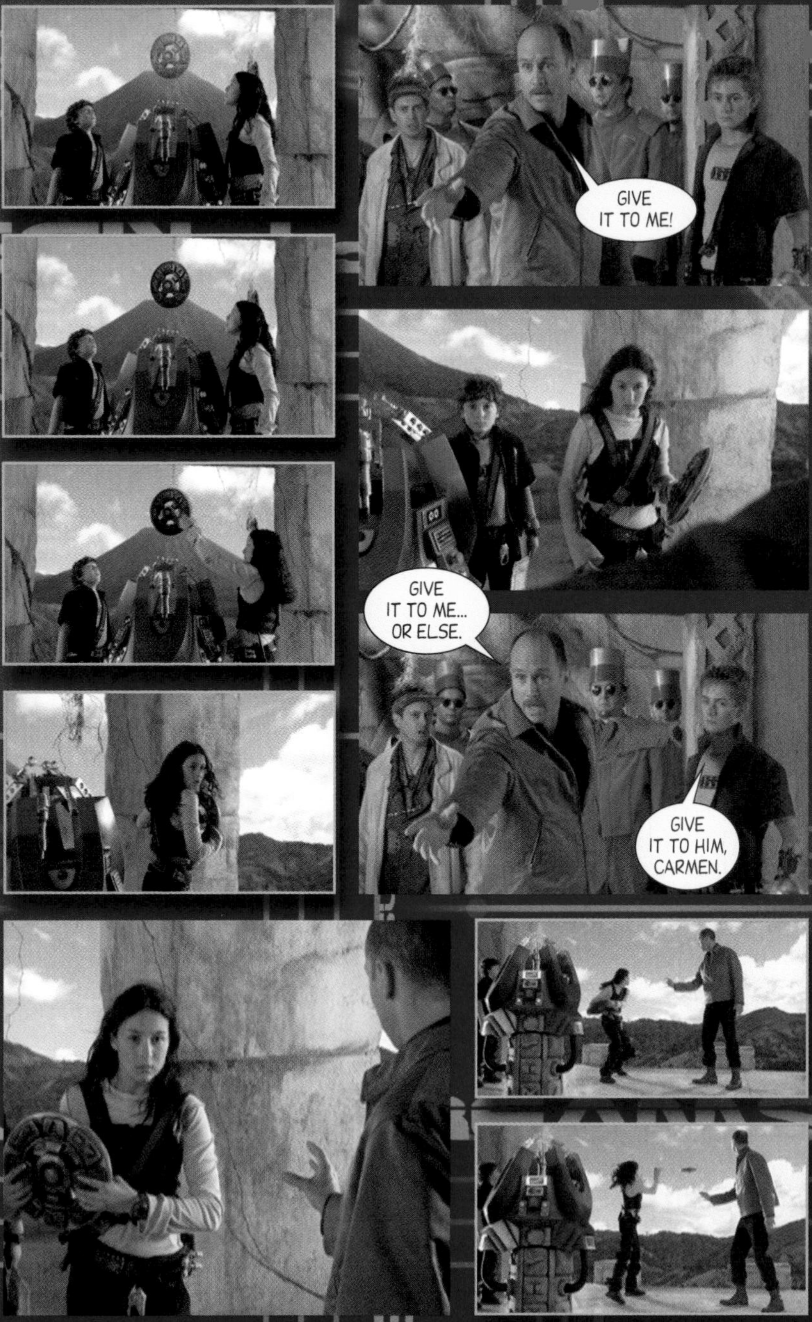
GIVE IT TO ME!
GIVE IT TO ME... OR ELSE.
GIVE IT TO HIM, CARMEN.

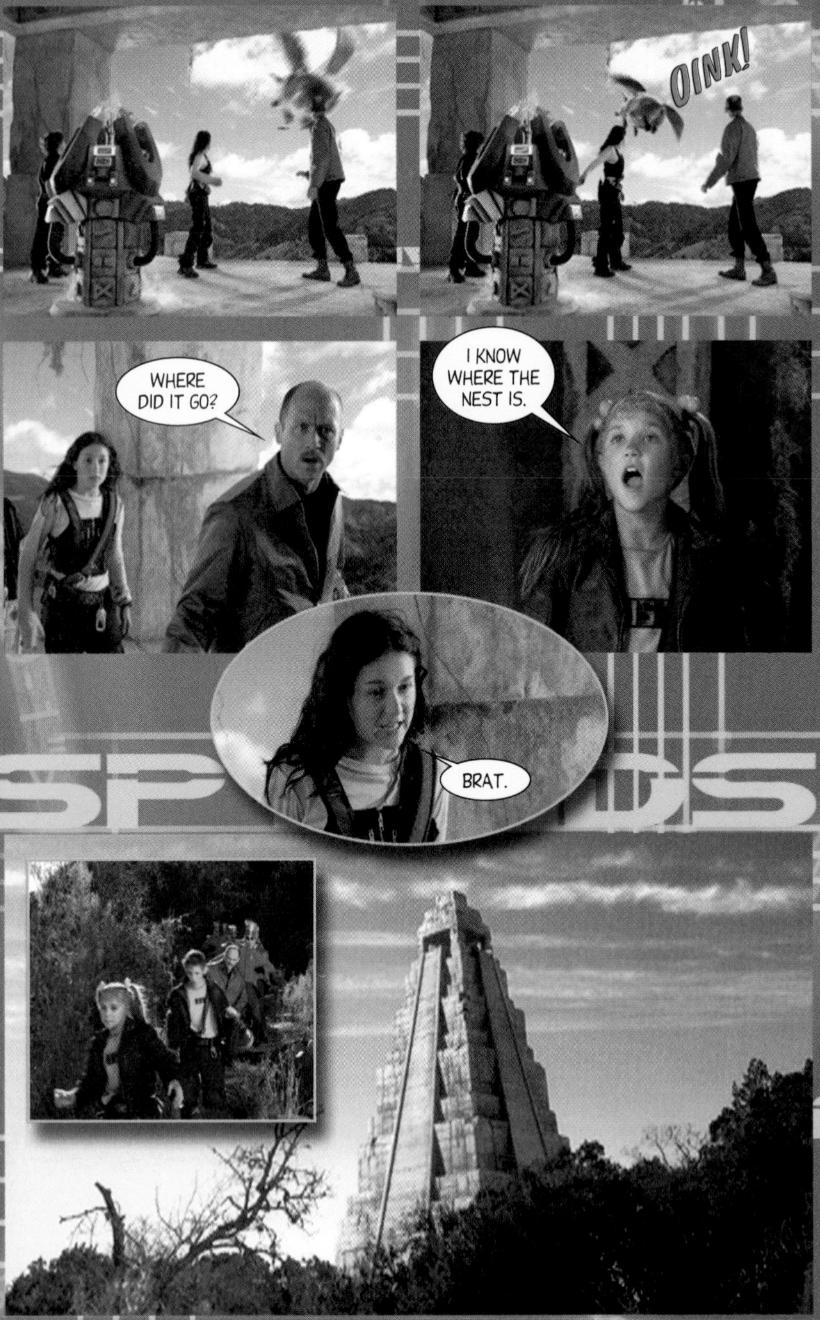
OINK!
WHERE DID IT GO?
I KNOW WHERE THE NEST IS.
BRAT.

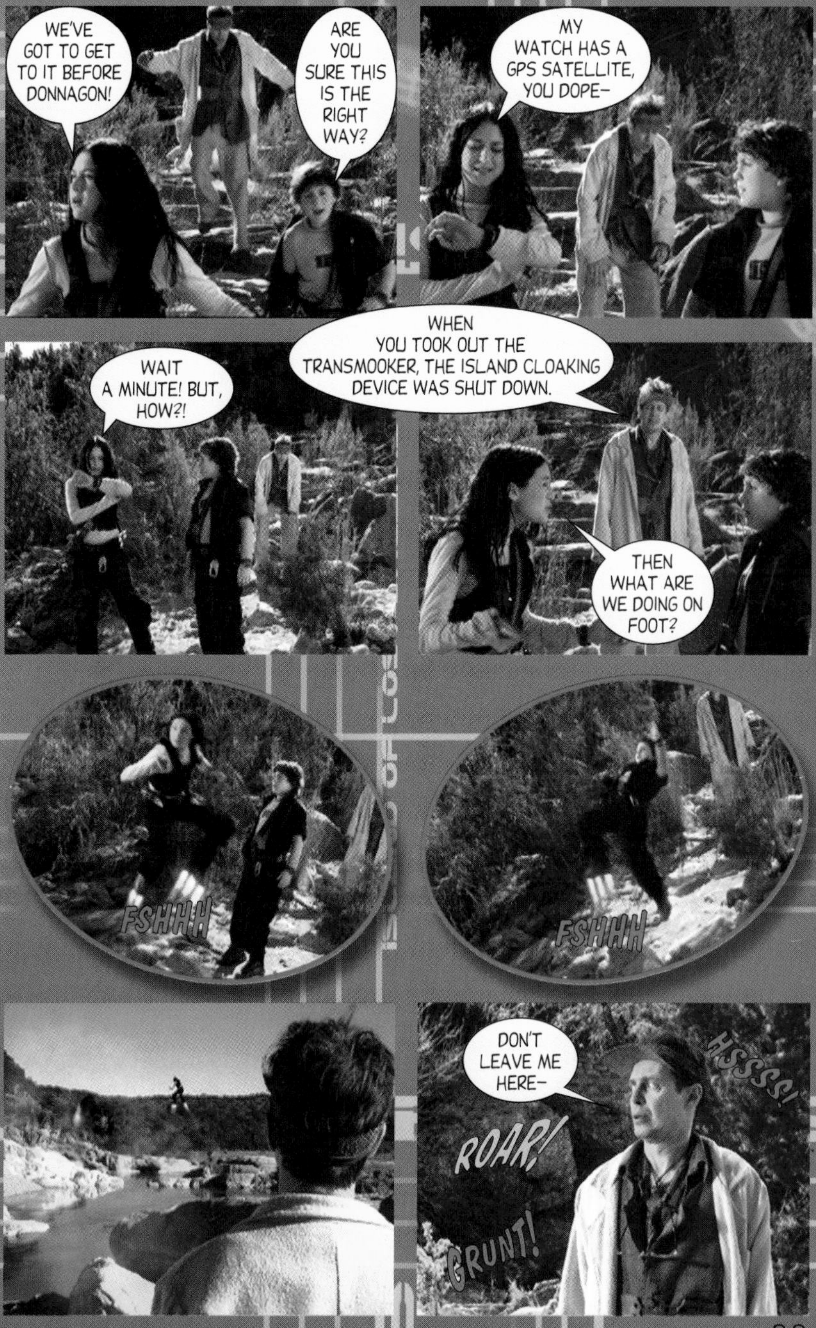
WE'VE GOT TO GET TO IT BEFORE DONNAGON!
ARE YOU SURE THIS IS THE RIGHT WAY?
MY WATCH HAS A GPS SATELLITE, YOU DOPE–
WAIT A MINUTE! BUT, HOW?!
WHEN YOU TOOK OUT THE TRANSMOOKER, THE ISLAND CLOAKING DEVICE WAS SHUT DOWN.
THEN WHAT ARE WE DOING ON FOOT?
FSHHH
FSHHH
DON'T LEAVE ME HERE–
HSSSS!
ROAR!
GRUNT!

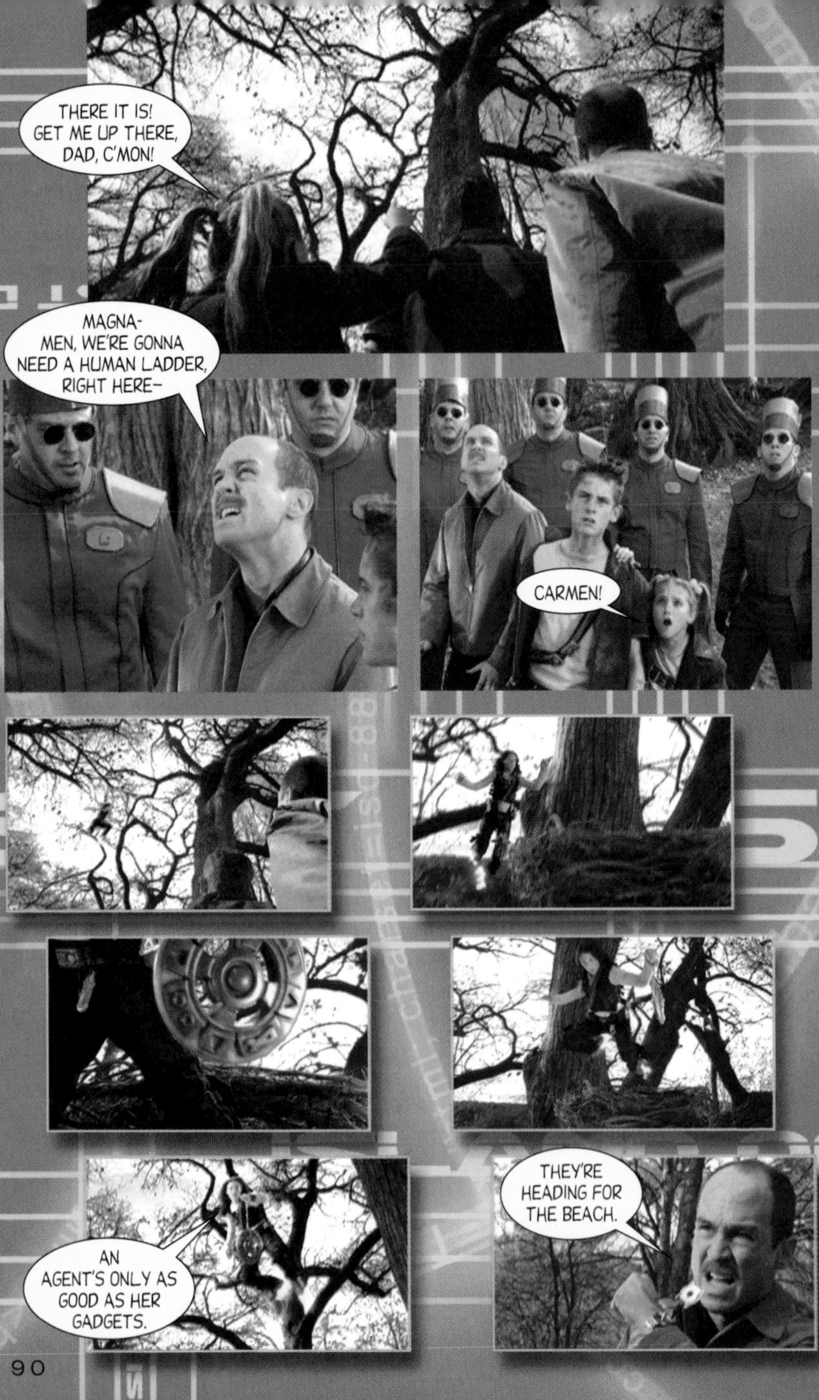
THERE IT IS! GET ME UP THERE, DAD, C'MON!
MAGNA-MEN, WE'RE GONNA NEED A HUMAN LADDER, RIGHT HERE–
CARMEN!
AN AGENT'S ONLY AS GOOD AS HER GADGETS.
THEY'RE HEADING FOR THE BEACH.

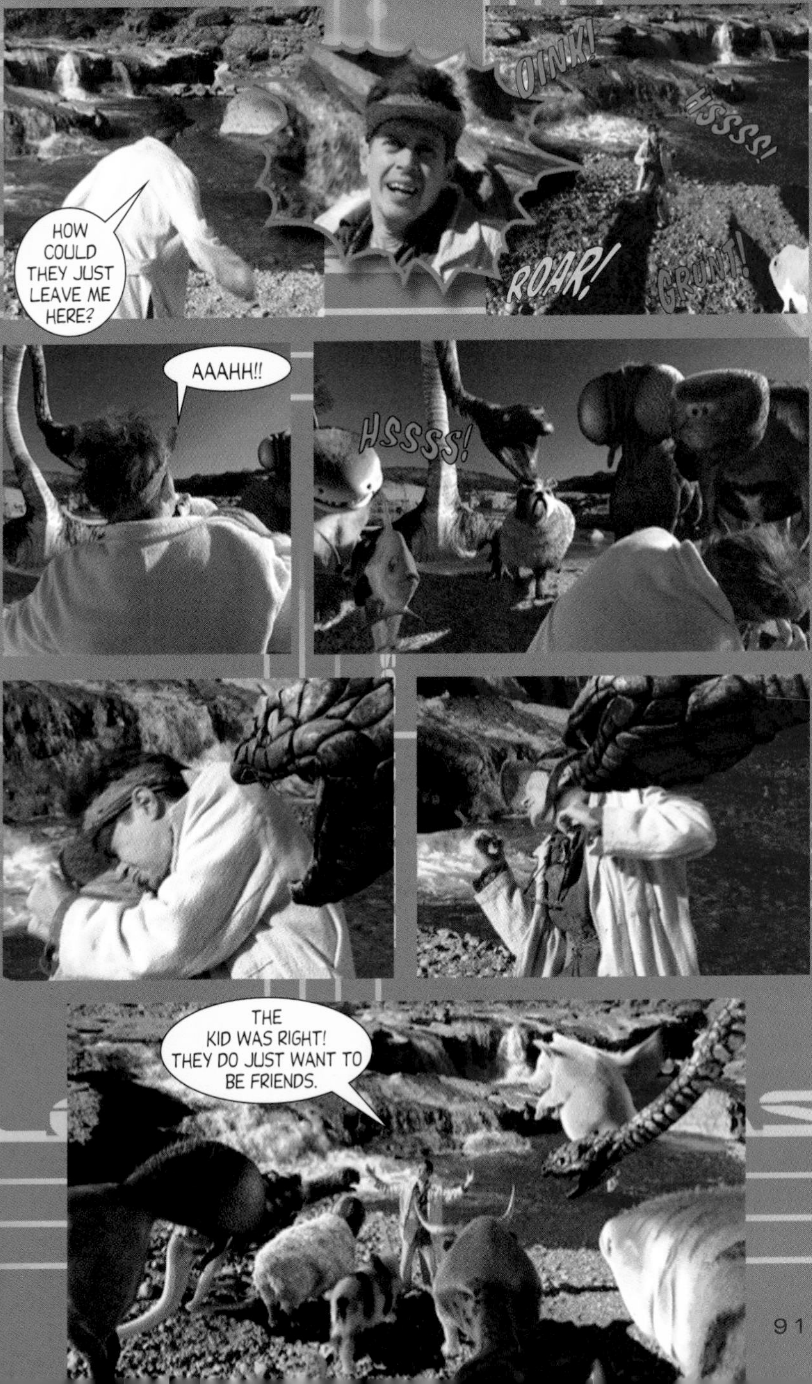
HOW COULD THEY JUST LEAVE ME HERE?
OINK!
HSSSSS!
ROAR!
GRUNT!
AAAHH!!
HSSSS!
THE KID WAS RIGHT! THEY DO JUST WANT TO BE FRIENDS.

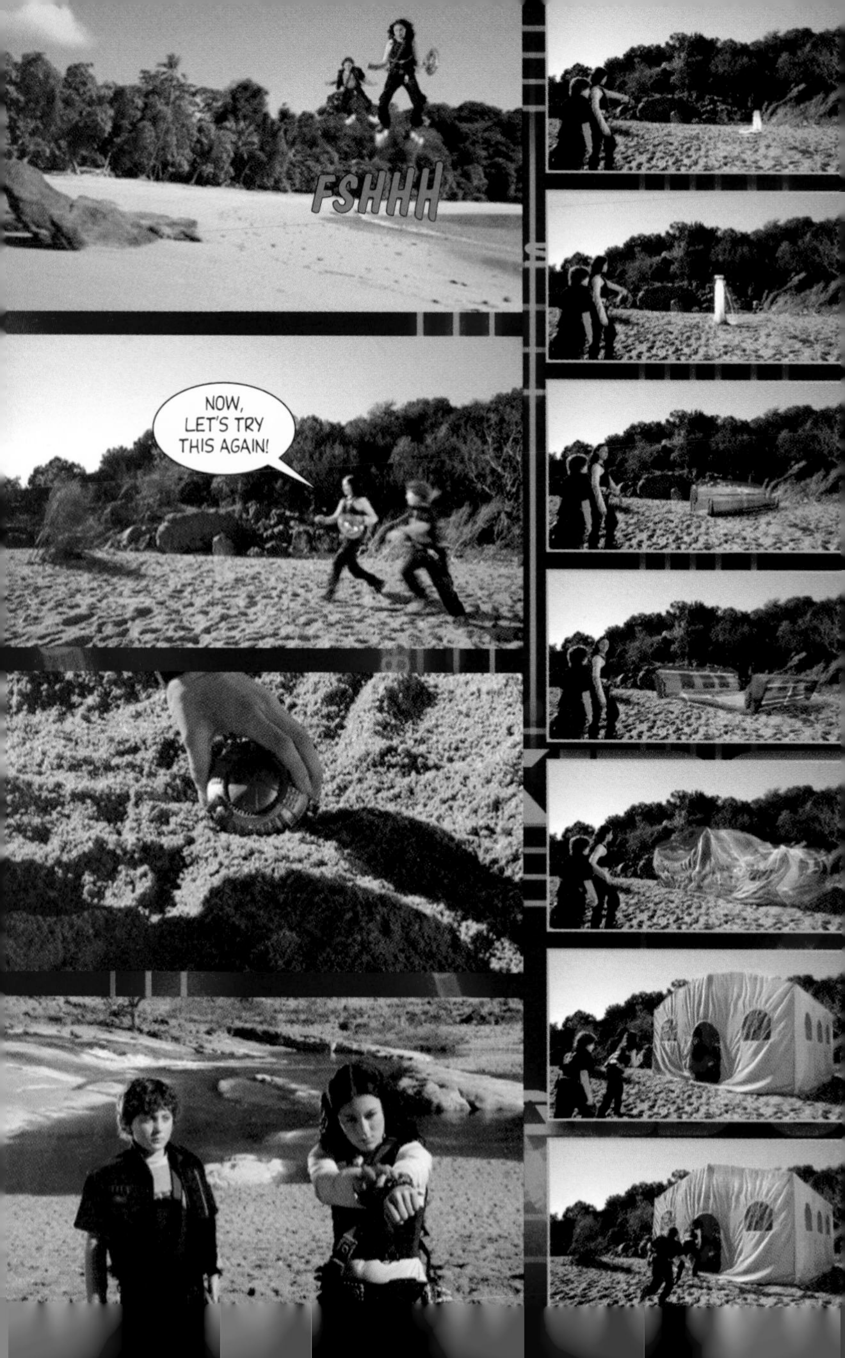
FSHHH
NOW, LET'S TRY THIS AGAIN!

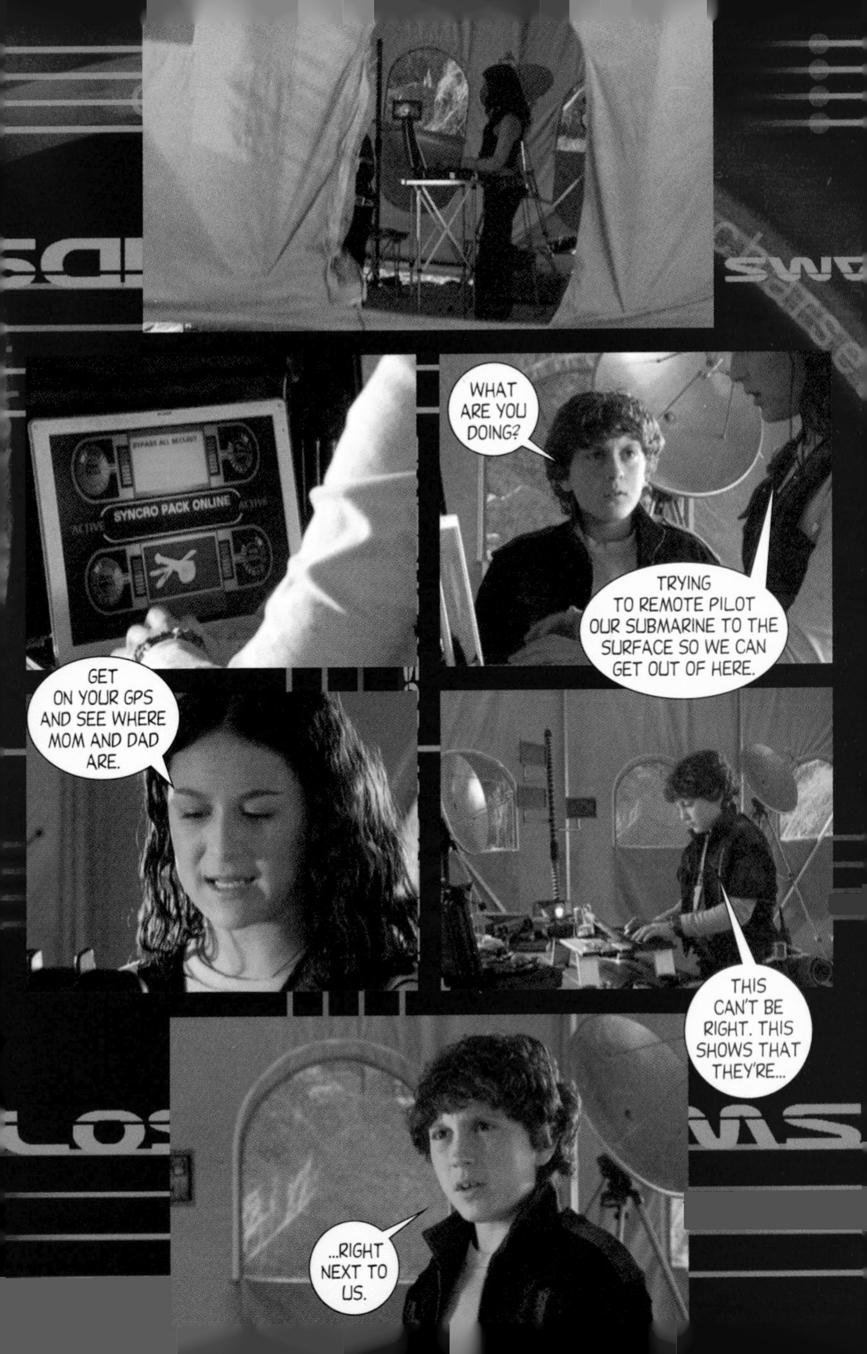
SYNCRO PACK ONLINE
ACTIVE
WHAT ARE YOU DOING?
TRYING TO REMOTE PILOT OUR SUBMARINE TO THE SURFACE SO WE CAN GET OUT OF HERE.
GET ON YOUR GPS AND SEE WHERE MOM AND DAD ARE.
THIS CAN'T BE RIGHT. THIS SHOWS THAT THEY'RE...
...RIGHT NEXT TO US.

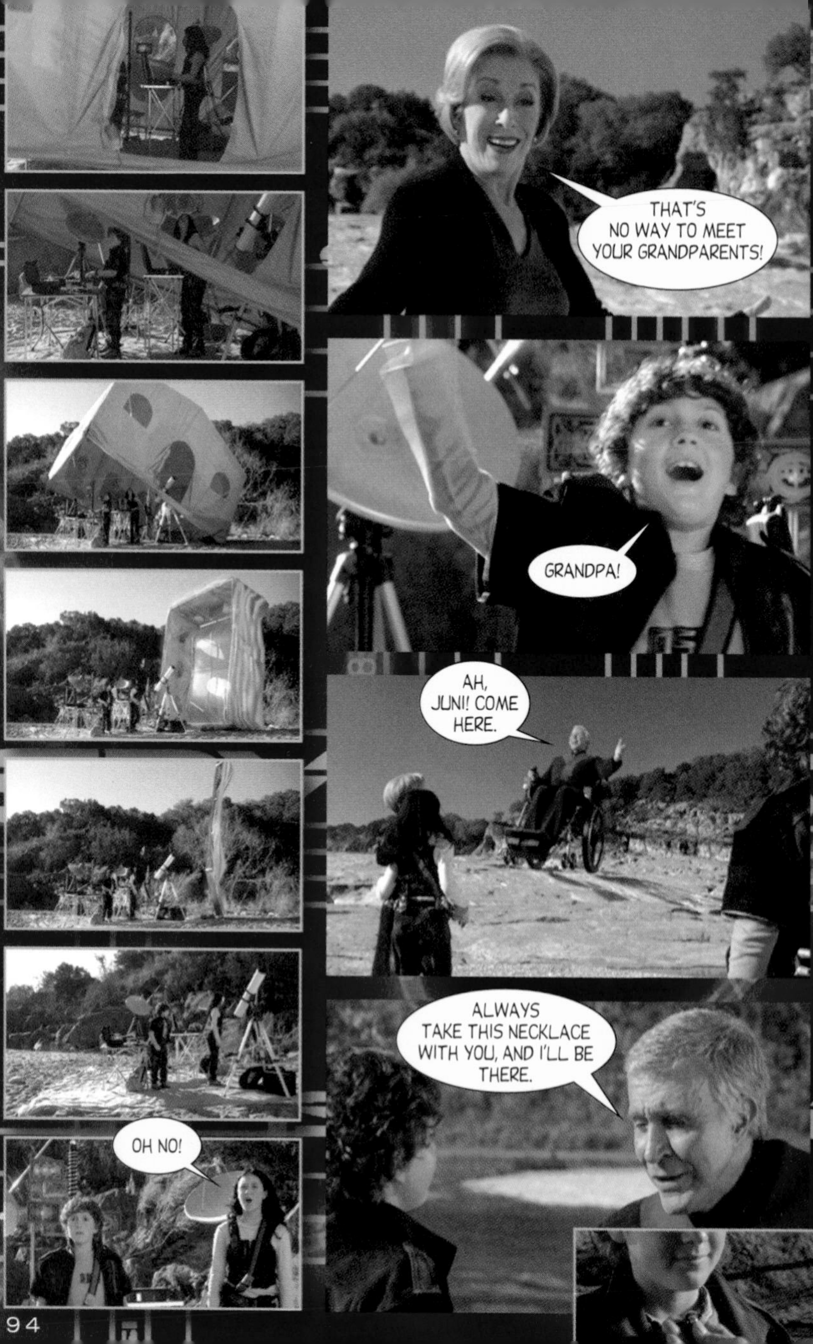
OH NO!
THAT'S NO WAY TO MEET YOUR GRANDPARENTS!
GRANDPA!
AH, JUNI! COME HERE.
ALWAYS TAKE THIS NECKLACE WITH YOU, AND I'LL BE THERE.

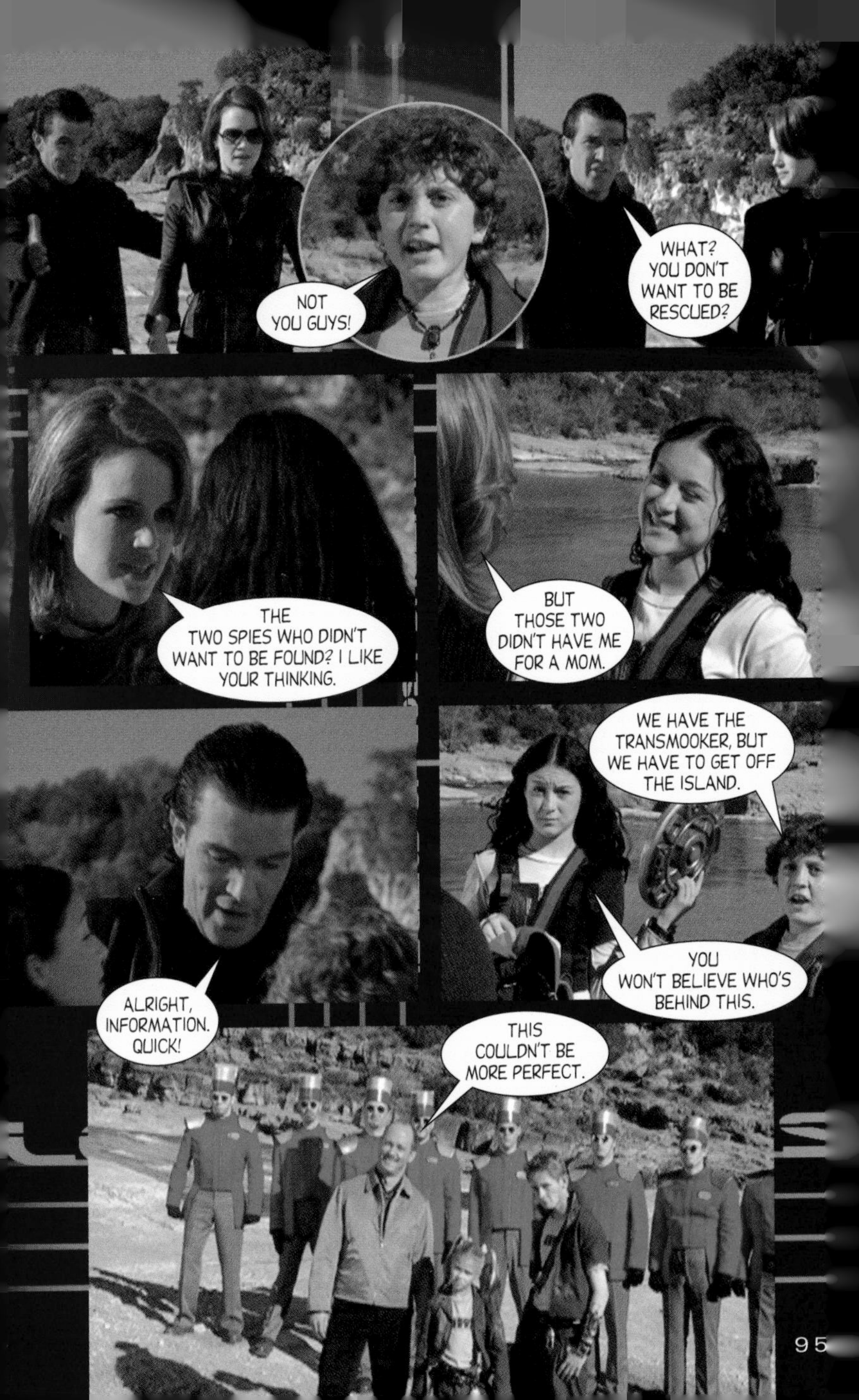
NOT YOU GUYS!
WHAT? YOU DON'T WANT TO BE RESCUED?
THE TWO SPIES WHO DIDN'T WANT TO BE FOUND? I LIKE YOUR THINKING.
BUT THOSE TWO DIDN'T HAVE ME FOR A MOM.
ALRIGHT, INFORMATION. QUICK!
WE HAVE THE TRANSMOOKER, BUT WE HAVE TO GET OFF THE ISLAND.
YOU WON'T BELIEVE WHO'S BEHIND THIS.
THIS COULDN'T BE MORE PERFECT.

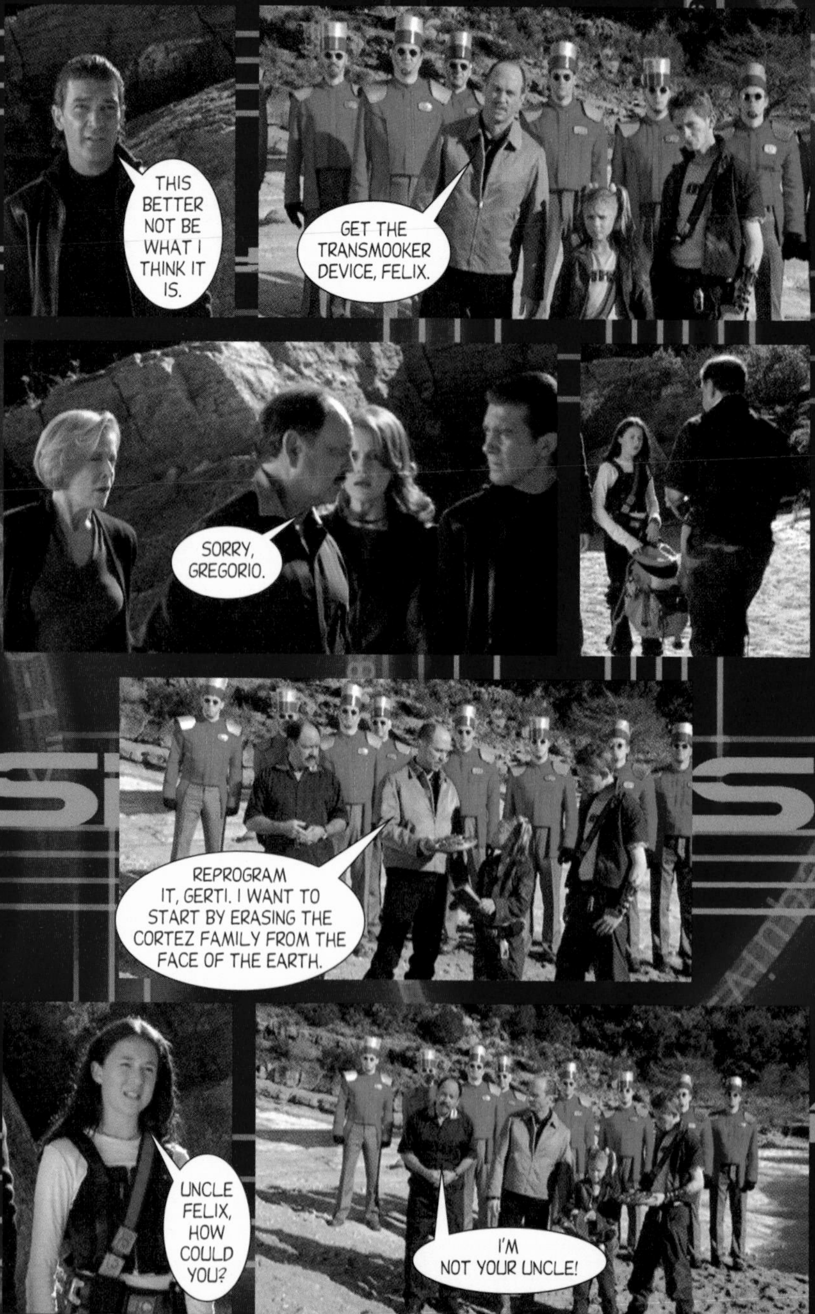
THIS BETTER NOT BE WHAT I THINK IT IS.
GET THE TRANSMOOKER DEVICE, FELIX.
SORRY, GREGORIO.
REPROGRAM IT, GERTI. I WANT TO START BY ERASING THE CORTEZ FAMILY FROM THE FACE OF THE EARTH.
UNCLE FELIX, HOW COULD YOU?
I'M NOT YOUR UNCLE!

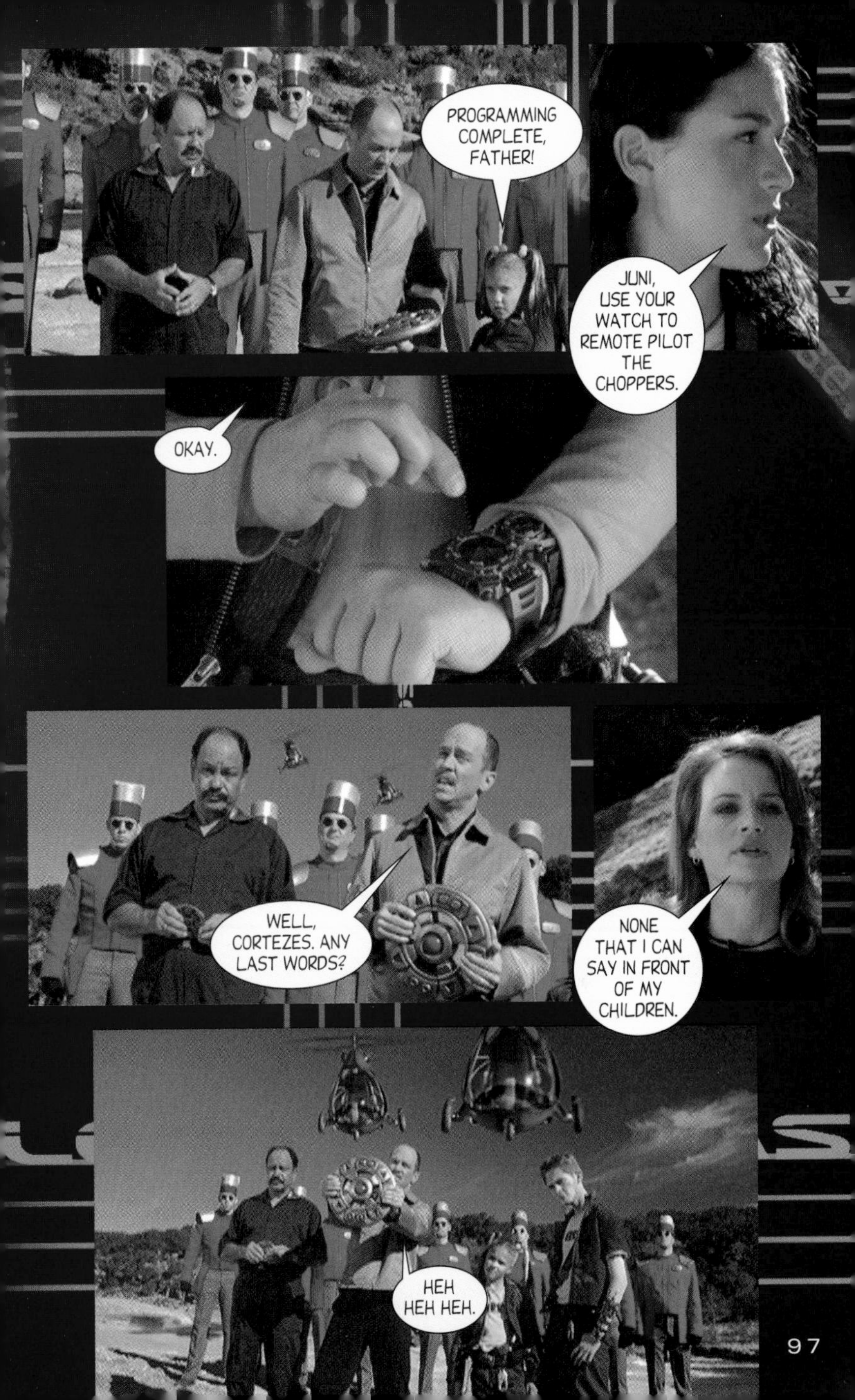
PROGRAMMING COMPLETE, FATHER!
JUNI, USE YOUR WATCH TO REMOTE PILOT THE CHOPPERS.
OKAY.
WELL, CORTEZES. ANY LAST WORDS?
NONE THAT I CAN SAY IN FRONT OF MY CHILDREN.
HEH HEH HEH.

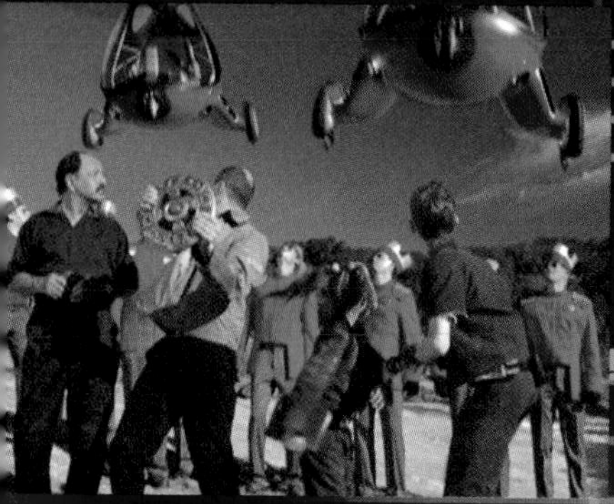
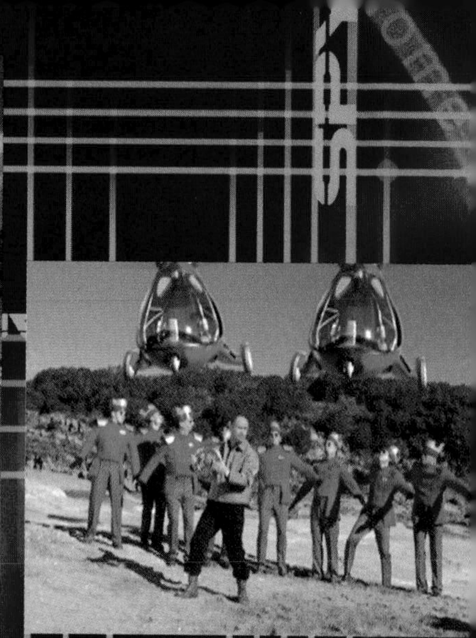
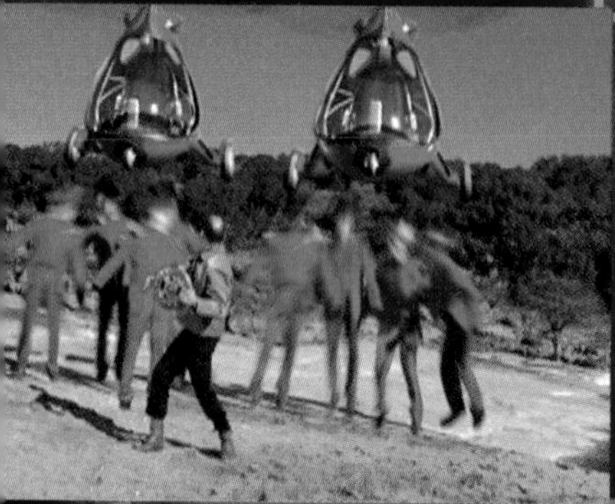
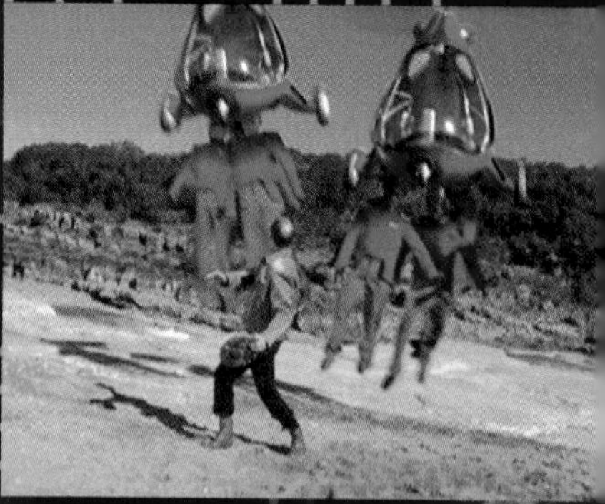
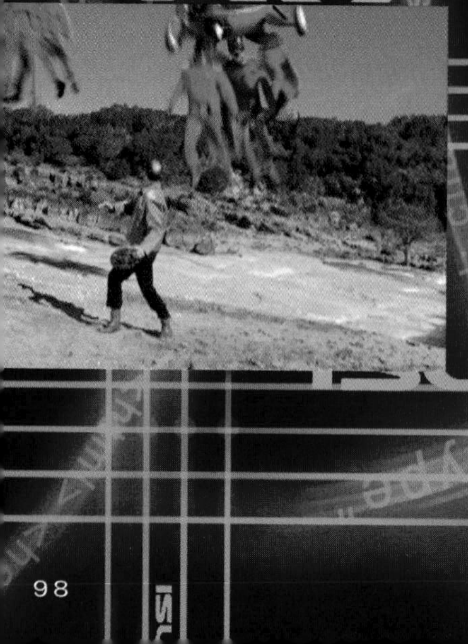
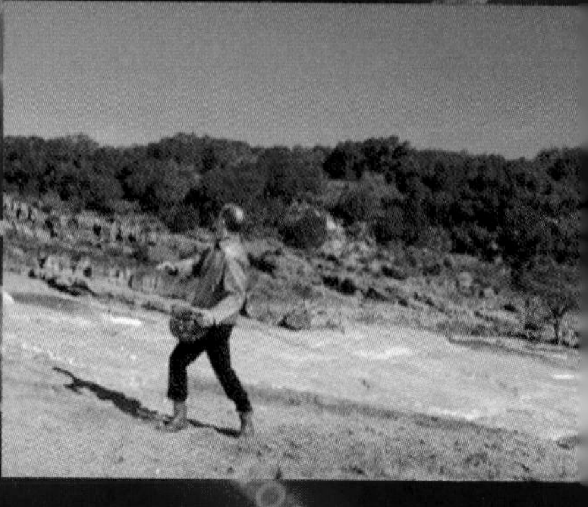

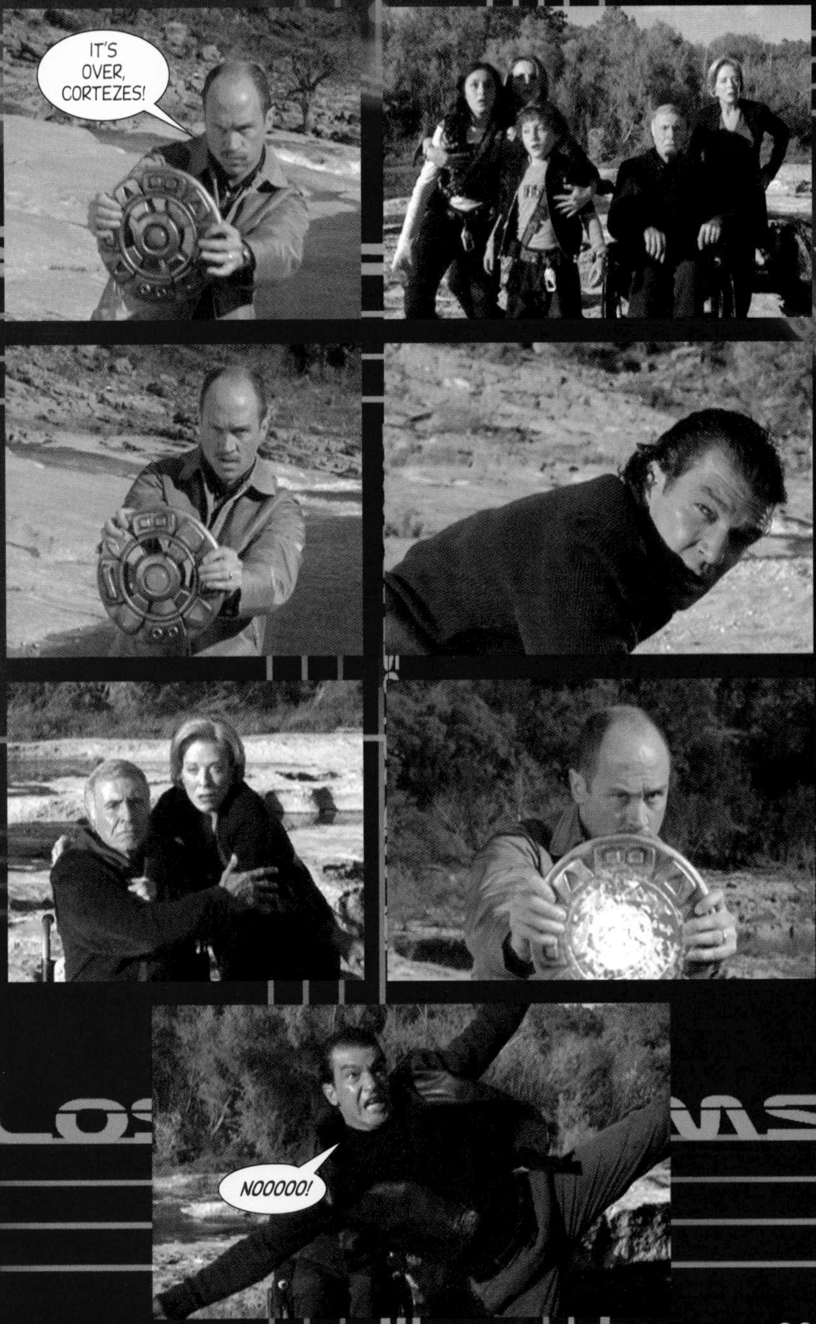
IT'S OVER, CORTEZES!
NOOOOO!

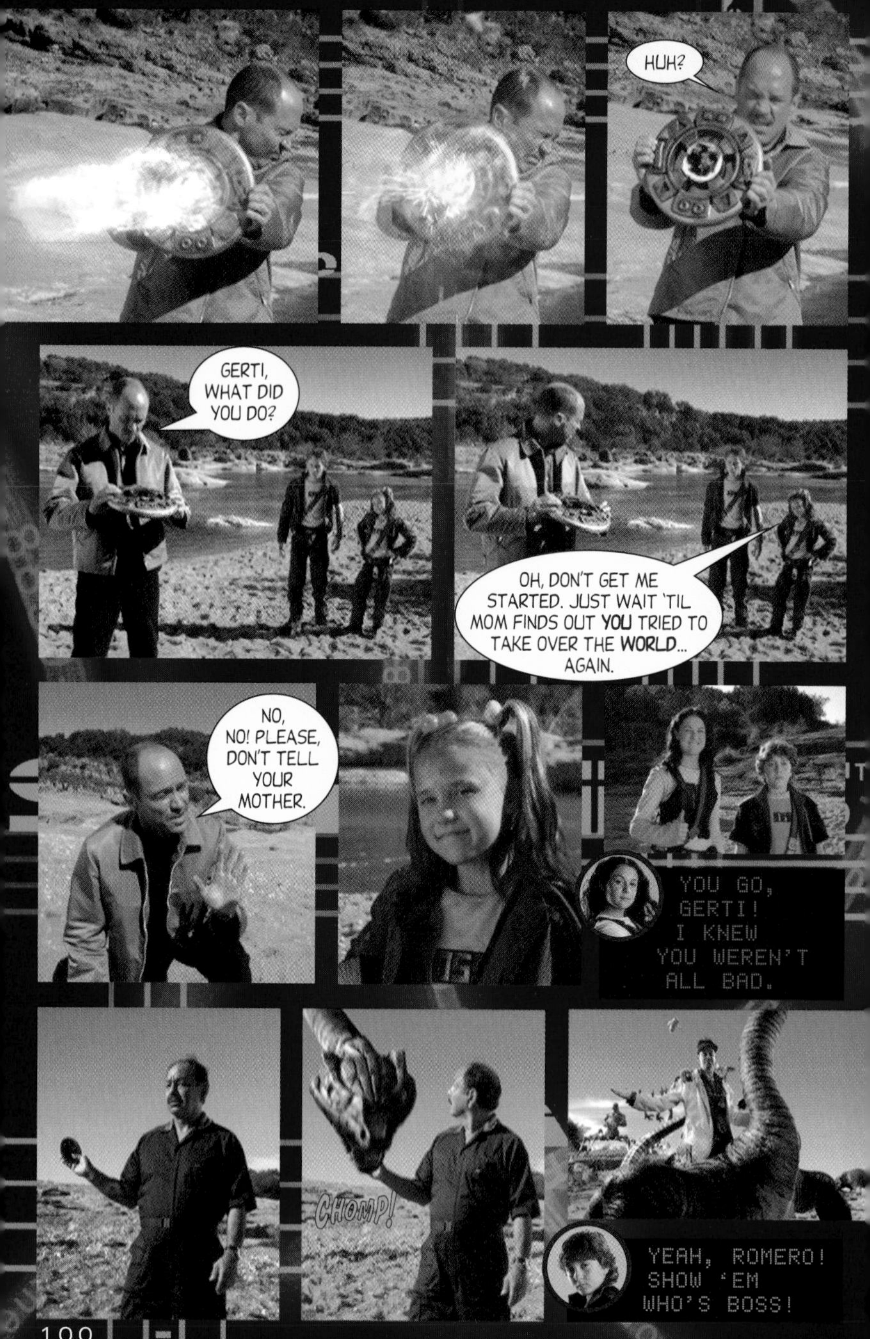
HUH?
GERTI, WHAT DID YOU DO?
OH, DON'T GET ME STARTED. JUST WAIT 'TIL MOM FINDS OUT **YOU** TRIED TO TAKE OVER THE **WORLD**... AGAIN.
NO, NO! PLEASE, DON'T TELL YOUR MOTHER.
YOU GO, GERTI! I KNEW YOU WEREN'T ALL BAD.
CHOMP!
YEAH, ROMERO! SHOW 'EM WHO'S BOSS!

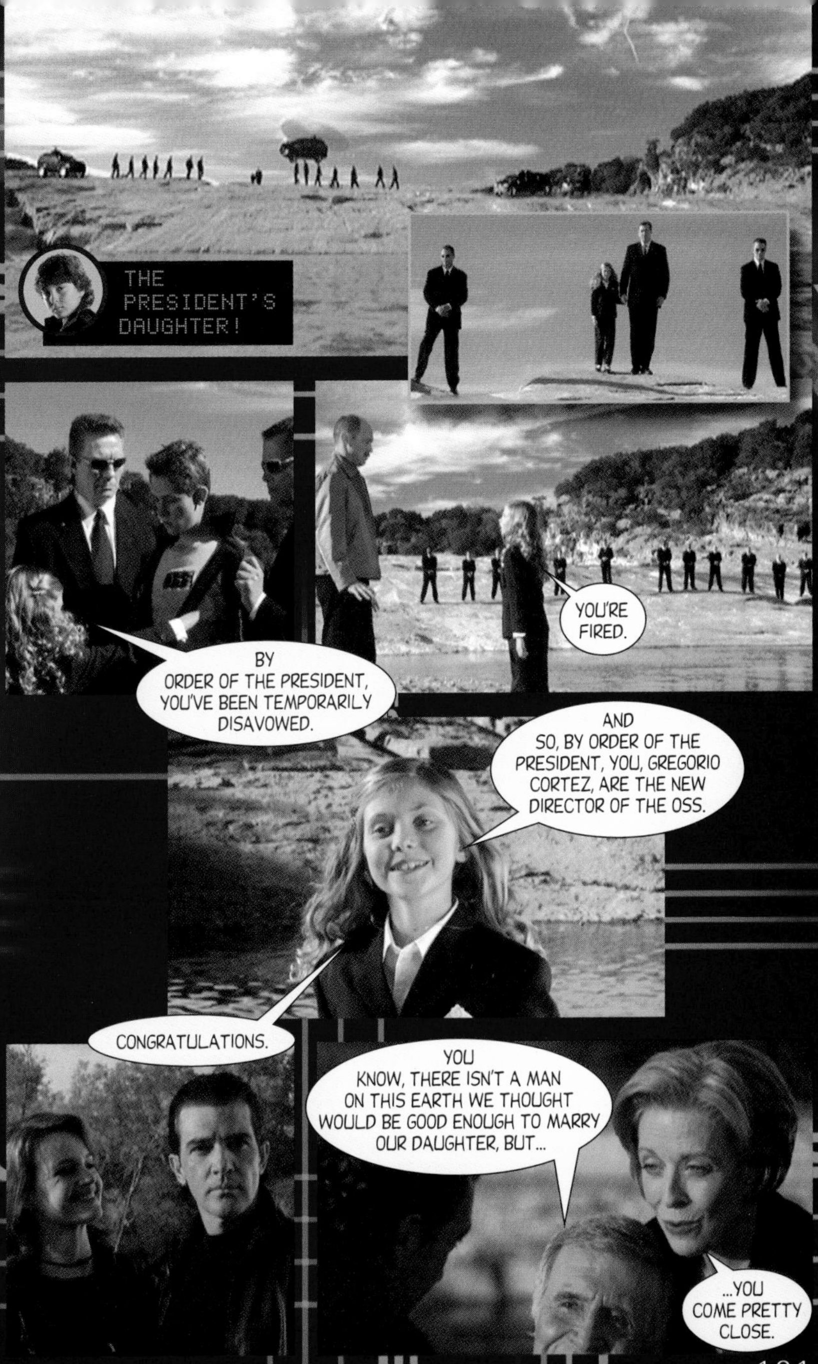
THE PRESIDENT'S DAUGHTER!
BY ORDER OF THE PRESIDENT, YOU'VE BEEN TEMPORARILY DISAVOWED.
YOU'RE FIRED.
AND SO, BY ORDER OF THE PRESIDENT, YOU, GREGORIO CORTEZ, ARE THE NEW DIRECTOR OF THE OSS.
CONGRATULATIONS.
YOU KNOW, THERE ISN'T A MAN ON THIS EARTH WE THOUGHT WOULD BE GOOD ENOUGH TO MARRY OUR DAUGHTER, BUT...
...YOU COME PRETTY CLOSE.

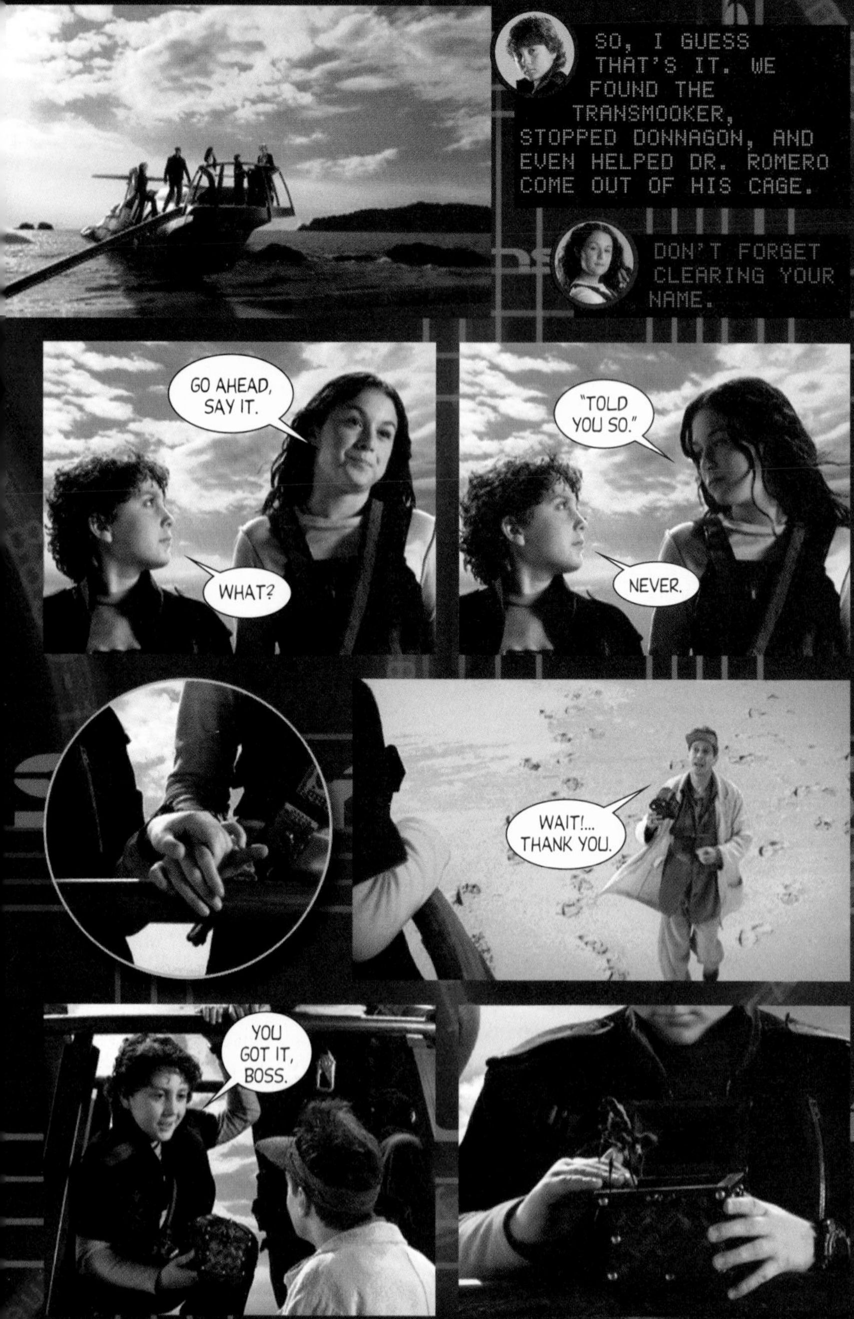
SO, I GUESS THAT'S IT. WE FOUND THE TRANSMOOKER, STOPPED DONNAGON, AND EVEN HELPED DR. ROMERO COME OUT OF HIS CAGE.
DON'T FORGET CLEARING YOUR NAME.
GO AHEAD, SAY IT.
WHAT?
"TOLD YOU SO."
NEVER.
WAIT!... THANK YOU.
YOU GOT IT, BOSS.

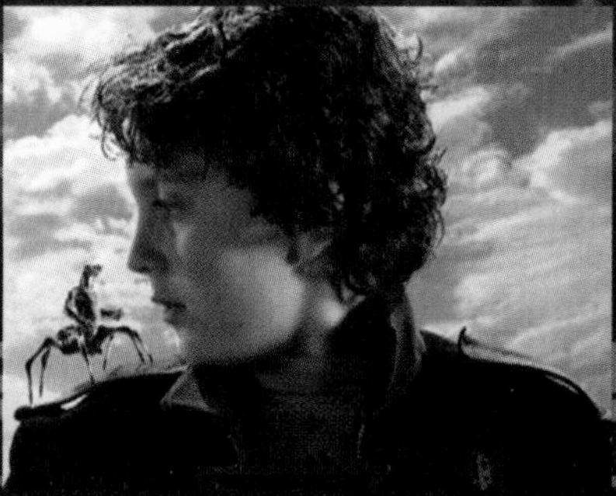

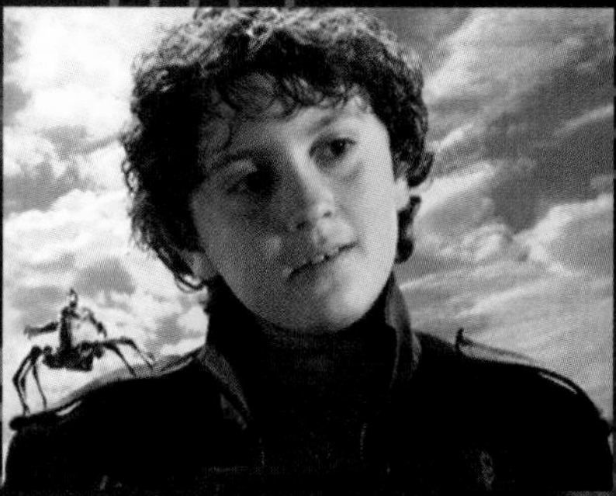

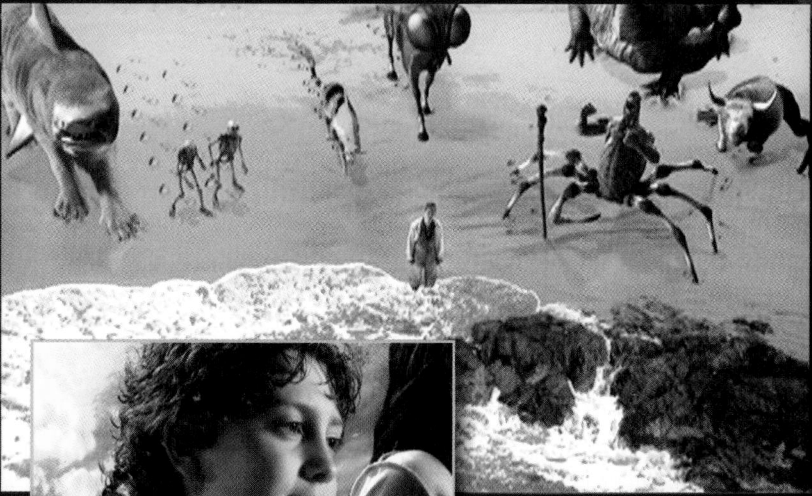

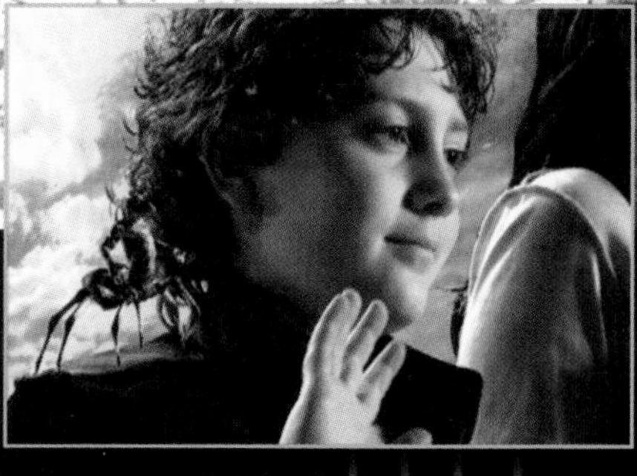

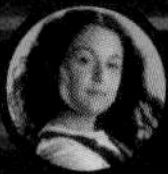

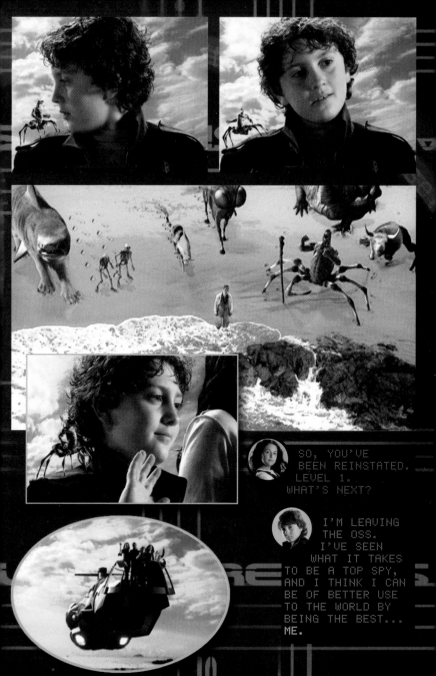

SO, YOU'VE BEEN REINSTATED. LEVEL 1. WHAT'S NEXT?

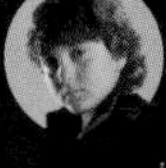

I'M LEAVING THE OSS. I'VE SEEN WHAT IT TAKES TO BE A TOP SPY, AND I THINK I CAN BE OF BETTER USE TO THE WORLD BY BEING THE BEST... **ME.**

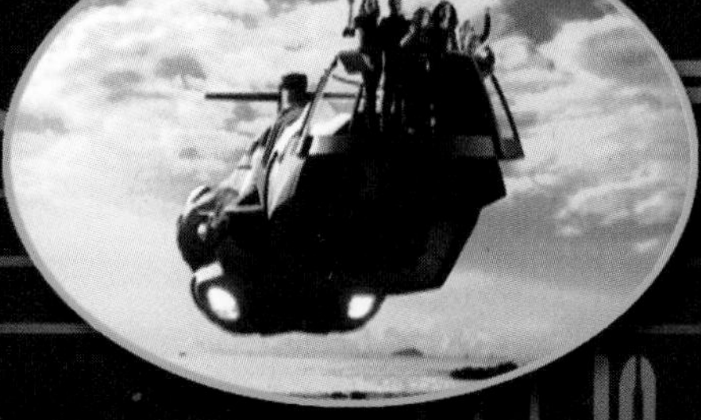